D1285533

THE HOW AND WHY OF LOVE

An INTRODUCTION *to* EVANGELICAL ETHICS

BY MICHAEL HILL

The How and Why of Love: An Introduction to Evangelical Ethics
© Matthias Media, 2002

Matthias Media
PO Box 225
Kingsford NSW 2032
Australia
Ph (02) 9663 1478
Fax (02) 9663 3265
Int. ph +61-2-9663 1478
Int. fax +61-2-9663 3265
email: info@matthiasmedia.com.au
Internet: www.matthiasmedia.com.au

Distributed in South Africa by:
Christian Book Discounters
Ph (021) 685 3663
Email: peter@christianbooks.co.za

Distributed in the United Kingdom by:
The Good Book Company
Ph (020) 8942 0880
Email: admin@thegoodbook.co.uk

Unless otherwise indicated, all Scripture quotations are from The Holy Bible, English Standard Version, copyright © 2001 by Crossway Bibles, a division of Good News Publishers. Used by permission. All rights reserved.

ISBN 1 876326 45 X

Cover design and typesetting by Joy Lankshear Design Pty Ltd

Dedicated to the memory of

Christine Harden Hill

1944–1992

• • •

Wife and closest friend for over twenty-six years—
a woman who expressed her faith in love

GALATIANS 5:6

Contents

Preface

IN THE COURSE of teaching Christian ethics in local churches and in a theological college I discovered the need of a simple, clear and concise introductory text. I found two books that were brilliant. One was written from the perspective of Natural Law and would have been superb if I wanted to teach traditional Roman Catholic doctrine. The other was written from a liberation theology perspective and did not suit the needs of conservative evangelical Christianity. Both books were excellent from the point of view of clarity and logic. The text was simple and unambiguous. The logic was impeccable. Basic assumptions and presuppositions were stated and the arguments flowed sequentially. I looked for something comparable from an evangelical perspective but could find nothing.

What was needed was a book that explained and accounted for morality from an evangelical perspective in the same simple and clear fashion. In my search for such a text I discovered that there were many good books on Christian ethics from an evangelical perspective. Some were not written at an introductory level. Those that were did not meet the criteria that I had established. Evangelicals are committed to the belief that the Bible is the Word of the one true and living God. An implication of this understanding of Scripture is that it has to be understood as a unit. The message as a whole has to be understood if the bits and pieces are not to be taken out of context and distorted or misunderstood. Many of the evangelical texts on ethics that I read used a part of the Scriptures to develop an ethical theory. Some based Christian ethics on creation, others on the Ten Commandments, and still others on the Sermon on the Mount or the vision of the Kingdom to come. A part of Scripture was taken to represent the whole. The validity of this approach to Christian ethics was called into question by the fact that these theories disagreed at significant points.

My study of the Bible confirmed what others had both perceived and proclaimed. The Bible has its own hermeneutic or way of understanding itself. The key to this understanding was the idea of promise and fulfilment. At the time of creation the Garden of Eden was full of possibilities and hope. The promise of these possibilities was thwarted by sin. Nevertheless God remained faithful to the promise. He worked in history to overcome the consequence of sin and to reveal his purposes for humankind. The revelation of his purposes was revealed in a number of stages. After the fall the assurance of redemption was expressed in his promise to Abraham. God's Kingdom was then foreshadowed in the nation of Israel, who, while being the people of God, were still slaves to sin. The sin of Israel and her kings could not frustrate the purposes of God. He eventually sent his only Son, the one true Israelite and promised king. Christ's death, resurrection and exaltation secured the forgiveness of sin and the redemption of creation. The substance of God's salvation was realised in Jesus' earthly ministry but it awaited consummation at his return.

The idea occurred to me that if the Bible was the Word of God and should be understood as a unit, then an ethic based on just part of the Scripture would be inadequate. The likelihood of an inadequate ethic was increased by the fact of progressive revelation. The earlier stages would be incomplete and the latter stages, taken by themselves, may require an understanding of the foundations laid in the earlier stages. Who knows what distortions would be contained in an ethic that took part of God's message as the whole? It was at this point in my search that I decided to turn my own hand to the task. I was determined to discern the ethical approach or approaches taken in the Scriptures and on the basis of this knowledge develop a theory of Christian ethics consistent with the Bible.

In outlining a biblically-based Christian ethic I have not tried to justify my presuppositions. I have simply adopted a conservative evangelical approach to the Bible in the hope that others have successfully undertaken the apologetic task of defending that approach. My explicit assignment has been to develop an ethic consistent with an evangelical understanding of Scripture. The analysis and justification of all my presuppositions and assumptions would defeat the purpose of writing a simple introduction. The more scholarly work will have to wait for another time. Nor have I tried to address all the issues facing Christians today. My emphasis has been on the *method* of doing ethics and not on the *content*. In order to keep the text within a reasonable length for an introduction I have not specifically addressed the issues of social ethics. The book is limited to the area of personal ethics. It tackles the question—what should I do? The framework is set in place so that readers can address the question— what social structures ought we to have in our society? The issues of the nature of social justice, the structures of government, education, family etc, have been left for another time.

The number of topics in the domain of personal ethics is, as indicated above, limited. Detailed attention has been given to five issues. The first three topics are explicitly mentioned in the Scriptures. The other two topics are not taken up in the text of the Bible. The reason for this selection has to do with methodology. A different method has to be employed when examining issues not mentioned in the Scriptures. The nature of the different methodologies is discussed in the text. The discussion is clarified by the examination of both types of issues. The hope is that the reader, through the scrutiny of both theory and issues, will be able to test and approve what is "good and acceptable and perfect" to God (Romans 12:2).

I wish to thank Dr. Peter Jensen, Dr. Royle Hawkes, the Rev. Andrew Cameron, Dr. Megan Best and my wife, Wendy, for reading a draft of the text and offering comments and corrections. Their assistance has been most helpful. The faults and deficiencies in the text remain mine.

Section One

UNDERSTANDING ETHICS

This section provides insights into the basic
ideas and concepts used in ethics. It furnishes
a framework for ethical thinking.

CHAPTER ONE

What's Ethics All About?

FROM THE DAWN of history humans have engaged, successfully or otherwise, in the task of giving an account of the reality they experience. As rational beings, people need to be able to understand their experiences and control the outcomes as far as possible. The management of life seems to be an aspect of the human capacity to choose from the various options possible.

Over time, the knowledge accrued from the endeavours of life became so extensive that it was eventually broken up into a number of subject areas. Each of these areas takes up an aspect of reality and develops an account of that reality on which people can operate. Today people study a huge range of subjects ranging from astronomy to zoology.

This book is an attempt to give an account of one aspect of human life. Our attention will be focused on the area of understanding called ethics. Ethics is the study that attempts to give an explanation of people's moral experience. The accounts people have given of human moral experience are called ethical theories, and the fact that these accounts are called 'theories' indicates that they need to be justified. Reasons and evidence are demanded if people are going to adopt these accounts and commit themselves to operating on them. This book will attempt to give an account of human moral experience based on a biblical understanding of reality. It will be an evangelical account in so far as the author believes that the gospel is central to the Bible's understanding of reality. In the Bible the gospel has to do with the problem of sin and God's promise of salvation. The gospel maintains that God's promise is fulfilled in the person and work of Jesus Christ. With this in mind let us turn to an examination of morality.

Morality

Definitions

There is the wonderful story about the ancient Greek philosopher, Aristotle (384–322 BC). He came up with a definition of man (that is, mankind in general). He declared that man was a featherless biped. Another Greek philosopher of the time, Diogenes (c. 400–325 BC), plucked a chicken and ran it through the streets of Athens crying out, "Make way for Aristotle's man". No doubt the great Aristotle was embarrassed. But he wasn't the last person to be embarrassed by trying to give a definition of some word or concept.

Definitions are notoriously difficult to get right. Yet this will not present a great problem if we realize that people can know things without being able to give an explicit verbal account, a definition, of what it is that they know. Young children can pick out humans from other animals such as dogs and cats from a very early age. They can do this without being able to give an account of what a person or human is. The fact that they can continually pick out humans without making a mistake is enough to convince us that they know what a human is.

As humans we know more than we can tell. This fact has not always been recognized. One group of eminent philosophers who influenced a great deal of educational theory in the western world actually defined knowledge as that which could be made verbally *explicit*. According to this view the young children we spoke about earlier did not really know the difference between a human and a dog. The claim of these philosophers that real knowledge had to be explicit is obviously false. It seems more reasonable to argue that people have knowledge or know something when they can use it or act upon it. There does not seem to be a need to require that people can make what they know verbally explicit. Our educational system recognizes that some knowledge and skills cannot be passed on verbally. In these areas people are required to do apprenticeships and pick up knowledge and skills by watching and copying.

Likewise, in order to get you to understand what morality is I do not have to come up with a watertight definition. It will be enough to provide several examples and anecdotes for you to pick up the concept and be able to use it.

Some Examples

Some time ago I was on a family camp. We were playing cricket with the children. At the camp it was decided that the younger children could get out twice before they lost their turn at batting. The adults only had to be dismissed once. One young boy missed the fact that he had been caught. The catch had been taken behind him and he did not see it. Later, when he was bowled and asked to surrender the bat to someone else, he was most indignant. "Every other child had to get out twice", he declared. When the adults insisted that he finish his turn he shouted, "That's not fair". He saw the whole incident as an injustice. His fervent indignation was moral indignation.

Our young boy's experience is not unique. We have all been engaged in, and continue to be engaged in, moral activities. A moment's reflection on our experience will confirm this truth. People feel moral outrage, for example, when someone cheats them or betrays them.

In our modern world various moral issues have gripped our attention. The feminist movement has caused the issue of sexual discrimination in the workplace to occupy our minds. Newspapers reporting the views of medical experts calling for the legalization of heroin have provoked heated debate. Accounts of vicious rape-murders on the TV have aroused our moral passions. Morality may not be easy to define, but moral experience is such a universal thing that we can point to examples and people will know what we are talking about.

Morality and the Bible

The Bible is full of morality. The ingredients are scattered throughout its pages. Moral rules, moral injunctions, and moral judgments abound. Moral values and moral virtues are explicitly adopted and promoted. For example, when Israel comes together as a people to proceed into the Promised Land they are given commandments which include the following moral rules:

You shall not murder

You shall not commit adultery (Exodus 20:13-14).

These commandments are re-iterated for Christians in Romans 13:8-10 where the moral principle behind the rules is identified. These rules are specific applications of the general principle—love your neighbour as yourself. Besides moral rules and principles we find lists of virtues and vices in the Scriptures:

Whoever is righteous has regard for the life of his beast (Proverbs 12:10).

By insolence comes nothing but strife (Proverbs 13:10).

Now the works of the flesh are evident: sexual immorality, impurity, sensuality, idolatry, sorcery, enmity, strife, jealousy, fits of anger, rivalries, dissensions, divisions, envy, drunkenness, orgies, and things like these. I warn you, as I warned you before, that those who do such things will not inherit the Kingdom of God (Galatians 5:19-21).

But the fruit of the Spirit is love, joy, peace, patience, kindness, goodness, faithfulness, gentleness and self-control (Galatians 5:22-23).

Morality and Ethics

By now we should have some idea of what morality is all about. Later in the book we might attempt some kind of definition of morality, realising that it is bound to be inadequate at points. However, for the moment we can work with the intuitions and understanding about morality that we have picked up from the sections above.

This book is not just a book about morality. It is a book about ethics. Hence we need to be clear about the difference between morality and ethics. Ethics is the *study* of morality. As such, ethics has three distinct aspects. These areas are known as descriptive ethics, normative ethics and meta-ethics.

Descriptive Ethics

In the study of ethics we begin with the *descriptive* task of trying to identify the moral standards and rules that people adopt. Prior to World War II, the majority of people living in Australia would very probably have shared a common morality. It would have generally been agreed that divorce and homosexuality were morally wrong. Had we been alive then we could have ascertained the moral beliefs of the population by taking a survey. In doing this study of morality we would have been engaged in ethics; that aspect of ethics we call *descriptive ethics*.

Christians engage in the task of descriptive ethics when they study the Bible. For example, a person might go through the Gospel of Mark and list all the moral rules, principles and values found there. As a consequence of this study the person would locate the morality of Mark's Gospel.

A study of various societies and cultures will show that there appears to be a variety of moralities. That is, there are groups of people who have different sets of moral beliefs and values. The significant point to notice here is not that many moral values overlap but that some do not. Some, for example, believe that monogamy is a moral virtue and others believe that polygamy is. It does not appear that both can be right. *Descriptive ethics is not concerned to locate the right set of values but simply to ascertain the moral standards that people have or have had.*

Normative Ethics

The conflict of moral values allows me to introduce the second aspect of ethics. This is the aspect called *normative ethics*. The fundamental task of normative ethics is to locate moral standards that we can operate on and live by. In doing normative ethics we go beyond the descriptive task. *Normative ethics is not satisfied with locating standards that people have or have had. It is concerned to locate standards to live by. It attempts to locate a set of moral values that are right and true.*

One aspect of the task of normative ethics is that of *analysis*. In normative ethics we analyse the rules, principles, values and virtues of a particular morality and see how all the parts or aspects fit together. Analysis will allow criticism of a particular morality but it will also lead to the next task of normative ethics, which is the task of *justification*. Justification is the task of demonstrating that we have the right values and virtues, principles and rules. That is, in normative ethics we attempt to show that a particular set of moral values meshes with reality in a way which is more adequate than other sets. In this way we attempt to vindicate our morality. If we are looking for standards to live by it will be important that we have the right set.

Meta-ethics

Sometimes the study of ethics goes beyond analysis and justification and asks questions that are raised by the very analysis of morality itself. Questions like:

> What is moral value?
> Can moral values be justified?
> Are moral values objective? (That is, are there true and false values?)

In asking these questions we are not focusing on any particular moral rules or values but taking up an examination of the *kinds of things* we are dealing with in the study of ethics. These are the kinds of questions that can be asked of all normative theories. This aspect of ethics is generally called *meta-ethics*. As a discipline it deals with the second-level questions that come up when we study ethics. Talking about moral values prompts questions about the nature of values. The examination of the nature of values does not help us to locate particular values that might operate as norms. It is, therefore, not part of the task of normative ethics. Nor does it help us to justify any particular set of values as such. *Meta-ethics focuses on and examines the assumptions made and concepts used by any and all ethical theories.*

Focusing on Normative Ethics

Analysis is a fundamental part of doing normative ethics. The following anecdote illustrates the type of analysis in which normative ethicists engage.

> Grandma was planning to visit a friend in the country, which required her to stay overnight. Her instructions to Grandpa before leaving, were: "turn off the soup when you come home from golf". Next day she returned to find the soup (luckily!) still simmering in the stockpot. Grandpa's flustered explanation was, "...but it rained, and I didn't go to golf".

It is not hard to understand the thinking behind Grandma's injunction. She knew that the soup had to be cooked for several hours. She calculated that the time would be up when her husband returned from golf. Hence the particular instruction to turn off the soup when he got home. Grandpa thoughtlessly failed to go behind the instruction to the reasoning that produced it. He failed to understand the intention of the command and so failed to see how to fulfil the intention when circumstances changed.

Many people are like Grandpa in this anecdote when it comes to Christian morality. They take the moral commands and instructions from the Bible and obey them, but they do not go behind the command to see the reasons for them. Morality becomes simply a matter of obeying rules and directives. Normative ethics, on the other hand, looks behind the particular injunctions to see what is going on. As a result it helps us to be morally consistent in changing conditions and circumstances.

A number of the biblical writers do go behind the moral commands and attempt to give an account of some aspect of morality. James, the brother of Jesus, engages in normative ethics when he suggests that morality is unified. In his letter he writes,

> If you really fulfil the royal law according to the Scripture, "You shall love your neighbour as yourself", you are doing well. But if you show partiality, you are committing sin and are convicted by the law as transgressors. For whoever keeps the whole law but fails in one point has become accountable for all of it. For he who said, "Do not commit adultery", also said, "Do not murder". If you do not commit adultery but do murder, you have become a transgressor of the law (James 2:8-11).

The moral commands of the Bible fit together because they all issue from the same person. God is offended if any of the commands are broken. One cannot be selectively moral.

The apostle Paul also engages in an aspect of ethical theory when he ties several of the commandments together in Romans 13:8-10. Like James, he takes up the rules not to commit murder or adultery. Paul sees these rules as expressions of the principle of loving one's neighbour. The rules are unified by the fact that they have the same purpose—that of loving one's neighbour. We can fit both Paul's and James' thinking together and conclude that God's general purpose is that people should love one another and that this finds particular expression in not committing adultery or murder etc.

A number of biblical scholars have argued that the biblical writers were not interested in normative ethics. In a sense this is true. The biblical writers were not interested in theorizing about morality *per se*. They were not interested in analysing and justifying their moral values in the systematic way a modern ethicist might. Nevertheless they understood their moral rules and values as having a rationale, or reason for being. As we have already seen, both Paul and James understood their normative material to have a place in a broader understanding. When they point out this broader context and the way the moral material relates to it, they are implicitly doing normative ethics. This book is an explicit attempt at normative ethics. It is an attempt to construct an ethic on the basis of an evangelical understanding of the Bible.

THE HOW AND WHY OF LOVE

Terminology

For the purposes of this book we will use the words 'ethics' and 'morality' to refer to different things. Admittedly in everyday usage we frequently use the words 'ethics' and 'morality' as if they refer to the same thing. We might say that so-and-so has no ethics or no morality, in which case we probably mean that the person in question does not appear to have moral standards or values. In this book, however, we will use the word 'ethics' to refer to the study and analysis of morality. Adopting this sense of the word 'ethics' will have its consequences. While it may be true that everyone has a morality, it is certainly not true that everyone has given explicit thought to seeing that the moral standards and rules they operate on are consistent or justifiable. Not everyone has an ethic.

The Need for an Ethic

At this point it will be helpful to introduce another distinction. This is the distinction between synthetic and analytic knowledge. A child, three or four years of age, might be able to pick out bulls from other animals and objects, and not make a mistake, in which case we would say that the child knew what a bull was. We would claim that the child had a certain knowledge. I want to call this knowledge *synthetic* knowledge. At such an early age the child might not be able to give a verbal account of the difference between a bull and a cow, in which case we would claim that the child does not have an *analytic* knowledge of cows and bulls. Analytic knowledge is knowledge that one can make explicit through language. Despite the lack of analytic knowledge we would still want to insist that the child knew what a cow was.

Getting back to ethics, we have seen that people can have a morality without having a normative ethic. People can hold moral beliefs and operate on moral rules without ever having analysed how they all fit together. That is, people can have a synthetic knowledge of ethics without having an analytic knowledge of it. People might have an intuitive apprehension of how their morals fit together, without being able to explicitly state how. What is more, people can operate quite adequately without this analytic knowledge until they are faced with a conflict of values or until their morality is challenged by another moral system. Down through history there have been communities that have operated for a relatively long period of time on a traditional morality without feeling the need to analyse or question it. Fortunately or unfortunately, ours is not one of those communities nor one of those times. We must have an ethic as well as a morality.

It is extremely unfortunate that some Christians take a 'tell me what to do' attitude when it comes to studying Christian ethics. They are happy to study particular moral issues like abortion and homosexuality, but unwilling to put the time and effort into studying the theory that enables them to understand why certain ethical conclusions are reached. 'Just treat the issues' is the cry. An analogy may be drawn between helping the hungry and teaching ethics. The 'just treat the issues' attitude is similar to the attitude of the hungry who say 'don't bother to teach me how to grow food, just give me the food'. Not only is this attitude shortsighted, it is morally irresponsible.

C. Stephen Layman gives three reasons for developing an analytic account of morality or ethical theory (Layman, 1991). Firstly, theories tell us the sort of thing we need to know to settle moral issues. This need is strongly felt in a society like ours where traditional rules will not cover the situations generated by modern technology. Traditional rules do not cover issues like sperm donation, surrogate motherhood and the ozone layer. Secondly, theories present us with a general picture or vision of the moral life. A theory will give us a sense of the general direction we ought to be heading. This sense can give us rough moral guidance and set the parameters of our moral search and research. From this point we can go on and spell out the details. Thirdly, having a theory helps us to be consistent and avoid bias. Our capacity for moral outrage can be selective. We can be violently opposed to abortion on demand and not concerned about an unjust war in which our nation has some participation. Consistency is a virtue in morality. These three reasons alone are enough to drive us to study ethics.

CHAPTER TWO

The Various Accounts
of Morality

IN THE EARLY 1960's I stayed in a village just outside the town
of Maprik in the Sepik District of New Guinea. One morning we
were disturbed by a commotion at the edge of the village. We went
over to see a young woman convulsing on the ground. My friend
and I both concluded that she was having an epileptic fit. The local
villagers, however, were convinced that she had been possessed by a
'*sanguman*'—a spirit that lived in the trees nearby. There was only
one event, but different people had provided two diverse accounts
of what was happening. We supplied a medical account in terms of
body chemistry while the locals provided a religious account.

It should be no surprise to find that throughout history people
have given various accounts of morality. The various types of
accounts can be broken up into two main groups. One of these
groups has explained morality in terms of what people do. Ethics is
seen to be about determining what actions are right or wrong, good
or bad. The other group has explained human moral experience in
terms of people's character. For this group, ethics is not ultimately
about whether actions are right or wrong but whether human
beings are virtuous and have a good character. The focus of this
group is not the detached actions of people but the moral agent
who performs the actions. According to the first group of thinkers,
ethics is basically about the moral evaluation of actions. Their
concern is to locate the actions or types of actions that people have
an obligation to do or to avoid doing. Because this group is
interested in discovering actions or type of actions that form the

moral duties that bind people these theories have been labelled the 'ethics of duty'. The second type of theory considers the task of ethics to be the discovery of morally good traits of character. Morally good traits of character are called 'virtues'. Theories of this type are classified under the heading 'the ethics of virtue'. When either of these broad general categories are used they inform the reader that the account of morality under consideration is oriented towards explaining morality in terms of either the action or the agent—whether ethics is seen as a matter of doing or being.

Both the ethics of virtue and the ethics of duty can be broken up into further categories. For example, under the category of ethics of duty we find a number of different sub-types. The three major sub-types are *deontological, teleological* and *consequentialist.* An outline of these three sub-types will be provided below.

An examination of some examples of each category and sub-category of ethical theory will help us to clarify our understanding of the logic of various theories and accounts. Hopefully this exercise will lead on to examination of the biblical material. Armed with the traditional categories, we might be better able to locate the logic of biblical ethics. Of course it is always possible that the biblical material might not fit any of the categories. Yet even this discovery will advance our understanding of biblical ethics.

Morality Explained in Terms of Actions: The Ethics of Duty

With the ethics of duty an attempt is made to locate the actions or the types of actions that people 'ought' to do. In other words these theories endeavour to discover our moral duty or obligations. For this reason this approach has also been labelled 'the ethics of obligation'. Remember the *evaluation of actions* is fundamental to morality, according to this type of theory.

Deontological Theories

The word 'deontological' comes from a Greek participle meaning 'it is binding'. Deontological theories argue that there are certain features of actions like murder or adultery that make them right or wrong, and therefore binds people to do them (or not). All deontological theories agree that people ought to do the right thing simply because it is right, and not because of any consequences or outcomes that might follow. One well-known deontological theory argues that an action is right if God commands that it be done, and wrong if God commands that it not be done. According to this theory the feature that makes an action right or wrong is that God commands it or forbids it. For this reason the theory has been called the Divine Command theory.

The German philosopher Immanuel Kant (1724–1804) proposed another famous deontological theory. He understood the essence of human nature to be the capacity to think rationally. As a consequence he argued that moral directives were right if they were in accordance with reason or right thinking. Right thinking was universally applicable, so Kant argued that any rule or imperative had to be universally applicable if it was to be moral. Kant provided a number of tests for moral directives that would enable people to tell whether directives were right or wrong. But the basic test was that people should only act on moral directives that they could choose, by an act of will, to be a general law for everyone. No one, he argues, could choose the maxim (rule of conduct) 'I will make promises, but not keep them' as a universal law. Reason tells us that if everybody adopted it as a rule of conduct then the very convention of promising would break down. The only maxim in regard to promise-keeping that could be a universal law is the one 'always keep your promises'. This would be a moral rule of conduct not because God commanded it, but because it was in accordance with right thinking.

We have only examined briefly two examples of deontological ethics. A more detailed account of these two theories would be profitable as would a more comprehensive account of this group of theories. However we have seen enough to understand that a theory is a deontological theory if it suggests that a feature of the action or type of action binds people to do them or not do them as the case may be.

Teleological Theories

Teleological theories differ greatly from deontological ones. The English word 'teleological' is derived from the Greek word *telos*, meaning end, goal, or purpose. Teleology is the study of ends or goals. A teleological ethic gives accounts of why actions are morally right or wrong in terms of the goals envisaged. In a theistic context the term '*telos*' refers to 'the purposes and goals which are inherent in things because of the way God made them'. In a non-theistic context it means 'the natural goals which are simply part of the reality of things'.

Some of the ancient philosophers, observing the evidences for design or purpose in nature, developed a doctrine that everything was designed to serve a purpose. Moreover they held that the nature of a thing, its design, enabled it to move towards its appropriate goal. The notion of goal or end was developed in several different ways. From Aristotle we get the traditional example that the goal of an acorn is to become an oak tree. Correspondingly the goal of any human, a rational creature, according to Aristotle, was to think. It was thought that each kind, or type, of thing found in the world had its own goal. In a sense the goal was part of its nature. Aristotle's mentor and teacher, Plato (428-348 BC), arranged the various kinds of things in the world in a hierarchical order, linking the goal of one kind to another. The goal of vegetables, for example, was to grow luxuriantly in order to serve animals as food. Plato devised a chain of order. Vegetables were to serve the animal, the animal was to serve the rational, and reason to serve divine truth.

Careful note ought to be taken that while the subject of the sentence "the goal of an acorn is to become an oak tree" is in the singular, it refers not just to one particular acorn, but to all acorns. The reference is *generic* in that it refers to every seed of the same kind. Teleological theories are based on the fact that there are various kinds of things found in nature that have their goals built into them.

One teleological theory with a long history is the doctrine of Natural Law. Dwyer (1987, pp.15–16) puts forward this description of the doctrine of Natural Law. The doctrine of Natural Law makes three basic claims. The first is that some things, especially persons, have a purposiveness that is part of their very being. This claim is foundational to the doctrine. The second is that the purposiveness embedded in reality can be discovered by an intelligent examination of the world. If the purposive nature of reality could not be known then it would be of no help in trying to determine moral criteria by which to live life. The necessary moral factor is given by the third claim, that the purposiveness revealed in reality is normative in moral decision-making. That is, the goals built into the very nature of things provide the moral criteria for life. These goals become the standard by which we judge actions to be right or wrong.

Thomism is a classical example of the doctrine of Natural Law. "The starting point for all advocates of Natural Law is to work out the *purpose* of human life" (Vardy, 1994, p. 53). According to Thomism, human thinking can work out the purpose of human existence. Even though human nature is not perfect the Thomistic tradition maintains that it is a reasonable guide to what people should be. Reflection on human experience reveals that the purpose of human life is manifold and includes 'to live, to reproduce, to learn, to have an ordered society and to worship God'. Given this goal as the standard of human action, one is able to come to a number of conclusions. Because the purpose of life is to live, suicide is morally wrong. Likewise, because the purpose of life includes reproduction, any sexual activity that does not allow the possibility of conception is wrong.

It is obvious that Natural Law theories will vary according to the various understandings of the purpose of human life. If someone believed that the proper goal for all action was the creation of a harmonious community, then any action or type of action which contributed towards this goal, or was consistent with it, would be morally valid. Since the rules forbidding murder and adultery would clearly contribute to the production of a harmonious community then they would be valid moral rules. There may be intermediate goals along the way to this final goal of a harmonious society, and these intermediate goals would also give moral direction. However, the doctrine of Natural Law is not necessarily committed to a social or communitarian comprehension of humanity.

An individualistic approach could also be embraced.

For the benefit of later discussions we might draw aside from our argument and recognize a distinction between two different forms of teleology. We have seen how teleological theories in ethics locate the *telos* by looking at the nature or the design. For obvious reasons this type of teleology is called natural teleology. By way of contrast, we might set ourselves goals (*teloi*) in our lives. These would be goals that we would strive to reach in the future. This type of teleology is called historical teleology. Teleological ethicists locate the good by examining the design of nature (or the nature God has given them). This process involves natural teleology. Once the nature of the good has been established people will make it the goal in their lives. The good will be achieved by a historical process. This is historical teleology. Later we will see why it is important not to confuse these two types of teleology.

We can observe a clear difference between deontological theories and teleological accounts. For deontological theories, an action is either right or wrong depending on the properties or features of the action. For teleological theories rightness is defined in terms of the goal to which the action may contribute. The reasons for thinking certain rules or principles are valid moral rules vary with each type of theory. Both types of theories might conclude that murder was wrong but they would do so for different reasons.

Consequentialist Theories

An easily recognizable difference between purpose and consequence enables us to separate off another group of theories. Whereas teleological theories are concerned with the task of recognizing and responding to the purposive order detected in creation, consequentialist accounts of morality focus on the fact that individual agents have needs and desires that anticipate fulfilment. As a result of this focus, the morality of actions or types of action are evaluated in terms of how well those desires are met. Those actions or types of actions productive of the satisfaction of human needs and desires are deemed to be morally good, and those that inhibit or harm satisfaction are regarded as evil.

One can discern why consequentialist theories have been classified as teleological in the past. Certain regular consequences of human action are used to establish the goal of action. These intended consequences become the goal or *telos* of moral action. Teleological theorists would argue that the consequentialist approach to ethics confuses purposes with outcomes. A simple illustration will highlight the point. Natural Law theory is, you will remember, a teleological theory. It argues, for example, that the purpose of sexual intercourse is procreation: to have children. Nevertheless the theorists who adopt this approach acknowledge that one of the outcomes of sexual intercourse might be satisfaction and pleasure. According to Natural Law theory, an act of sexual intercourse is only moral if it leaves open the possibility of conception. Conversely, one well-known consequentialist theory argues that actions are morally correct if they bring about the maximum satisfaction of human need for the greatest number of people. The implication of this theory is that sexual intercourse is morally justified by the fact that it is productive of pleasure and satisfaction. One must note that this consequentialist theory does not promote haphazard and random intercourse. Sexual intercourse would need to be regulated so that it produced the maximum pleasure for the greatest number of people. Because indiscriminate sexual intercourse would produce emotional pain it has been argued that the institution of marriage provided the necessary regulation. Teleological theorists would maintain that the purpose of sexual intercourse has been confused with an outcome, or reduced to an outcome, by the consequentialists. Consequentialists would plead that it is proper for the consequences to be the measure of morality.

Purposes are detected by the mind examining the nature of things found in creation. This is a purely reflective process. Consequences are discovered by the empirical examination of particular actions and events. One has to move from case to case to see what the outcome is. One could see how the two different approaches would yield two different accounts of morality. The teleological approach would take the basic design of human nature and locate the purpose. This understanding would be untrammelled by the contingencies of time and wear. The consequentialist, on the other hand, would observe human desires and needs and set the goal accordingly. For consequentialists, an act is good because of, and only because of, its consequences. This 'only' precludes any consideration of nature and design. The fact that the design may have been compromised by time or wear or human will would not be taken into account. The goals determining moral behaviour would be completely different.

Classical or Hedonistic Utilitarianism is a good example of a consequentialist theory. According to this theory actions or types of action are right if they produce the greatest amount of pleasure for the greatest number of people. The theory is classified as utilitarian because morality is defined in terms of things which satisfy the desires and needs of people; things that people can use. With Classical or Hedonistic Utilitarianism ('*hedone*' is the Greek word for pleasure), pleasure is considered to be the ultimate good and pain is the evil to be avoided. There are other forms of utilitarianism that recognize more than one good. Knowledge and power, for example, are understood by some scholars as basic goods. Just as consequentialist theories can differ according to what is perceived as the goal of moral action, so they can differ in regard to what is considered harmful. Other things besides pain might be listed. These differences would be due to the different understandings of the needs of humanity.

In order to prevent confusion at this point we need to clarify two different uses of the word 'good'. A valid distinction can be drawn between moral good and non-moral good. Truthfulness, for example, is a moral good, while food and pleasure are non-moral goods. This distinction is vital to both consequentialist and teleological theories. Both types of theories maintain that morality is all about securing non-moral goods. Truthfulness is a moral good, according to classical utilitarianism, because it secures the greatest amount of non-moral good (that is, pleasure) for the greatest number. Truthfulness is also a moral good for teleological theories but for a different reason. It secures the purpose for which speech was given. For example, for some teleological theories the purpose might be right personal relationships. Whether the goal of action is determined by the purpose or consequence, both types of theories envisage that right action moves toward some non-moral good—be it pleasure or purpose. The securing of non-moral goods determines that an action or type of action is morally good.

A further question can be raised about the recipients of the non-moral goods in the case of consequentialist theories. Classical Utilitarianism argues that the non-moral good produced should go to the greatest number of people possible if the action is to be morally valid. Other utilitarian theorists have argued differently. Egoists, for example, hold that the non-moral good should go to the self, while altruists maintain that it ought to go to others. The question of who should be the recipients does not arise with teleological theories. Anything of a certain type ought to move towards its purpose. Everything of the same type will have the same purpose. All will be included.

The reasons for moving away from the traditional approach of classifying consequentialist theories as teleological are several. One is to avoid confusion by highlighting the differences. Another has to do with the way the two types of theories operate and the criticism that can arise from the different ways of operating. With teleological theories, the goal tends to restrain the types of action possible. Consequentialist theories, on the other hand, maintain that the goal or end justifies the means. Let us take an extreme example to highlight the difference. Murder might become a valid moral option for a utilitarian approach if, for example, it produced the greatest possible pleasure for the greatest number of people. By way of contrast it is difficult to see how murder would be a possible moral option if the purpose of life included living.

Further Nuances

No doubt you will have noticed that reference has been made to *types* of actions, and not just to actions. There is a good reason for this. Some people believe that every individual action is unique.

That is to say, all actions are particular. As a consequence it is argued that each action has to be morally evaluated separately and individually. Conversely, others believe that many actions are similar to others and that one can locate types of actions. The belief that actions are unique has certain implications for ethics. If it is true then there will be no place for rules. One could not, for example, have an absolute rule that truth-telling is always right. Each individual case of truth-telling would have to be considered separately. Given the various theories, a particular case of truth-telling may be morally right for different reasons. According to one theory it might be right because God commanded it. According to another it might be right because it produced the greatest pleasure for the greatest number. But if all actions are unique, an examination has to be made in each case. One cannot follow a rule.

Regardless of whether this belief that every action is unique is true or false, it is obvious that operating on such an ethic would be time-consuming and clumsy. Most people do not concede that every action is unique. They recognize similarities between individual actions. For this reason they are happy to operate on the basis of rules which cover actions which are of a similar type.

At this point a further distinction can be drawn. Some scholars argue that moral rules are of such a nature that they are absolute. Absolute rules are unconditional. They apply to every case no matter the time or the circumstances. Other ethicists affirm that moral rules are only general rules. They apply to the majority of cases but there will be cases where the rule does not apply. Three basic options are available in regard to the place of rules in ethics. Theorists can adopt no rules, general rules or absolute rules. Whichever position is embraced, it will make a distinct difference to the shape of the theory and its operation.

Motivational Theories

One can hardly reflect on the basic teaching of Jesus in the Sermon on the Mount (Matthew 5–7) and believe that morality is only concerned with the outward act. An internal element or motive seems to be an essential part of morality. Fairweather and McDonald provide us with a pertinent illustration (Fairweather, 1984, p. 65). They describe a situation where some young children are playing on an electrified railway line. Another child observes their play, and goes and tells their parents. What is the motive for the child's action? Is it because he is concerned for their safety, or is it because he bears a grudge against the children and wants to get them into trouble? Most of us would agree that if the action was out of concern for the children's safety then the act of informing was morally praiseworthy, but if it was to get them into trouble then it may be morally blameworthy. Another distinction seems justified when we examine this example. We can distinguish *intention* from *motive*. The child's intention was to tell the parents. His motive might be to get the other children into trouble. Roughly speaking, the intention has to do with the shape of what is to be done, and the motive is the reason for doing the action.

Careful consideration is required when dealing with motives. Motives can sometimes be confused with *dispositions*. People as moral agents have dispositions or general tendencies to act in particular ways in certain types of situations. In our example of the boy telling on the other children, it might be that the boy in question had a kind disposition. That is to say, he usually was compassionate and generous in the way he treated others. However, for some particular reason on the occasion in question, he may have acted in a different way. His particular motive, to get the children into trouble, would stand in contrast to his general disposition. Motives are more specific and directive than dispositions, since they relate to particular actions.

It is often conceded that a person has done the morally wrong thing for the right reason. Conversely, we can imagine someone doing the morally right thing but for the wrong reason. Actions and motives have to be evaluated separately. However, if, contrary to fact, motives and actions *could not* be separated then motives would become a feature of the action. In that case, the motive or motives could be listed as features of the action and what were previously called 'motivational theories' would be just another form of deontological theory. As it is, all we have to note is that morality is not limited to the consideration of whether actions are right or wrong. There are other dimensions, such as motives, to consider. This very fact might press us to conclude that the ethics of duty (or ethics of obligation) approach is both incomplete and inadequate, and press us to move towards a theory of virtue where the character of a person is assessed.

Mixed Theories

Mixed theories that attend to both features of the action and outcomes or goals are found in the history of ethics. Such theories have a foot in both camps displaying both deontological and teleological aspects. The trend in recent times has been to call theories that evaluate action in terms of a feature of the act, deontological. Any other type of theory is classified as teleological, hence mixed theories are now categorized as teleological. There is a convenience to this practice of only recognizing two types of theory but this practice has its cost. It leads to a lack of precision and the creation of ambiguity.

Criticisms

Fault has been found with the deontological approach to ethics because in some circumstances it seems manifestly clear that the consequences of an action *are* morally relevant. An example of such a situation is found in the stories coming out of the Second World War. Christian people hiding Jews in their attics were questioned by the Gestapo and asked if there were Jews in the house. Some lied and felt justified in doing so, for the consequences for the Jewish people had they been found would have been horrific. The people would have suffered in concentration camps and may eventually have been put to death. The criticism is that the deontological approach ignores both consequences and purpose. This criticism seems to have the support of Scripture at points. When the disciples of Jesus plucked heads of grain as they walked through a grain field on the Sabbath, Jesus dismissed a deontological interpretation of the fourth commandment with the words 'the Sabbath was made for humankind and not humankind for the Sabbath'. At the very least, Jesus' words indicate that Christian ethics cannot be exclusively deontological. Jesus seems to imply two things. The first is that the Pharisees have ignored the purpose of the commandment. The second is consequentially focused. It is that it is proper for the hungry to be fed on the Sabbath.

Teleological theories, on the other hand, have been condemned because the end or goal seems to justify the means. Many actions that intuitively seem wrong appear to be morally validated. While the criticism may be true of consequentialist theories, it does not seem to be true of teleological theories. Although teleological theories avoid this particular problem, we are still left with the question of whether or not a teleological approach to ethics is enough to encapsulate biblical morality. Many sections of the Bible, like the Ten Commandments, come across with great deontological force.

There is also a wider question in relation to the whole 'ethics of duty' approach, which covers both deontological and teleological ethics. Is an account of morality solely in terms of actions adequate enough to cover all the biblical material? The narrow focus on actions or types of actions yields a picture of the moral life that is less than adequate. Virtue theorists have criticized the 'ethics of duty' approach to morality on the grounds that on this type of account an individual's moral life seems to be made up of a thread of particular actions. Strung together like a string of beads, these pellets of moral activity by themselves cannot account for the moral nature of the agent. The 'ethics of duty' approach seems to give no unity to the moral life. More particularly, it does not account for the moral development of the agent. It seems to say that the history of the moral agent consists of just right or wrong actions at particular points. By way of contrast, the biblical notion of sanctification seems to allow for some sort of moral development. If sanctification does include moral development, then the 'ethics of duty' approach that restricts itself to mere actions clearly does not give an adequate account of morality.

Morality Explained in Terms of the Agent: The Ethics of Virtue

It is most appropriate that we turn at this point to the other major approach to ethics. Traditionally this strand has been called the ethics of virtue. Instead of focusing on action, the ethic of virtue centres on the agent. If the ethics of duty is about *doing*, then the ethics of virtue is about *being*. Character and disposition, rather than action, is the object of examination and analysis.

Aristotle presents the classical example of an ethic of virtue. Like the doctrine of Natural Law, Aristotle's theory of ethics is based on a teleological understanding of reality. Reason was the distinguishing mark of human nature, and happiness was the goal. While reason was the distinguishing feature of the human soul, it was not the only component. The soul was made up of rational and irrational elements (Vardy, 1994, pp. 40-42). Aristotle divided these two elements into two parts. The rational or thinking segment had a scientific part and a calculative part. The scientific part had to do with logic, facts, and truth. The calculative part had to do with evaluating and choosing. According to Aristotle, the irrational part of the soul also had two parts: the desiderative and vegetative. The desiderative or appetive part was associated with all the various particular desires and needs that people have. It is important to understand that these desires and needs could be channelled and controlled by the rational part. The vegetative part was the source of nutrition and growth and accounted for all those instincts necessary for survival such as eating, drinking, resting and procreating.

Both the rational and irrational elements of the soul gave rise to virtues. Virtues were those qualities that enabled a person to achieve directly or indirectly the *telos* or goal of life. The rational element gave rise to the intellectual virtues, and the irrational portion to the moral virtues. Vardy's fruitcake example explains the operation of the soul and the integration of the various elements:

> Let us suppose that the vegetative part of me needs sustenance or nutrition and growth. Now, the desiderative part of me desires cake rather than fruit. However, the

scientific part of me knows the fact that, given my current waist size, fruit will do me more good than cake will. So, finally, the calculative part of my mind thinks about the advisability of cake over fruit or vice versa, and comes to a decision: How about fruit cake? The scientific part of my mind will then be able to follow the precise instructions on how to make a reasonably respectable fruit cake of the health-food variety. Thus the vegetative, desiderative, calculative and scientific parts of my 'soul' have all come into play (Vardy, 1994, pp. 41-42).

Aristotle saw humans as social beings that lived together in community. The goal of happiness could only be achieved by individuals-in-community. The moral virtues were those traits or dispositions that allowed one to live happily in community. There were intellectual virtues associated with the rational element of the soul and these were cultivated through instruction or education. The moral virtues arising from the irrational component of the soul were cultivated by habit. To be a moral person one had to habituate oneself to have those traits or dispositions that would allow one to find happiness in community. Aristotle's theory of ethics included such moral virtues as patience, truthfulness, courage and modesty.

The ancient Stoics also developed an ethic of virtue, but it was quite different to Aristotle's. Since humans lived in a law-governed universe over which they had no control, it was not possible in the Stoic's view to set objective goals and achieve them. However, as rational beings, humans had control over their minds and emotions, so they could set subjective goals. The aim was to develop the thoughts, desires, and emotions that could live in a deterministic world without getting frustrated or disappointed. Subduing and controlling one's emotions was central to life. Whereas Aristotle favoured such virtues as temperance and justice, the Stoics prized virtues like self-control. In both Aristotelian and Stoic ethics the development of the character of the person who engages in moral action is uppermost. The traits or dispositions formed through the constant repetition of right behaviour enabled a person to live morally in the world. Instead of asking which action is right or wrong, this approach to ethics presses one to consider the kind of person who will be able to achieve the goal. However, the ethic is not limited to developing the right kind of being. Given that the trait of kindness is appropriate to the goal of a happy community, for example, then it will follow that all actions ought to be acts of kindness.

Modern Christian ethicists, like Stanley Hauerwas, who adopt an 'ethic of virtue' approach, see character as a basic aspect of human existence. For Hauerwas character is the manner in which the formation of the self takes place, and it shapes the nature and the content of the self. It is the integrity and consistency of the self that allows for stability and growth. Character is the basic expression of the orientation of life that gives unity and principle to the self as an agent of action. Because character is deliberative, it orders a person's desires, affections, and actions according to certain reasons rather than others. It is made up of a person's fundamental values, commitments and beliefs. These values, commitments and beliefs grant an understanding of the world from a particular perspective and this particular perspective helps the individual to interpret actions in the right way. It is only when the right (Christian) beliefs and commitments are in place that an individual will see and understand situations in the proper light. Obedience to the values and beliefs of the community of faith must precede understanding, for Hauerwas. If the question is asked 'Why should I, as a Christian, adopt honesty as a virtue?' then the answer would be 'Because it is necessary for my part in the community of peace'. The point to note is that character is the determinative element in moral behaviour for those who adopt the virtue approach to ethics.

Elements of the ethic of virtue are found within the pages of Scripture. Not only does the Bible provide us with information about human nature but it also locates and delineates the goal of human life. Moreover, in numerous places we find lists of virtues and vices. It may be significant to note in passing that many of the New Testament virtues are virtues of personal relationship and community. The lists include virtues like compassion, kindness, hospitality, gentleness, generosity, peaceableness, truthfulness, humility, patience and forbearance.

Conclusions

The options we have examined make the development of a vast array of theories possible. Deontologists can have differing sets of moral rules and different reasons for adopting the rules. Teleologists can have different goals and consequentialists different non-moral goods. Any group may operate on general rules, absolute rules or no rules at all. Virtue theorists may develop different accounts of human nature and locate divergent goals and as a consequence press for the maturation of different traits or dispositions. Historically speaking, however, only a limited number of theories have won widespread acceptance.

The fact that moral material contained in the Bible is spread across the range of approaches may seem to leave us with a dilemma. But in reality it does not. As we have seen, each type of theory displays weaknesses, and this fact may establish that by themselves each type of theory is inadequate. It may be that we need to take up complementary aspects from each type of theory. William Frankena pushes us towards such an approach when he discusses the relationship between the ethics of virtue and the ethics of duty:

> I propose therefore that we regard the morality of duty and principles and the morality of virtues and traits of character not as rival kinds of morality between which we must choose, but as two complementary aspects of the same morality. Then, for every principle there will be a morally good trait, often going by the same name, consisting of a disposition or tendency to act according to it; and for every morally good trait there will be a principle defining the kind of action in which it is to express itself. To parody a famous dictum of Kant's, I am inclined to think that principles without traits are impotent and traits without principles are blind (Frankena, 1963, p. 65).

There seem to be two gates into the moral field. One gate is through consideration of actions and the other through reflection on character. Problems occur when theorists are content with one half of the field, and isolate duty from virtue and principles from traits. Virtue theorists like Hauerwas make a strong point when they argue that actions are only ever interpreted in the light of a person's values and beliefs. But this does not imply that a principle cannot be drawn from the values and beliefs and used to morally evaluate particular actions or types of actions. The important point will be to understand the principle in the context of belief, and use it in the appropriate context. In the end I suspect that it does not matter which gate one enters through, as long as one keeps the whole field in sight.

Equipped with a basic understanding of what ethics is all about, and some idea of the type of accounts of morality that are possible, we can now focus our attention on the moral material found in the Bible to see what approach it takes.

Section Two

THE BIBLE AND ETHICS

Evangelicals believe that the Bible as a whole is the Word of God. This section interprets the Bible as a unit that reveals God's plan of salvation in history. The integrated story of salvation history provides the basis for an ethical theory.

CHAPTER THREE

Using the Bible in Ethics

Biblical Morality and Christian Ethics

A general distinction was made in Chapter One between morality and ethics. A more particularized version of this distinction must now be introduced. This is the distinction between biblical morality and Christian ethics. Biblical morality has to do with the morality found in the Bible. Israel's morality at the time of the Exodus is an example of biblical morality. It is encapsulated in the Ten Commandments (Exodus 20:1-17). Detailed accounts of this morality are spelt out in other parts of the book of Exodus, Leviticus, and Deuteronomy. One moral obligation, for example, placed upon the people of Israel at that time was the obligation to care for the poor and needy. Some provision for the poor was made by a law instructing the land owners to leave the gleanings, the ears of corn and other grain dropped by the reapers as they harvested, for the poor and the aliens (Leviticus 19:9–10).

If we were to list all the moral obligations and virtues found in Exodus, Leviticus and Deuteronomy we would simply be describing the morality of Israel. The question of whether this morality was obligatory for Christians today is not answered by describing the morality of Israel. We can still ask the question whether or not it applies to Christians today. Christians disagree on the answer to this question. Using Paul's statement that Christians are not under the Law, some ignore the morality of Israel. Others argue that while we are not under the whole package of the Law, we are still bound by the moral rules and principles contained in it. For the moment it does not matter who is correct. The task of Christian ethics is locating what is normative for Christians in this present age.

Some unreflective Christians believe that the revelation of God is exactly the same in any part of the Bible. These Christians would claim that the morality of Israel was normative for Christians today. For them, biblical morality and Christian ethics are identical. Christian ethics is rather easy for these people. They can take a moral rule, principle or virtue from any part of the Bible and without further interpretation apply it directly as moral guidance for Christians today.

Simple deliberation about some of the contents of Israel's morality would also suggest that this unreflective position is wrong. The rule about gleanings in Leviticus 19:9-10 is a case in point. One can imagine that this rule was adequate for the ancient people of Israel who lived in an agriculturally based society. The villages and towns were not far from the farms. But it is highly unlikely that this rule would be satisfactory for poor people living in huge modern cities such as London or New York. People in these cities do not live close to the places where the farming is done. Even if the poor could get transport to the farming areas they would lack the facilities to process and use the grain. The aphorism 'Time has made some ancient good uncouth' is applicable here.

A simplistic hermeneutic (way of understanding the Bible) that assumes that the revelation of God is exactly the same in any part demands that the Bible be used in this way. We need to note that the Bible does not declare that the revelation of God is the same in any and every part. In fact there are statements in the New Testament that suggest that parts of the Mosaic Law *cannot* simply be placed upon the Christian as a moral burden. Paul says that Christians are not under the Law (Romans 6:15). Indeed they are delivered from the Law (Romans 7:6). On the surface, these statements suggest that this unreflective approach is wrong. We will see later that the Bible does not see all its parts as interchangeable. Rather, the Bible sees God's revelation as progressive, moving through stages until it is completed in Christ. The moral elements of the Old Testament may well reveal a true morality, and still ring true to Christians today. But this may be because they are parts of a greater whole. We may need to base our Christian ethic on the greater whole. Only a proper understanding of the whole Bible will answer the question about the validity and application of the moral elements of the Law.

Hermeneutics, the Bible and Ethics

As previously mentioned, the study of this process of under-standing is called 'hermeneutics'. In general it is true that the shape of a Christian's ethic is determined by the way he or she understands the Bible. The ethic follows the hermeneutic.

Over the centuries, Christians have employed various hermeneutics in relation to the Bible. Arriving at an overall under-standing of the Scriptures, each of these understandings locates a dominant feature that sets the pattern for understanding the pur-poses of God. This pattern is then applied to ethical matters. Spohn (1984) has provided a useful summary of several of the more recent positions that will serve as illustrations and models of what a hermeneutic is and how one's hermeneutic determines the shape of one's ethic. The first model we will examine focuses on those pas-sages in Scripture that describe God's call to specific individuals like Moses or Elijah and infers that this pattern of relating to God is the pattern to be followed by all Christians. The understanding of the Bible that is arrived at in this way is one that sees the Bible as a book through which God speaks to people directly. God comes and speaks directly to individuals through the Bible and tells them what they ought to do. We shall call this approach to Christian ethics the Divine Command theory.

Since ethics is about what people ought to do, the command of God should provide the substance for ethics. Now it must be emphasized that the Divine Command theorists do not imply that God comes and speaks literally and directly to each individual. Rather the theory states that as Christians read God's word and reflect on their own situation they understand what God is commanding them to do. For many of these people the command of God comes as the voice of conscience. The content of the command does not come directly from God, it involves thought and deliberation, but the force of the command comes from God. To disobey the command is to disobey God. The sense of moral 'ought' that the Christian apprehends comes from the voice of God.

The hermeneutic employed by the Divine Command theorist is a simple one. The Bible is seen as the Word of God. When people of faith read the Bible, God tells them what to do. Since ethics is about what people ought to do, it is concluded that people ought to do what God commands. Now while there is truth in this theory, it is too simple. It leaves too much to the individual subject who is reading the Bible. It ignores the fact that the Bible itself presents a hermeneutic. The Bible as the objective Word of God gives many clues as to how it is to be understood. If the individual reading the Bible misses these clues he may well end up following a false command. The old Sunday School joke about the person who read in the gospels that Judas went and hanged himself, and then turned to another section of Scripture that said 'Go and do likewise', is crude, but it does illustrate an intrinsic weakness in the Divine Command theory. The theory does not help people to understand the Bible. The theory's great strength is that it understands moral injunctions as having the force of the command of God. That is to say, the theory appreciates that the obligatory nature of moral injunctions—the sense of 'oughtness' which comes with moral imperatives—comes from the fact that it is the Creator God who sets the direction and the goal of human activity.

Another influential hermeneutic that has generated its own peculiar ethic is that found in liberation theology. Arising out of the situation in the third world, this hermeneutic takes Israel's exodus from Egypt as the paradigm or pattern of God's relating to the world. The understanding of the Bible is that it is a book about how God liberates the poor and oppressed. According to this view, the big picture presented by the Bible is that God is on the side of the poor and oppressed, and works for their liberation. The conclusion drawn from this understanding, or hermeneutic, is that Christians must join in the struggle to liberate oppressed people for that is where God is to be found at work. God is committed to liberate the poor and oppressed, and those who serve him must display the same commitment. A more detailed analysis of the big picture would show, according to this view, that sin may be evident in the hearts of individuals, but that it is most evident in the social structures or arrangements that advantage some people and disadvantage others. True and lasting conversion will come only, according to this view, with the changing of wrong social structures. The task of the Christian is basically the task of changing wrong structures. This is the task of social engineering. If the structures of government or of the family, for example, are wrong and oppressive then the Christian's moral duty is to act to change them.

There are elements of truth in this perspective also. Of course Christian people are obligated to help the poor and change wrong social structures where it is within their power. But the hermeneutic of liberation theology seems to have adopted the Marxist perspective of collectivism. Collectivism is the view that society is more than the sum of the individuals who belong to it. According to this view the parts of society, the individuals who make it up, can only be understood in terms of the whole. Little significance is given to the individual members, for it is the social structures, laws, and attitudes that are significant. The weakness with this hermeneutic is that it does not, in the end, seem to be biblical. There is a great deal of evidence that suggests that the Bible does not hold that society is to be understood in purely collectivist terms. Also, the New Testament writers, while not disinterested in structural sin, seem to give a far greater weight to personal sin. (The particular issue of personal versus structural sin will be dealt with in more detail later in the book.) Again the point to note here is the link between hermeneutic and ethic.

One final illustration of a hermeneutic is seen in the case of Natural Law. Proponents of the Natural Law approach to ethics mentioned in the previous chapter believe that an understanding of the Bible, the big picture as it were, shows that there are purposes and goals inherent in things because God has made them. Moreover, this biblical picture of reality indicates, as does common experience, that ordinary people are able, without the help of the Bible, to discover the purposiveness embedded in reality. This discovery takes place by way of an intelligent examination of the world. The significant factor for ethics arising from this hermeneutic is that the God-given goals and purposes set the standard for behaviour. We ought to note that the big understanding of the Scriptures advocated by this approach contains many other elements. On this view, the Bible is basically concerned with how God saves his people. But this big picture includes the elements essential for an understanding of ethics. The key element of purposiveness provides the logic for an understanding of sin and the need for salvation. Sin is the failure of people to achieve God's purposes. Salvation is lifting the consequence of this failure.

Again one would have to concede that there are many elements of truth in this hermeneutic and ethic. Nevertheless, this approach has been rightly criticized. Perhaps the major criticism has been that the Bible actually teaches that sin has adversely affected human reason and that people cannot read off the pattern of God's purposes without the help of Scripture and the power of the Holy Spirit. The consequences of a Natural Law approach to ethics is that it lessens the importance of Scripture. The Bible now becomes just a moral reminder. God's general purposes, that are the substance of morality, can be known by anyone anywhere just by the application of reason. Advocates of Natural Law see this universal availability of moral standards as a positive feature. However, Paul and other biblical writers deny fallen human beings can understand the big picture of reality without the help of revelation. Moreover the Bible teaches that the original order established by God in Eden has been fractured and disordered by sinful humanity. Even if people could read off the order of the present world it would not be God's good and undefiled order.

An important observation can be made at this point. All the hermeneutical approaches we have discussed above have one thing in common. Since biblical hermeneutics is concerned with interpreting the Bible, these approaches are all concerned with locating or finding the meaning or significance of the Bible as a whole. Each of the above approaches has a different understanding of the significance of the big picture presented in the Scriptures.

Each locates what is the ultimate significance of the Bible and then draws out consequences for our understanding of morality. As a consequence each ends up with a different account of morality. Each produces a different ethic.

The difference in understanding and the difference in the big pictures drawn have to do with the way the various approaches interpret the Bible. That is, the variation has to do with differences in hermeneutics. Hermeneutics has to do with the principles they use to arrange and integrate the various bits and pieces of Scripture and the significance that is given to the various parts. If we are going to develop an evangelical approach to ethics we must now examine the principles that evangelicals use to interpret the Bible and then go on to observe the understanding or big picture this hermeneutic produces.

An Evangelical Hermeneutic

Since our understanding of the overall message of the Bible will shape and determine the nature of our ethic, we must give careful attention to the way we put this 'big picture' together. Putting the bits and pieces of the Bible together in many ways is like putting a jigsaw puzzle together.

The pieces of the jigsaw cannot be put together in any old fashion. Evangelicals believe that the Bible is the Word of God. Because it is the Word of God, there is an essential unity to the Bible. It is the story of one God working towards one ultimate goal and purpose. He may have immediate and intermediate goals and purposes along the way, but these all feed into his ultimate and final purpose. The Bible is God's message of how he has graciously acted in history to reverse the effects of sin and establish a new creation. Although human hands wrote the Bible, it was inspired or God-breathed. God was and is the author of the message. Moreover it is a living word. It is the message by which God continues to reverse the effects of sin and establish a new creation. When people read the Bible with an open heart, they engage themselves with the living God, not only as he has revealed himself in history but as he is today. Evangelicals believe these things precisely because it is what they discover when they read the Bible.

Several hermeneutical principles follow from a commitment to the Bible as a unified message from God. The first is that the Bible has to be understood in its own terms. Statements in the Bible must be understood in the biblical context in which they are found and proper account must be taken of the Bible's own structure. Let me illustrate these two points by use of analogy. Imagine someone receiving a 'Dear John' letter. (A 'Dear John' letter is a letter written by a person who wants to break off a romantic engagement.) Suppose that in this particular example a woman has written a letter that has two clear sections. In the first section she describes her affection for the man she had previously dated. She uses the word 'love' by which she refers to the emotional attachment she feels for him. In the second section she outlines the reasons why she does not want to have a permanent relationship with the man. The particular reasons mentioned are the facts that he cannot control either his money or his temper. She argues that this lack of self-control in these two areas would make any permanent relationship painful. Now if the recipient of the letter took the statement 'I love you' from the first section and concluded that this meant that the writer was anxious to share life with him on a permanent basis he would be taking the statement out of context. By ignoring the second section and isolating the statement from the context of the whole letter, he would attribute the wrong meaning to the statement and draw a wrong conclusion. In essence he would make the word 'love' mean more than it does in its original context.

Two factors help in locating the significance of a text. The first has to do with the type of literature and the second with the apprehension of the author's intentions. These factors are usually linked together. There are many different types of literature or genre in the Bible. Within the Scriptures there is a rich variety of material including narrative, prose, poetry, legal documents, letters, gospels and so on. Various authors adopt different literary genre to suit their purposes. The selection of one genre rather than another often has to do with intention or purpose. One would not, for example, use poetry to write a scientific report, or legal language to express feelings of love. Because the logic of each genre differs each piece of literature has to be understood in its own way. When the psalmist writes in Psalm 65:13 that the hills, meadows and valleys "shout and sing together for joy", the language is not meant to be taken literally. In this section of the psalm, the writer is using poetry to paint the richness of the scene when God visits a land and blesses it. The remarkable abundance is such that it is as though the hills and valleys shout and sing for joy. The use of such metaphors enriches our understanding by providing the appropriate emotional colouring; a suitable response to God's exuberant graciousness. While the language of poetry is suitable in the Psalms it would be unsuitable for framing a legal agreement where clarity and precision was paramount. A legal agreement would require words to carry their plain and literal sense.

Understanding the Bible is a complex matter. Gaining an overall understanding of the Bible is a three-stage process. The process begins with the exegesis of the bits and pieces that go to make it up. Exegesis is not limited to the study of word-meanings. It includes the structure of sentences, paragraphs, chapters and the text as a whole. Each of these linguistic units only reveal their meaning when they are integrated in the appropriate way. The study of the way linguistic units are integrated is significant for a proper understanding. Grammar and syntax are vital to an understanding of the structure of the text at this stage.

The careful student will note that there was another exegetical factor embedded in the 'Dear John' illustration. Mention was made of the historical context. The woman writing the letter and the recipient had been involved in a romantic relationship. Knowledge of this historical background made the letter easier to understand. Indeed some of the details of the letter provided clues to the nature of the historical background. The fact that the woman gives reasons for not wanting a permanent relationship indicates that they did have a relationship. Cultural background is also exegetically relevant. Different cultures have different ways of expressing themselves. The parable of the Unforgiving Servant in Matthew 18 may be a good example here. A man seizes his fellow slave by the throat. Given the culture this action may not signify that the man was trying to choke the fellow slave. In the prevailing culture it may have been a way of claiming a debt. Cultural elements will intrude into the exegetical process.

Beyond the exegetical phase comes biblical theology, the second step. This is the process by which the logical structure of the overall message is located. We will see later that the biblical revelation moves through a number of distinct phases. If we do not engage in doing biblical theology we might end up giving the wrong value and significance to the content of the various stages. For example, without understanding the progressive structure of the Bible we might conclude that Christians still have to offer animal sacrifices and worship at a temple in Jerusalem. Biblical theology is vital in the process of understanding the Bible as a whole and on its own terms.

Finally we reach the stage of systematic theology. This is the stage where particular bits and pieces from all over the Bible are collected together in a systematic way to form a more complete picture. If we did not go through the stages of exegesis and biblical theology before collecting the parts together, we run the risk of imposing our own understanding on the Bible. Without the two previous stages, bits and pieces of the Bible can be given the wrong significance and put together in an inappropriate way. Suppose, for example, we wish to have a fuller picture of the nature and character of God. If we neglect the first two stages of exegesis and biblical theology and move straight to the task of systematic theology, we can take bits and pieces about the nature and character of God and put them together in our own way. Without the controls of a biblical theology we might conclude that there were three Gods, or that there was one God who wore three different masks at different periods in salvation history. We would not be forced to formulate the doctrine of the Trinity, the belief that there is one God and three Persons, if we ignored the second stage of the process.

It needs to be recognized that understanding the Bible is an ongoing activity. The more we read it the better we understand it. This is because the three-stage process feeds back on itself. It is a recursive process. As we build our systematic understanding through the process of exegesis and biblical theology we find that our systematic theology throws light on our exegesis and biblical theology. As we get to understand the various parts of the Bible through exegesis we discover that we see the significance of the parts better in the light of the emerging fuller picture. In the same way our better understanding of the parts enhances our understanding of biblical theology and this, in turn, again improves our understanding of the more integrated and comprehensive picture derived from systematic theology. Again the analogy of the jigsaw puzzle is helpful. The more bits we put together the better we can imagine what the whole picture will look like. The more we understand what the whole picture looks like the more we are able to see where the rest of the bits and pieces might go. Scholars liken this process of understanding to a spiral—the hermeneutical spiral. The idea is that a line representing our understanding moves both upward and inward as it curves back upon itself. As the line moves along it curves closer and closer to a full and correct understanding represented by the axis of the spiral. In the same manner the more familiar we become with the Bible using this three-staged process the better our understanding develops.

An evangelical hermeneutic, or evangelical way of understanding the Bible, is multi-levelled. This three-stage process of understanding the Bible presupposes (i) that the Bible is one unified message from God revealing his nature and his purposes and (ii) that his nature and his purposes are revealed in progressive stages. Some may argue that evangelicals are imposing these two key ideas on the Bible. However, our argument is that these presuppositions are not imposed on the Bible, but discovered in the plain reading of the text itself. They are adopted in an attempt to let God's word speak for itself. If God is going to speak he must be allowed to speak for himself.

The detailed exegetical work underlying the biblical and systematic theology found in this book will not be recorded. Space will not permit it. The reader must trust, to some degree, that it has been done adequately. But this trust can be augmented by some examination. One test of the adequacy of the underlying exegesis will be the shape of the biblical and systematic theology presented. If these do not seem to fit the reading of the text then there will be room for challenge. But even if the exegesis is deemed to be inadequate the exercise of developing an ethic will not prove fruitless. The book will still provide the reader with a sound way of proceeding to develop an ethic from the Bible as a whole.

We have spent some time on the discussion of a biblical hermeneutic. The reason for this, you will remember, is that the hermeneutic determines the ethic. We must turn our attention now to the content of the big picture of the Bible emerging from the employment of our hermeneutic. This content will provide the shape of our ethic.

CHAPTER FOUR

The Schema of Biblical Theology

Developing a Biblical Theology

If the argument in the previous chapter is correct then we will need to focus on the second stage of our hermeneutic and discover the logical structure of the Bible as a whole before moving on to outline a systematic theology from the Bible. Many students of the Bible have noticed a basic structure to its overall message. A number of scholars have outlined this structure. (See Dumbrell, 1985; Hebert, 1950; Robinson, 1955; Goldsworthy, 1981 and 1991.) This structure becomes apparent if one focuses on the biblical themes of promise and fulfilment.

The themes of promise and fulfilment are set against the background of Genesis 1-11. The logic requiring the implementation of the process of promise and fulfilment is caught up in the movement from creation through the fall to a disordered and destructive world. God creates a paradise where humankind can walk and talk with him. To use Goldsworthy's description, in the garden we see God's people, under God's rule, in God's place. These three elements are the essence of the notion of the Kingdom of God. Despite the Creator's gift of life in a setting where all humankind's needs and desires are met in abundance, Adam and Eve violate God's just order. The breach of this order in the context of the Creator/creature relationship can only be seen as an attack on the majesty of God and the rejection of his Lordship. Genesis 4-11 records the disorder and destruction that follows humankind's disobedience. The thing that unites humankind in this period of history is its opposition to God (Genesis 11:1–9). Despite humankind's rejection of God's rightful majesty and his just order in creation, God immediately takes the initiative to restore things.

The attitude that rejects God's majesty and right to rule is called sin, and it leads to actions that are called sins. The story of God's activity in history to save people from the consequences of their sin, and reinstate his order and lordship, can be divided up into three basic stages. The first epoch runs from the promise to Abraham (Genesis 12) to the realization of this promise in the establishment of the historical Kingdom of Israel under Solomon. The second epoch commences with the decline of the Kingdom after Solomon and terminates at the end of the period of the prophets. The final period begins with the coming of Christ and concludes with the consummation of the age at his return.

The promise to Abraham that God would make him a great nation and bless him must, in the context, be understood to be an assurance of salvation. Moreover, this salvation would be extended to 'all the families of the earth'. The two great events of this first stage of salvation history are those of exodus/redemption and land/inheritance. The realization of the promise in history includes escape from bondage in a foreign land by way of the Passover, and the presence of God in the midst of his people through the instruments of covenant, law, tabernacle/temple, and priesthood. In a diminished way, the majesty of God is restored through the practice of worship, and God's just order is re-established through obedience to the Law. Many indicators are provided to show that this fulfilment of the promise can only be a foreshadowing of something greater to come. Unlike the situation in Eden, the sanctuary where God resides in the temple is veiled off from the people. The people continue to sin and sacrifices for sin need to be offered repeatedly. The archetypical rulers, David and Solomon, whom God has appointed through the symbolism of anointing, in the end, fail to obey God and keep his order. Like the rest of humanity they are slaves to sin.

The climatic significance of Solomon's reign has often been passed over or ignored. Without an awareness of the historical fulfilment of the promise to Abraham in the reign of Solomon, the idea that the Kingdom of Israel is a foreshadowing of God's greater Kingdom will not seem feasible. It is important that the notion of historical fulfilment be secured at this point. Robinson (1997, p. 10) supplies three compelling reasons for accepting the climactic significance of Solomon's reign. The first of these reasons comes from 2 Samuel 7, where God reveals that through David's offspring the Kingdom will be established. The second comes from 1 Kings chapters 3 to 10, where Solomon and his Kingdom are described at length. Not only has the whole of the Promised Land been captured and occupied but God has also given peace to Israel in fulfilment of this promise (8:56). Moreover Solomon excels all the kings of the earth and the whole earth seeks "the presence of Solomon to hear his wisdom" (10:24). Finally in a psalm 'Of Solomon', Psalm 72, the prayer is not only that "all nations serve him" (v. 11) but that all nations be blessed in him (v. 17). Clearly Solomon, in some way, fulfils the promises made to Abraham.

Because of Israel's failure to keep God's laws, the latter prophets project the fulfilment of God's promise to Abraham into the future. They predict a new exodus, a new Passover, a new inheritance, a new David, a new temple. In this new era, there will be a new covenant and the people of God will have new hearts. The significance of this last point should not be lost. The heart in the Old Testament is the inner being where the emotions, will and mind are located. Through the integration of these various aspects of the heart people formulate intentions. Unlike the people of Israel who were slaves to rebellion (Romans 6:17), the new people of God will be committed to obeying God's rule and maintaining his just order. All this will happen on the coming 'Day of the Lord'.

The New Testament writers identify Jesus as the promised Lord—the one designated as the true king. He is "the son of David" (Matthew 21:15; 22:45), "our passover" (1 Corinthians 5:7), the one who "dwelt among us" (John 1:14), and he offers up his "blood of the covenant" for the sins of many (Mark 14:24).

However, this final epoch of salvation history does not arrive all at once. There is a tension between that which has arrived and that which is still to come; a tension between the 'now' and the 'not yet'. The manner of God's rule being exercised over God's people in God's place has several facets. The nature of this tension is made apparent by Goldsworthy:

> In his first coming he (Jesus) is revealed as the last Adam, the seed of Abraham, the faithful Israel, the son of David. In his resurrection he, as the covenant keeper, is justified and accepted into the eternal presence of the Father. This representative and substitutionary role of Jesus only touches others if the Kingdom somehow comes to them also. This happens with the coming of the exalted Christ in his word and by his Spirit. Those who are united to him by faith find that they now experience the Kingdom tension in themselves. They are in the Kingdom in their representative, but in themselves they are strangers and pilgrims in the world. The resolution of the tension is promised in the return of Jesus to consummate universally what is already a reality in him (1997, pp. 42–43).

According to the New Testament writers, the death, resurrection and exaltation of Jesus as the Christ secures the long-awaited redemption: the goal of God's activity. In this way Christ establishes the rule of God and God brings people into his presence through Christ. The preaching of the events of Christ's life and death is the evangel or gospel; the good news by which all peoples are called to enter into the Kingdom. The redemptive pattern of sacrifice, forgiveness and restoration found in the Old Testament foreshadows the pattern found in the gospel. Hence the true significance of the practice of animal sacrifice in Israel is only discovered in the light of the gospel. Since the basic theme of salvation history is the redemption secured by God for his people, the gospel becomes the hermeneutical key to the Bible.

Two things become apparent from this brief outline of God's activity in the world. The first is the unifying theme of the notion of the Kingdom of God. The second point is that the nature and establishment of this Kingdom is revealed progressively. Although the phrase 'the Kingdom of God' is not used frequently outside the Synoptic Gospels, the underlying elements of God's rule over God's people are to be found everywhere. The rejection of God's rule in Eden, and the consequent fracturing of his order in creation, are followed by a series of revelations concerning the re-establishment of his rule and the restoration of his order. At a basic level the stages of revelation could be reduced to four. This would include Eden, followed by the Fall and then the Kingdom foreshadowed by Israel and the Kingdom established in Christ. But our brief outline of salvation history would suggest that it is a little more complicated. Goldsworthy (1981) suggests six stages are necessary to cover the picture revealed in the Scriptures. These are:

1. The Kingdom Pattern Established EDEN
2. The Fall ADAM'S SIN
3. The Kingdom Promised ABRAHAM
4. The Kingdom Foreshadowed DAVID—SOLOMON
5. The Kingdom at Hand JESUS CHRIST
6. The Kingdom Consummated THE RETURN OF CHRIST

The inclusion of stage three is justified on the grounds that the promise to Abraham incorporates two levels of understanding. The first level is fulfilled under David and Solomon and the second under Christ. Stages 5 and 6 are warranted because of the 'now' but 'not yet' tension in the New Testament. Some aspects of the Kingdom are realized in the death and resurrection of Jesus. Other components await the new age that will come with his return.

The common themes that flow through each of these stages bind them together, and vindicate the presumption that the Bible is one unified message from God. Dumbrell (1985), for example, shows how the themes of Jerusalem, temple, covenant, Israel and creation are taken up and developed in the movement of God's revelation. These five themes find their final development and expression in the vision of the new heaven and new earth in the book of Revelation chapters 21-22. The message is that through the stages of salvation history God "is making all things new" (Revelation 21:5). In his study of these themes Dumbrell shows that "the entire

Bible is moving, growing according to a common purpose and towards a common goal" (1985, Introduction). The study of biblical theology is not only the study of major themes but also how various parts of the Bible relate to these themes.

The Claim of Biblical Theology

We need to be absolutely clear about what is being claimed on behalf of biblical theology. The claim is not that the stages of progressive revelation are found in each book of the Bible. The argument is that the pattern of progressive revelation is found in the Bible as a whole. The pattern established by the stages of revelation has to do with the logic of the story as a whole and not the logic of individual books or sections. Because of the unity of God's action and message the various parts of the Bible hang on the skeleton of the logic of the progressive stages. Some parts of the Bible refer to only one stage of revelation. Others cover several stages. Some books, like Romans, cover all the stages. Nevertheless the logic of each book or section fits into the logic of the story as a whole.

For the purpose of this book, we will modify Goldsworthy's six-stage schema. The reason for so doing is that the promises to Abraham (Genesis 12, 15) are very general and on most occasions provide no content in relation to ethics. They promise a great nation and a land but do not generally give us any understanding of and the nature of the moral order imposed. From this point of view the promises are not helpful for ethics on most occasions. By way of contrast Israel and its laws supply a great deal of information about the shape of God's moral requirements. I, therefore, propose to adopt the following five-stage schema in the rest of the book on most occasions. Where the promises to Abraham are relevant to the issue at hand I will drop back to using Goldsworthy's six-stage schema.

1. EDEN The Kingdom pattern established.
(God's people under God's rule in God's place.)
2. THE FALL The rejection of the Kingdom pattern.
(The rejection of God's majesty and order)

3. ISRAEL/LAW The Kingdom foreshadowed.
4. JESUS CHRIST The Kingdom at hand.
5. RETURN OF CHRIST The Kingdom consummated.

Developing a Systematic Theology

With a clear idea of the different stages of revelation and how they are related, we are in a position to systematically integrate relevant bits and pieces of the Bible without distorting their significance. We can collect together the material from each stage and see how it is related to the other stages. In this way we will give the right weight or significance to the material in each section. For example, we can put together Moses' instructions in relation to divorce (Deuteronomy 24:1-4) and Malachi's word that God hates divorce (Malachi 2:16)[1] without accusing God of inconsistency. A law restraining a people who are slaves to sin (Romans 7:14) cannot be equated with God's ideal purpose. Moses' instruction regulates the behaviour of a hard-hearted (Matthew 19:8) and disobedient people. It does not provide an insight into the ideal.

An outline of the overall picture of the Bible is vital to a proper understanding of the Scriptures. The big picture provided by systematic theology will be a vital part of the process of understanding the Bible. We must leave the development of this outline to future chapters. For the moment the implications of this three-staged process must be considered.

The Implications for Theology and Ethics

Since God reveals himself and his purposes through progressive stages in history then biblical theology will be a necessary part of any hermeneutic. The implications for the study of theology are straightforward. We will not be able to take any part of Scripture and claim that it contains the message of the whole. It will not do, for example, to take the God who is revealed at creation and use this information to deny that God is Trinity. This is because later stages of revelation reveal that God is three Persons.

Given a biblical understanding of salvation history, the weight of the material in the historical foreshadowing by Israel cannot be given the same weight as the material on the fulfilment in Jesus. The theological significance given to animal sacrifice in the time of Israel, for instance, cannot be the same as the significance given to Christ's sacrifice on the cross. Christians are not obligated to offer animal sacrifices on behalf of sin according to the New Testament. In fact, to continue to offer animal sacrifices after the death of Jesus would be to deny the efficacy of his sacrifice for sin.

Just as the theological material of the Scriptures has to be weighed according to the schema of salvation history, so the moral material unveiled at the various stages of revelation will have to be given its appropriate significance. The obligation to leave the gleanings of their fields, although morally binding on the people of Israel, may not have the same significance in the lives of Christians in the 21st century. If we are going to understand the moral material in the Bible correctly we will have to take into account the structure of the biblical message.

The task of this book is to provide a biblical account of ethics. That is, the purpose of this book is to build an understanding of morality on the basis of God's revelation of himself and his purposes. In the end, our ethic or account of morality will be built upon systematic theology. But if our systematic theology is to be consistent with God's revelation it will have to be a systematic theology arrived at through an understanding of biblical theology. Unfortunately, many books on Christian ethics develop a theology without giving heed to the inherent progressive structure of God's word. By ignoring biblical theology these books invalidate their foundations. The hope is that the approach taken in this book will correct this tendency.

An Evangelical Hermeneutic

We are now in a position to understand what we mean by an evangelical hermeneutic. An evangelical hermeneutic is a biblical hermeneutic, a way of interpreting the Bible. The way is defined in terms of presuppositions, principles and rules. These presuppositions, principles and rules come from the three levels of the process of understanding outlined above. The second level of the process establishes the nature of God's revelation as progressive revelation. Israel under the Law foreshadows a reality yet to come. The pattern of salvation is the same in each stage of history. Salvation is by grace through faith. The actual mechanism of atonement varies. Animal sacrifice is replaced by the death of God's Son.

The essence of an evangelical hermeneutic of the Bible is that it makes the gospel the key to a right interpretation and understanding. The gospel is the proclamation that salvation is by grace through faith in Christ. This was the message preached beforehand to Abraham. It was foreordained before creation that Christ would be the saviour of the world and that he would suffer for the sins of others. The grace of God finds its ultimate expression in the death of Christ, and salvation is through faith in him and his work of atonement. The use of the gospel as the key to understand the Bible is the defining characteristic of an evangelical hermeneutic and the distinctive attribute that marks it off from other ways of interpreting the Bible. The great virtue of an evangelical approach is that it allows the word of God to speak for itself. It does not allow the readers to rearrange the message of the Bible to suit themselves.

CHAPTER FIVE

Creation Order

Let us continue to develop the analogy between understanding the Bible and putting a jigsaw puzzle together. After we
have put the jigsaw together we can stand back and look at the big
picture. From a distance, the overall shape of things will capture
our attention. The bigger shapes will dominate the scene. Close up,
the details will display themselves. So it is with the Bible. Imagine
that we have understood all the bits and pieces of the Bible and
have been able to put them together in the right way using our
three stage hermeneutic. From a distance, as it were, the stages of
salvation history will dominate. Close up the details will be clearly
revealed. Both overall shape and details are necessary parts of the
big picture. We cannot build an ethic on the mere skeleton of
salvation history. We need to include the details to fill out the
account. We need to construct our ethic from a fuller understanding of the Bible.

If this book were an exercise in systematic theology and not
ethics, I might attempt to provide an extensive understanding of
the Bible. Undoubtably this would take many volumes. Moreover,
the number of volumes would be greatly extended if I attempted to
justify my understanding and not just recount it. I shall not
endeavour to make explicit a full understanding of the Bible (if that
were possible) as attempts at recounting the fuller picture as well as
justifying it would take us away from our purpose. I shall merely
recount and draw on such aspects of the big picture that are relevant to developing an ethic.

In my judgment, the material relevant to developing an ethic
occurs at three different levels in the Bible. These are the levels of

creation order, personal relationships, and the Kingdom of God.
We shall deal with each of these aspects in turn.

Creation Order

In this book, I will argue that the original creation with its revealed
goals or purposes provides us with the basis for determining what
is morally good. Creation witnesses a plethora of individual things
come into existence, which are not found swimming in a sea of
chaotic disorder. The creation accounts emphasize the fact that
there is an intelligible arrangement to creation. The phrase
'according to its kind' is repeated some nine times to highlight the
fact that many of the created entities have certain properties in
common. Among the kinds mentioned in Genesis are plants
yielding seeds, fruit trees, birds and sea creatures. There is a
common nature found among things of the same kind. Birds share
common properties such as beaks and wings. Sea creatures share
characteristics that enable them to inhabit the sea. It is these
common characteristics or similarities that enable individual things
to be grouped together into kinds. Philosophers refer to this
arrangement, according to similarity, as 'generic order'.

There is, however, another kind of ordering that is evident in
the creation accounts. The various kinds of things are subsequently
arranged according to *purpose*. For example, mankind is given every
plant yielding seed, and every tree with seed in its fruit, for food.
The birds and the beasts and the creeping things are given every
green plant for food. It is clear that the purpose of plants and fruit
is to serve as food for other creatures. Moreover, mankind is given
an overall goal or purpose. Humans are to have dominion over the
earth. In the context of Genesis there is no doubt that this includes
multiplying in number and keeping the order which God has given
to creation. Dumbrell (1988, p. 20) reminds us that the word
'dominion' in the Bible means 'protecting the relationship for
which one is responsible; it is to serve others and to seek their
good'. Philosophers refer to this purposive order or arrangement as
'telic order' because it involves being ordered towards a goal or *telos*.

No complete account of the generic and telic ordering of creation is supplied in Genesis. Nevertheless the meagre account presented achieves its purpose. It creates the overwhelming impression that creation is ordered according to God's plan. God gives everything a nature, and this nature is in accordance with his purposes. Put another way, a thing's design is governed by God's purpose and his purpose becomes its goal. The relationship between nature and purpose, or, generic and telic order, is an intrinsic one. The goal governs the nature of the design. The goal is, in a sense, included in the design. God created kinds with certain purposes in mind. By the very act of creation these purposes were built into the nature of things. Things can be used for purposes that were not intended, but the nature or design of those things limits the range of uses. A stone cannot be food for humans and a tree cannot fly like a bird. Their design or nature will not allow this. The examples found in the creation accounts will illustrate the point.

Human beings are given a number of goals. One is to be fruitful and multiply. Another is to fill the earth and subdue it. In order to achieve this second goal, humans are given dominion over every living thing. In relation to the first goal humankind was separated into two sub-kinds: male and female. The different sexual natures given to these two sub-kinds were in accordance with God's purpose that individual males should be united with individual females to become one flesh (Genesis 2:24). Out of this unity would come the issue of children. According to Paul, the rejection of God's authority and the consequent violation of God's order (Romans 1:18) is clearly illustrated when women exchange natural intercourse with men for intercourse with others of the same kind and when men commit sexual acts with men (Romans 1:26-27). The different natures of male and female are such that they are designed to meet God's primary purpose for unity. Sexual intercourse between a man and a woman binds them together psychologically. From this unity comes the possibility of reproduction. Human sexuality may be used in ways that God did not intend. Homosexual intercourse, on the evidence available, does not seem able to secure the unity of marriage. Nor is it capable of leading to reproduction. It, therefore, fails to achieve God's purposes.

In relation to the purpose of subduing the earth, God provides humanity with a suitable nature. In the course of our examination of ethics we will see that a doctrine of human nature, or anthropology, is central to ethics. Every ethic is based on some understanding of human nature. The biblical writers use a variety of notions to describe human nature (see Cooper, 1989, chapters 2–6). Basically, the biblical writers recognize that humanity may be described from two different but complementary aspects. Humankind has an outer and an inner nature. The outer nature is the body. The actions of the body can be observed by others. The inner nature is referred to in three basic ways, which highlight various aspects of the inner being. They cannot be construed as parts.

The three basic aspects of the inner being are the soul, the spirit and the heart. The soul refers to the inner self. Humans are conscious of the self. The spirit designates the internal force that enlivens the soul and gives it direction. The heart identifies the integrated components of the mind, the emotions and the will, which enable people to think, feel, and choose. The integrated activity of the heart formulates intentions and intentions lead to actions when opportunity presents itself. Thus while the inner being cannot be observed, some clues as to its nature can be inferred from the actions of the body. Only God sees the true and comprehensive state of the inner being.

The fact that the mind can be aware of creation, and reflect upon it, provides people with the capacity to understand God's order and purposes. The emotions or affections locate things of value, and people become attached to them. The will provides the opportunity of choice, such that people can choose to do the right or wrong thing. In this way, human nature is appropriate to the goal of subduing the earth. Humans have the capacity to understand God's commands and ways. They can attach themselves to the purposes of God, and choose to obey him, or they can set their affections on other things and rebel against him.

There is yet another purpose that God had planned.

Genesis 3:8 indicates that it was part of God's purpose that human beings should share a friendship with him. Appropriately, they have the capacity to walk and talk with him in the garden. This capacity for a personal relationship with God is unique amongst the creation. Being personal and relational beings makes humans like God, in one sense. God, being a Trinity, is personal and relational, and so it is no surprise that humans are also personal and relational. Using their minds, humans can understand God's character and purposes. Through the operation of the affections and the employment of the will they can respond in trust toward God. This human capacity for personal relationships opens up the possibility of friendship with God. If human beings had a different nature or design, the goal of friendship might not be possible.

Nature and purpose are logically related. The fact that human nature has the capacity to think, feel, and choose means that humans can understand God's plan and choose to follow it. Nature allows a thing to achieve its purpose. But the design supplied also limits what can be achieved. For example, a stone cannot have unity through sex as its goal. The nature of a stone limits the purposes it may be used for. Just as nature limits the possible goals so the purpose given by God shapes the nature of a thing. But this shaping still allows a range of possible goals. For example, people can use their sexuality in a number of ways. Bestiality, homosexuality, promiscuity, adultery, and rape are all options for those who have inherited a human nature. But God's purpose, which ought to be humanity's goal, is that individual males and females, when they give expression to their sexuality, might give themselves to each other in service and find the unity of marriage. Clearly the capacity given to individuals by nature does not necessitate that only one goal can be reached. Nature is not totally determinative. A person may choose to be single and celibate. However when a person does not act in accordance with their nature, damage of some sort follows. There is a price to be paid for not keeping nature and purpose synchronized. The principle that misuse leads to damage is embedded right across the created order. It is a principle that follows logically from the idea that everything has a nature.

Given the creation account's emphasis on nature and purpose, the theology of the Bible would seem to give partial support to the doctrine of Natural Law discussed in Chapter Two. You will remember that the doctrine of Natural Law contained three basic claims. The Bible seems to support two of these claims and deny the third. The first claim was that things, especially persons, have a purposiveness that is part of their very being. The third claim was that the purposiveness revealed in reality sets the standard for the moral life. The goals that God has built into the various kinds of things that he has created determine what is morally good for these things. The second claim was that the purposive nature of reality could be discovered by an intelligent examination of the world. The biblical writers reject this second assertion of Natural Law (e.g. Romans 1:21; 12:2). Romans 2:12–16 suggests that people can understand only bits and pieces of the picture of reality. They can know that fidelity in marriage is good and lying is wrong, but they cannot understand God's plans and purposes in an integrated and holistic way. To do this they require a revelation from God.

The evidence that natural teleology is deeply embedded in the biblical narrative goes on beyond the creation accounts. It is found in all the stages of biblical revelation. After the rebellion of humankind against the rule of God, people were not able to locate their true purpose. A gap appeared between generic and telic order. Nature was separated off from its true purpose. Creation experiences the futility of not being able to secure its proper goals (Romans 8:20). However all was not lost. God put a plan into action whereby nature and purpose would be united again. This was a plan that God had had before the creation of the world. The historical sequence of events that led to the achievement of this goal takes us into the area of historical teleology or eschatology.

It must be noticed that natural teleology determines one of the major ways we use the word 'good'. The good for any kind of thing is found in its God-given purpose or purposes. Sticking to the example we have been using, the good of human sexuality is found in marriage. We will call the use of the word 'good' in such cases objective. This is because this use is based on the objective nature of the kind of thing in view. There are other uses of the word 'good' that are subjective. I might want to buy an old dilapidated car to participate in a demolition derby. I find a big old car with little miles left in it and no comforts and I say, 'This is good'. By this statement I mean that the car suits my purpose. The 'goodness' is tied to my purpose, and not to the nature of cars. In the study of ethics it is important not to confuse the objective use of 'good' with its subjective use.

God's plan for creation has a complicated design. Various things are arranged according to various purposes. It appears that the multiple and various purposes found in the created order fit together. There is to be harmony in creation. All the bits and pieces are to fit together in the right way. The Bible labels this harmony as peace. This is the way things were in the Garden of Eden before Adam and Eve sinned. The order untouched by sin provides the ideal for fallen humanity in the rest of the Bible.

The important point being made in the creation accounts is that there is an order to creation. The creation accounts are not concerned to provide a detailed account of the shape of creation, but they do demonstrate an objective order of creation. This is important because it is the basis on which all moral values will be founded. The fact that we don't have a revelation of the complete order in the creation accounts is significant, but not overwhelmingly so. We will discover the basic shape of this order by an examination of the rest of the Scriptures.

The Fall

The creation accounts of Genesis 1 and 2 are followed by a passage that describes the Fall (Genesis 3) and its consequences (Genesis 4–11). The Fall takes us from the state of harmony of Eden in Genesis 1–2 to the state of disorder and death in Genesis 4–11. How did one tiny event have such catastrophic consequences? In Romans 1:18 Paul uses two Greek words to summarize the event. The English equivalents of these two words are 'godlessness' and 'wickedness'. 'Godlessness' refers to a rejection of the majesty of

God. It is an attitude or way of thinking that refuses to honour the majesty of God. It refuses to let God rule. 'Wickedness' refers to a violation of God's just order. It involves a refusal to arrange things in the way that God planned. Paul joins these two words together in such a way as to signify that they are two aspects of the same reality. Logic confirms this unity. The rejection of God's right to rule expresses itself in a denial of God's order. The reality we meet here is the reality of sin. The consequences are consistent with the action. Humans were given the task of keeping God's order in the world. Once humans had rejected that order, the world became disordered and damaged.

From an ethical point of view, the significance of the Fall is twofold. The first point is found at the subjective, or personal, level. The creature adopts an attitude and stance that does not honour the Creator. The second has to do with the objective order of creation. God's good order is fractured and disordered by the activity of humankind. God's purposes have been ignored and rejected, and humanity can no longer reach its true goal. Nature has been separated from its purpose. Consequently nature, including human nature, is subjected to futility. Humanity rightly faces destruction unless it is saved. But even in the darkness of the disorder of futility there is the foreshadowing of hope. Noah and his family are saved and their salvation is by God's grace. Nature and purpose have been separated but there is hope of reconciliation.

The Fall creates a problem for some of our terminology. Prior to the Fall, nature was ordered. It reflected God's ultimate will and purpose. After the Fall, the natural order is distorted—but it is not chaotic or totally disordered. God's design is still evident but creation is like a jigsaw puzzle with some of the pieces out of place. This means we can talk about nature in two senses. The first has to do with the unspoilt order prior to the Fall. The second has to do with the distorted order after the Fall. Perhaps we should talk about *original* nature in contrast to the *empirical* nature that can be observed after the Fall. This book contends that the original nature, and the goals or purposes embedded in it, is the basis of our ethic and determining what is good. A further contention is that aspects of the framework of this original order can be viewed in the creation accounts, in the Law and Wisdom of the Old Testament, and in the person and work of Christ. The revelation of this framework enables the believer to make sense of empirical nature and to use the observations of empirical nature to determine aspects of reality not revealed in Scripture.

Israel and its Law

In Genesis 12 we are introduced to Abram, later called Abraham. Abraham had a right relationship with God. He was designated as righteous. This was not because he did not fracture God's good order. Nor did he refuse to rebel against God's majesty at points. The biblical narrative records his sins. Rather, he was called righteous because he believed God and trusted him to fulfil his promises. And God did fulfil his promises to Abraham. His descendants became a great nation and occupied the land promised to them.

It is significant that from the time the people of Israel moved out of Egypt, they signified, in a formal way, by their religious and cultural structures, that they were the people of God. The tribes were gathered around the tabernacle in battle order, symbolising God's presence with them. God was their leader (Numbers 2). He was at the centre of their existence as a nation. Furthermore the nature of the relationship between God and his people was formalized with the giving of the covenant on Mount Sinai. Later covenants reasserted the basic shape of this relationship.

Although the people of Israel had been chosen by God and formally recognized as the people of God, the history of Israel is a history of national failure. The people never lived out the possibilities found within their relationship with God. The Law mapped out the basic order of life that God wanted them to adopt. Their salvation from slavery in Egypt gave them a reason to serve him. They knew that he was a gracious and loving God. Yet rebellion maintained a hold on their hearts. The people continued both individually and corporately to disobey the Law.

The significance of this stage in salvation history for ethics is often over-emphasized. The Law of Moses does not provide a complete and binding guide to Christian morality. On the other hand it should not be dismissed as irrelevant. The basic shape of God's rule, and God's just order established at creation, is confirmed and further delineated in the Law. Yet it is delineated in positive and negative ways. For example the people of Israel are told *not* to commit adultery, a negative command.

Nevertheless the Law gives us, as Christians, a glimpse of God's just order. Aspects of the configuration of his good order are revealed. There is good reason for the negative aspects being included. The revelation comes to a people who have rebellious hearts. Even though God has called them and dealt graciously with them they are still, as Paul points out, slaves to sin. The negative aspects address this rebelliousness. The negative pattern is exposed in the Ten Commandments. Only three of the commandments are stated in positive terms. The rest are asserted negatively. The sevenfold repetition of 'do not' presupposes a spirit of rebellion and disobedience.

While Christians are not under the package called the Law (a package designated as the 'Old Covenant'), the moral elements in the Law are part of a continuum that gives shape to an ideal. This continuum reaches from creation to Christ. Many people like to divide the regulations and laws that give shape to God's covenant with Israel into moral, cultic and civil elements. In this way it is hoped that the cultic and civil elements can be jettisoned with the coming of the New Covenant in Christ, and the moral component retained. However the Bible itself does not operate in this way. The Old Covenant is seen as a discrete unified package with a number of aspects, not parts. These various aspects cannot be unravelled and treated as parts. Moreover the Old Covenant and its Law is seen as a shadow of the reality to come in Christ. The partial gives way to the complete. This is true of the cultic and civil aspects as well as the moral.

Nevertheless, the way the Old Covenant foreshadows the New Covenant in Christ means that it can play a role in helping us to understand the New. Nature and its purpose have not changed; they have just been revealed in a complete and startling way. For this reason, the moral elements of the Law cannot be dismissed. Paul declares that the ideal of gracious sacrificial love demonstrated by Christ on the cross incorporates the fulfilment of the negative aspects of the Ten Commandments (Romans 5:8). After citing four of the negative commandments he proclaims that "love is the fulfilling of the Law" (Romans 13:10). Jesus argues that the outward behaviour prohibited by the commandments is linked to an inner being which displays attitudes that are also condemned (Matthew 5:17–48). The negative attitudes of anger and lust are to be condemned and replaced with positive ones.

One can only conclude that there is continuity between the moral elements of the Old Covenant and the New. Frequently these elements are stated positively and are included in the ideals of the New Covenant. More often, though, the moral elements in the Old Covenant are stated negatively, but these negative elements point to and find positive counterparts in the New Covenant. For example, in Exodus 20:15 the people are commanded not to steal. By way of comparison, in Ephesians 4:28 Paul tells his Christian readers that they must no longer steal but work so that they may be useful and have something to give to those in need.

The Kingdom at Hand in Jesus

The relationship between nature and purpose was fractured by sin, but the two are united historically in the person of Jesus Christ. He is the one true human who recognizes the majesty of his Father and is obedient even unto death. Unlike the rest of humanity, who are godless and wicked, he is godly and righteous. All the elements of the moral ideal are realized and revealed in him. In him we see God's just and good order. Unlike Platonic thought where the moral ideal is an abstract idea, in biblical thought the moral ideal is more than just an idea in the mind of God. It is a pattern built into creation and distorted by the Fall. Jesus is the perfect man who fulfils the role God had given to humanity. In perfect obedience to the Father, he restores right relationships to the whole of creation. The whole of creation and not just humankind is redeemed

(Romans 5–8). Fulfilling the role given to humanity, Christ is the one who restores, and therefore maintains, the order of God. Those who participate in his death and resurrection through faith are renewed inwardly and await the redemption of the body. We must note here that while God's ideal is set in terms of natural teleology his purposes are achieved in history. This is a matter of historical teleology or eschatology. "The time is fulfilled, and the Kingdom of God is at hand" (Mark 1:15).

Just as Adam sets the pattern of rebellion and sin for humanity, so Christ sets the pattern of trust and obedience (Romans 5:12–21). Fallen creation delivers disease and death. Christ, as the Lord of creation, heals and restores people to life. His outward actions and his inner character are completely in accordance with the will of his Father. All his actions spring from the virtues of love, patience, kindness, generosity, faithfulness, gentleness and self-control. Jesus only does that which is good. No evil practice finds its way into his life. By faith, believers participate in the death and resurrection of Christ. In Christ believers have died to sin (Romans 6). For those in Christ, the only thing that counts is "faith working through love" (Galatians 5:6). Love is the law of Christ (Galatians 6:2). Love does good to all (Galatians 6:10). And, as we have seen, the good is determined by the nature God has given to things and God's purpose for those things.

While Christ renews the minds of believers in the present evil age (Romans 8:5, 12:2), the creation is still subject to futility. Creation is still to be set free from its bondage to decay (Romans 8:21). Until everyone has the will and capacity to maintain God's order, this present world will be marked by disorder. Even though Christians may attempt to keep God's order, many other people will not. Nature and purpose will not be completely united. Believers will continue to suffer an ongoing sense of futility.

Jesus' Return and the Consummation of the Kingdom

At the consummation of the new order, nature and purpose will be united across the whole range of reality. There will be a new heaven and a new earth. Generic and telic order will be coupled in the way God intended. The resurrection of the body will usher in an eternal domain. In the Kingdom, people will delight in the joy of right relationships while those who have rejected Christ and his gospel will face the judgment of God. They will experience the eternal disorder they have chosen.

Conclusion

In regard to the nature of reality in general, we can conclude that God has created various kinds of things and given them a nature. To have a nature is to have a design. The design of a thing is related to its purpose. Or, to put it another way, generic order gives a clue to telic order. In this regard we could agree with the proponents of Natural Law. However, the biblical writers will not admit that God's order can be read off from creation. There are two reasons for this. The first is that sin has disrupted the order. The second is that the human mind has been corrupted and cannot read nature correctly. There is damage to both the objective reality and the knowing mind. A disordered reality and corrupted minds present a double barrier to a proper understanding of God's order. However, the order can be known, and this comes about objectively through the revelation of the Word of God, and subjectively by the renewal of the mind and the work of the Holy Spirit.

Knowledge of the nature of creation and God's purposes for it can be found in the creation accounts, in the Law and Wisdom of Israel, and in the person and work of Jesus Christ. While the basic shape of God's order and purposes are given in the revelation of Scripture, not all the details are spelt out. Nevertheless, given the schema and the details available in the Bible, many other details can be inferred. This enables us to move into new areas as new knowledge of the creation is uncovered by the sciences. The array of kinds and purposes is vast, and the order is complex, but the biblical framework allows us to infer the direction that God would have us go.

The order established by God at creation with its inherent purpose is fundamental to Christian ethics. The purpose or goal supplies us with the content of what is good. Knowledge of what is good is essential if people are to love one another. For, as we shall discover, love is constituted by a commitment to the good of others. Love has an objective basis. This basis is found in the schema of creation established by God but fractured and disordered by sin. On any particular issue we will need to put together the relevant sections of Scripture so that we can know what is good in particular cases. The basic creation pattern is the starting-point for this exercise. The Law and the Prophets point to the original shape and purpose of God's good order and highlight the fractures and disorder caused by sin. Finally, the revelation in Christ gives us a glimpse of the completed and perfected order. With minds renewed by the Spirit of God through the work of Christ believers can use this information to discern what is right and good. Such discernment is the substance of wisdom.

From the aspect of nature, Christian ethics may be summarized as 'do good' (Galatians 6:10, Titus 3:1). The notion of good is clearly defined. It is determined by God's purpose for the kind of thing in question. The biblical writers, however, take up other aspects of morality, and it is to these aspects of morality that we must now turn if our ethic is to be complete.

CHAPTER SIX

The Ethics of Personal Relationships

ONE PARTICULAR ASPECT of the order of creation is taken up and given a great deal of attention in the Bible. This is the area of personal relationships. The central theme of the Bible is God's relationship with his people. Developed at both the personal and corporate level, this theme provides the substance of salvation history. While this vertical relationship between God and humankind is primary, it has implications for personal relationships on the horizontal level. Those who love God should love their neighbours. The reason why the biblical writers give the central place to personal relationships will become evident as we move through the various stages of salvation history. It has to do with God's purposes for humankind and humankind's role as God's vice-regent. Humankind is charged with keeping the world in order and this order includes relationships between humans. Tracking the course of personal relationships through salvation history will reveal the standard that God had in mind.

Creation

The problem posed for us here at the beginning of the story of salvation history is the problem posed for all historical accounts. Unless a prior story has been told, characters are introduced about whom very little is known. It is only as the story progresses that the dimensions of character are spelt out. When we read a story for a second and third time, nuances surface which may have been missed on the first reading. For instance, as the story of God's activity in salvation history unfolds, the evidence accumulates to suggest that God has a triune nature. He is three persons but only one divine Being. These persons are eventually identified as Father, Son, and Holy Spirit. Consequently the early church seized the intimations in the biblical text and formulated the doctrine of the Trinity as part of the confession of the Christian faith. Its inclusion in the early creeds testifies to its importance. The doctrine of the Trinity declares that God is not three gods nor is he one God playing out three different roles. It proclaims that each person of the Godhead is a genuine person and that each person relates to the others. The God who creates is a God who is personal and relational.

Theologians use a Greek word to describe the nature of the relationships in the Trinity: *perichoresis*. Translated into English this word describes a 'mutual indwelling'. So intimate and strong is the relationship between the persons of the Godhead that it can only be described in this way. Each person of the Trinity understands completely the thinking and values of the other two. And each person of the Trinity commits themselves utterly to achieving the plans and purposes of the others. Even though the persons of the Trinity have different roles, the community of the Godhead is one in heart and mind. The Persons of the Trinity love one another (John 14). In the context of the Trinity, love must be understood as a commitment to please the other. As the three persons of the Trinity relate on the basis of absolute love, there is no exaggeration to claim that God is love (1 John 4:16). A study of the nature of God's love shows that it is steadfast love. It is gracious and unconditional. It is demonstrated in his treatment of rebellious Israel. God shows patience because he is other-person-centred. He desires that people enter into the good he has created for them. In this sense, God is humble and counts the good of others above his own interests. God's love finds its final and total expression in the love of Christ. Jesus humbled himself and was obedient even to death (Philippians 2:5–11). He died to save his enemies (Romans 5:1–11). God's love is multi-dimensional. The essence of love is a total commitment to the good of the other but it also embodies graciousness and humility.

If we let a circle stand for each person of the Trinity, and an arrow for the relationship of love, then we can draw the doctrine of the Trinity in the following way.

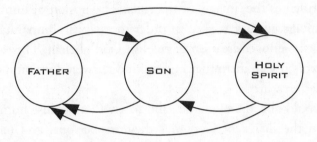

The essential pattern of personal relationships found within the Trinity may be drawn as follows. We will call this a mutual love relationship.

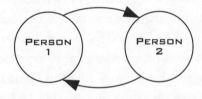

Human beings are also personal and relational. In this sense, and only in this sense, they are like God. In this regard we might say that humans are made in the image of God. But we must be cautious at this point. While Genesis 1:26-27 declares that humankind was made in God's image, it does not directly refer to the similarities between humans and God. To the modern western mind the word 'image' gathers up the notion of the repetition of an original pattern. A reflection in a mirror would be a good example of the modern notion of image. While the image may not be an exact replica, depending upon the quality and shape of the mirror, there would be clear points of similarity. If Genesis 1:26–27 did refer to a mirror image then we might be able to argue that humans are personal and relational beings because God is personal and relational. However the use of the word 'image' in the ancient Near East does not justify this inference. In its historical context, the word had to do with *function* and not nature. After conquering foreign nations, ancient kings would set up images or busts of themselves in the land they had conquered to remind their vanquished subjects that they, the conqueror, ruled their land. The conqueror exercised his rule through a vice-regent set over the foreign nation. The vice-regent ruled as the 'image' of the ruler. The notion of humankind as the image of God is used in order to establish humanity as the vice-regent set over creation to rule on God's behalf. The text goes on to explicitly confirm that humankind is given dominion over all the other creatures.

It would not, therefore, be valid to say that because humans are made in the image of God that they are personal and relational beings just like God. However there is no need to employ this inference, for the text goes on to say that human beings were created male and female. The particular male and female God creates go on to display all the features of persons. They think, trust, feel, believe, choose and act. It is clearly evident that human beings are personal beings. The fact that it is not good for man to be alone (Genesis 2:18) also indicates that humans are relational beings. However, only one type of personal relationship is specified in Genesis 2. We are told that a man shall leave his father and mother and cleave to his wife and the two shall become one flesh. Marriage is highlighted because it is the essential social unit. From marriage come new personal and relational beings. It is perfectly appropriate and fitting that new personal and relational beings, children, should issue from a personal relationship. Of course there are a range of personal relationships outside marriage, but these are not the concern of the writer in the first three chapters of Genesis. Chapters 4–11 will give some attention to other personal relationships.

The pinnacle of the six days of creation is reached on the seventh day (Genesis 2:1–4). At this point in the drama God rests. God ceases from his work and takes time to enjoy the order and relationships he has established. In Old Testament thought, the primary element in rest is not ceasing work, but enjoying the relationships set up by the creation. God's rest included walking and talking with Adam and Eve in the garden (Genesis 3:8). This notion of rest is delineated more clearly as the story of salvation unfolds. Adam and Eve, too, enjoyed rest. They walked and talked with God and lived in a garden that provided food in abundance without the exertion of work. Dumbrell reminds us that Genesis 2 provides a model of what the later Sabbath day was to represent (Dumbrell, 1988, p. 19). Rest is a time to enjoy the harmony of right relationships. Later disclosures in Scripture inform us that rest only comes when there is peace. The ancient Hebrew concept of peace was much richer than our modern idea. Our modern concept refers to a state of affairs where hostility has ceased; a time when there is no animosity or fighting. The biblical concept designates a more positive state of affairs where everyone delights in God, delights in their fellow human beings, and delights in the creation order.

It is not too much to assume that the relationship between God and the first humans was one of mutual love, even though the nature of the relationship is not specifically stated in these terms. Walking and talking with God in the garden does not necessarily indicate a mutual love relationship. All that we can say at this point in history is that the relationship appears to be a good one. But as we move through salvation history clear indications are provided that will justify our assumption. Later, well after the Fall, the dimensions of right relationships are spelt out. When God reveals his will for the people of Israel in the Law, right relationships are characterized by love. The Law may be summarized as loving God and loving your neighbour (Deuteronomy 6:5, Leviticus 19:18). Prior to the Fall Adam and Eve shared a right relationship with God. Hence we infer that they shared a love relationship with him. God's relationship to Adam in the garden may be represented in the following way.

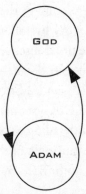

We will have to make a distinction between loving God and loving one's neighbour. As we have observed in the previous section, love is a commitment to the good of its object. Clearly humans cannot secure God's good. God does not have needs to be met in the way that humans do. Nevertheless God desires and wills the good of his creatures. By doing good to their neighbours, humans can please God. In this way they do his will and fulfil his desires. They can please him by obeying his will and sustaining his planned arrangement for creation. To love God is to please him. In this sense to love God is to recognize his majesty and worship him in obedience. Consequently we can say that humans can love God, and not imply that they are somehow fulfilling some inadequacy in God. On the other hand, to love one's neighbour is to be committed to his or her good, and meet his or her needs and desires. Keeping this in mind, we can represent the relationship between Adam and Eve in the garden before the Fall in the following way. Adam and Eve appear to share a mutual love relationship.

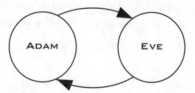

The rest and peace experienced in Eden is fractured and destroyed by the Fall. But rest and peace remain God's *telos* for creation and humanity.

It would be both appropriate and beneficial to make a comment on methodology at this point. It is clearly evident in this last section that in drawing up the big picture of the Bible, we are maintaining the shape and logic of the story by following the temporal order of salvation history. This is the order discovered by biblical theology. At the same time, we are filling in details of the picture that are not given in the text of Genesis 1 and 2 but are given in other parts of the Bible. This is the function of systematic theology. Our argument has been that provided this 'detailing' is based on sound exegesis and does not distort or devalue the logic of the progressive revelation of salvation history, then it is authorized by the Scriptures.

The Fall

In his account of the fallenness of humanity in Romans 1, Paul provides us with theological insight into the nature of the Fall. Adam and Eve's action in eating the apple was a manifestation of both ungodliness and wickedness. The Greek word for 'ungodliness' refers to an attitude that rejects God's majesty. Ungodliness denies the Creator's right to rule. The English word 'ungodliness' today generally refers to wrong behaviour. But the Greek word refers to an attitude that questions the majesty of God and his right to order reality. The Tempter denies God's word and order, and suggests that the power of choice has placed the right to order reality in human hands (Genesis 3:4–5). The power to choose is a seductive one. Surely Adam and Eve, the Tempter suggested, have the wisdom and discernment to know what is right and good.

Temptation is perverse. In order to question God's majesty one has to take the right to rule out of God's hands in order to see if it belongs there. The fact that humanity can question God's majesty, and appear to take the right to rule out of his hands, incites an attitude of rebellion. The power to choose whether or not to obey God is seductive. It implies that power could be in the creature's hands, and with it a right to re-arrange reality in the creature's own way. But for the creature the power to choose leads to either obedience or disobedience. It is a very limited choice.

Wickedness is the violation of God's order. Ungodliness and wickedness go together. They should not be separated. The rejection of God's right to rule inevitably leads to the infringement of God's proposed arrangement. The ungodliness of Adam and Eve fractured the right relationship that they had with God, as well as the right relationship they had with each other. They hid from the presence of God in the garden, and they concealed themselves from each other by the use of clothing. The general order that God had arranged had been fractured. And while the attitude of ungodliness prevailed, it would remain fractured.

There is another aspect to ungodliness. The attitude that fails to accept God's majesty and right to rule also fails to *trust* God. Paul gives us another insight into the nature of sin in Romans 14:23 where he declares that "whatever does not proceed from faith is sin". Adam and Eve failed to believe that God's order was for their good and consequently did not trust in that order. In essence, they did not believe that God loved them, and they saw no grounds for trusting God. They did not believe that God was totally and utterly committed to their good. The consequent lack of trust shattered their personal relationship with God, and they were appropriately dismissed from his presence.

Here we need to note an important implication. Immorality is not only an offence against God's general order and purposes; it is a personal injury and affront to God. Stealing from a neighbour is clearly a sin against the neighbour, but it is primarily a sin against God. It manifests an attitude that denies God's right to rule. This idea that all immorality is an offence against God is not only found in the account of the Fall. It emerges again at numerous points in the Old Testament. Two examples will be enough to illustrate and endorse the point. In 2 Samuel 11 and 12, we read of the account of David's adultery with Bathsheeba and the consequent killing of Uriah. When David is confronted by Nathan the prophet over the matter his reply is "I have sinned against the Lord" (2 Samuel 12:13). David's confession is made even more emphatically in Psalm 51:4: "Against you, you only, have I sinned". Proverbs 14:31 also confirms the point when it declares that "Whoever oppresses a poor man insults his Maker, but he who is generous to the needy honours him". The same idea is found in the New Testament. For example, James points out that all the moral laws come from God and to break one law is to offend him (James 2:8–11). God's role as Creator means that it is God's order that is fractured and God's purposes which are denied. Generic and telic order are inextricably tied to the person of the Creator. Consequently, immorality is chiefly an offence against God.

Given that morality has to do with the general nature of the various kinds of things in the created order and their God-given purpose or goal, it is easy to see how secular ethicists can claim that morality has nothing to do with religion. Secular ethicists can observe some order in creation and use it as a basis for ethics. However they do not believe it is the Creator's order. They can isolate this order from God's creative act and purposes, and declare that morality is independent of God. Many ethicists today go even further in their secularization of ethics. They declare that there is no telic or purposive order in creation, and that the generic order is open to manipulation or change. Since there is no God, and creation is inanimate, there is no fixed purpose to things. People are free to establish their own goals. In the area of human sexuality, for example, it is argued that people are not bound to use their sexuality in marriage. They are free to be homosexual, promiscuous, bisexual or whatever. The Bible, however, does not allow us to go in any of these directions. Proverbs 16:25 seems apt at this point: "There is a way that seems right to a man but in the end it leads to death".

Adam's choice sets the parameters for the rest of humankind. The Psalmist laments, "They have all turned aside; together they have become corrupt; there is none who does good, not even one" (Psalm 14:3). Likewise in Romans 5:12 Paul proclaims that "sin came into the world through one man, and death through sin". Later in 1 Corinthians 15:22 he argues that just "as in Adam all die, so also in Christ shall all be made alive". The assured implication of these verses is that human beings after the Fall were not free to desist from sin. In some way, all humanity participated in the original sin of Adam. Coming into consciousness through conception and birth, all human beings are seduced by the power of choice, and all choose for self and not for God. Removing themselves from a right relationship with the loving God, humans cannot but choose for self. They wilfully confirm the choice of Adam in their own lives. All people become aware of an order they did not create, yet they refuse to seek and to serve the One who created that order. At the basis of this choice is an attitude that refuses to trust God. Reference to this attitude should be written with a capital 'S'. It is (S)in that leads to the actions we call sins. It is this attitude that fractures a right and proper relationship with the living God.

We can capture the important elements of the Fall concerning personal relationships in a diagrammatic way. Using the symbols of circles and arrows adopted above, God's relationship with Adam can be represented in the following way. We must remind ourselves that this is the pattern that all humanity followed.

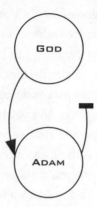

As we observed, the relationship between Adam and Eve was also affected by the Fall. This was indicated by the fact that they covered their nakedness. The openness found in the unity they previously enjoyed was marred by their new attitude to God and others. If God cannot be trusted, then neither can one's neighbours. Distrust is endemic. We can represent the relationship between Adam and Eve after the Fall in the following way.

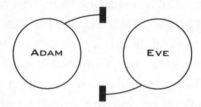

This pattern is applicable to all human relationships after the Fall. Humans will not graciously commit themselves utterly and totally to the good of others. They may be willing to do good at points, but not in the total way required by God. God must now set about redeeming the situation.

Israel and the Law

As we have seen, in Genesis 12 we are introduced to Abraham, who is to be the father of the nation of Israel. Previously in Genesis 6:8 we have been informed that Noah found grace in the eyes of God. Consequently he and his family were saved from the flood. In chapters 10 and 11 we discover a genealogy that traces the line of God's grace from Adam's son, Seth, through Noah, to Abraham. In his grace God made a promise to Abraham that his offspring would be as numerous as the stars in the heavens. We are told that Abraham "believed the LORD, and he counted it to him as righteousness" (Genesis 15:6). Abraham trusted that God would deliver what he promised. The element of trust lacking in Adam and Eve is found in Abraham in relation to the promise of God, and this is seen to constitute a right relationship with God. Trust is of the essence of right relationships. God loves Abraham, and Abraham trusts and obeys God in relation to his promise. In this regard Abraham is committed to pleasing God and fulfilling his purposes.

At other points in his life Abraham fails to trust God and he is not faithful to God's order (see Genesis 20). His trust seems to be selective and partial. Or perhaps it is that after his faith fails he repents and recommits himself to God. Nevertheless, despite Abraham's moments of unfaithfulness, God remains faithful to Abraham. The relationship between God and Abraham may be diagrammed in the following way. The dotted line indicates an incomplete or partial commitment to please God. It represents the condition of faith exercised by a person who is habituated to sin. There is willingness marred by incapacity.

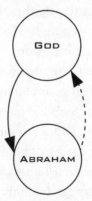

In Genesis 15 we read that God made a covenant with Abraham. Before we turn to the content of this covenant we need to consider its form. A covenant in the ancient Near East was a ritual by which the terms and shape of an existing relationship were given formal recognition. Abraham had a relationship of trust in God before the covenant was made. Likewise God had been gracious to Abraham and his ancestors before the ritual was performed. The terms of the relationship are spelt out in Genesis 15. God will give Abraham an heir. In fact, his offspring shall be like the stars of heaven in number and they will occupy a particular land: the Promised Land. The land is marked out in terms of the people who occupy it. Before all this would happen, however, Abraham's offspring will be aliens in a foreign land where they will experience slavery and oppression.

God kept his promise, and by the end of the Pentateuch we read that Abraham's offspring were a great nation waiting to enter the Promised Land. Numbers 2 informs us that there were six hundred thousand males over the age of twenty in the group that moved through the wilderness. Before the nation moved into the Promised Land, God made a covenant with the people at Mount Sinai. In this covenant, delivered through Moses, the terms of the people's relationship with God are spelt out. God had shown his love for the people of Israel. He had brought them out of the land of Egypt, out of slavery (Exodus 20:2). After hearing all the terms of the covenant all the people declared their allegiance to the Lord and affirmed their obedience. They declared: "All the words that the LORD has spoken we will do" (Exodus 24:3). In the light of this commitment, we might anticipate that the children of Israel would maintain God's order by keeping his Law, but the notion of original sin leads us to another conclusion.

By the time of Jesus, the thrust of the Mosaic Law was encapsulated in the two great commandments (Matthew 22:34–40; Luke 10:25–28; Mark 12:28–34). The Mosaic Law was seen to be God's fatherly instruction, and in it he decreed that the people should love God and love their neighbours. There is no doubt that the aim of the Law was to establish mutual love relationships. Yet the history of Israel demonstrates that this ideal cannot be achieved without God's divine intervention. Even though, unlike the rest of the nations, the people of Israel had insights into what is good and right through the Law, they continued to rebel against God's rule. While they had knowledge of what was good for them, they failed to prosper because they were slaves to disobedience. Much later in the history of Israel, Jesus used the notion of 'hardness of heart' to describe the condition of the children of Israel in the days of Moses (Mark 10:5). He indicated that they were corrupt in their inner being. By the exercise of the mind, emotions, and the will, they formulated intentions that were not in accordance with the Law of God. Moreover, these intentions were fixed and unchangeable. They would not or could not change their ungodly attitude.

Before we go on to observe the indications in the prophets about how this condition could be redeemed and transformed, we need to notice that God's covenant with Israel recognized and took account of Israel's sin. By his grace God was present with his people. His presence was located in the sanctuary of the tabernacle and later in the temple. Unlike Adam and Eve in the garden, the people of Israel did not meet with God face to face. God was present, but hidden. The people's access to God was partial and incomplete. Once a year the High Priest, representing the people, could enter the Holy of Holies and make a sacrifice of atonement for their sins. Because of sin the people's fractured relationship with God could only be maintained by a system of sacrifices. Under this regime the life of faith was a constant repetition of sin, repentance, sacrifice and atonement.

In the temple, there was a veil or curtain between God and his people. Because of the attitude of their hearts the people of God were denied direct access to God. As a consequence their relationship was not a full-blown mutual love relationship. It could be represented in the following way:

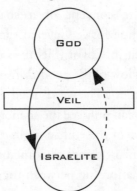

There are numerous indications in the Old Testament that God would one day take action to redeem the fragmented and futile condition caused by sin. Jeremiah, for example, predicts that God will make a new covenant (Jeremiah 31:31). Unlike the Old Covenant at Mount Sinai, the pattern of God's order revealed in the Law would be written on their hearts. The indication here is that people would know and understand God's order for creation and be committed to bringing it about. Their minds and wills would be renewed. The spirit of rebellion against the authority and majesty of God would be replaced by a spirit of obedience. Internal motivation would replace external constraint. The prophet Joel also predicts God's divine intervention in the future (Joel 2:28–32). He declares that God will pour out his Spirit on all flesh. During the period of the Law and the Prophets, the Spirit of God had come powerfully upon individual people and empowered them to undertake particular tasks and roles. Priests, judges, kings and prophets were among those who received this gift of God's empowering presence. But the Spirit of God was given sporadically and only for a brief period of time. It did not remain after the task or role had been accomplished. The prophet declares that the future downpour of the Holy Spirit will be on all flesh. The predictions of both Jeremiah and Joel are amongst the many elements of Old Testament prophecy that are taken up in the preaching of the gospel of Jesus Christ.

The Kingdom at Hand in Jesus

When speaking about the ministry of Jesus, the writer of the letter to the Hebrews uses the concept of a shadow to describe the relationship between the Mosaic Covenant found in the Pentateuch and the New Covenant in Christ (Hebrews 10:1). He declares that "the Law has but a shadow of the good things to come instead of the true form of these realities". The words used in this passage create the image of a people who can only see the shadow of a structure and not the form and substance of the edifice itself. The Mosaic Law is seen as a witness to the shape of things to come but not the substance of the thing itself. The relationship between the shadow and the reality to come is spelt out in terms of an incompleteness that implies an inadequacy. The sacrifice of the blood of bulls and goats was not adequate to take away sin for it had to be repeated year after year. But Christ offered a single sacrifice for all time and this sacrifice "perfected for all time those who are being sanctified" (10:12, 14). In the same manner the writer proclaims that the sanctuary in the temple was but "a copy and shadow of the heavenly things" (8:5).

In our outline of biblical theology, we have used the notion of model rather than shadow. This has been a conscious decision, and one that does not distort the understanding of the relationship between the New and the Old Covenants. The basic idea that the fundamental shape of the future reality is revealed in the Mosaic Law is carried by both these images. Both transport the idea that while the general shape is revealed, the details and substance remain hidden. In regard to human relationships with God the general pattern of things is contained in the Law. Humanity's relationship with God is broken by sin. The price of human wrongdoing and rebellion is death. This death is both physical and relational. After an allotted time, people cease to be at the level of bodily existence, and are cut off from a direct and intimate relationship with God. This is spiritual death. By God's grace, under the Old Covenant, people are able to have an indirect relationship with God through the temple. The price of sin is paid by the death of a goat or a bull substituted on their behalf. But the substitution is only temporary. It points to a substitute that is necessary for final and complete forgiveness of sin.

In the New Covenant it is revealed that the substitute is Jesus. When the New Testament writers reflect upon the forgiveness of sins and the re-establishment of a right relationship with God, they do so in terms of personal relationships. If the person of God is offended by personal beings then the price must be paid in personal terms. Within the framework of personal relationships, the price and nature of forgiveness must be personal. When a person forgives the wrong and hurt that another person has done to them, the cost is personal. The forgiving person has to absorb the wrong and the hurt of the other and not put it back upon the wrongdoer. The New Testament interprets and explains the death and resurrection of Jesus, the Son of God, in these terms. Jesus died for the sins of humankind. Jesus undergoes the physical and relational death that all humanity deserved. In doing this he represents humankind. Because God is Trinity and Jesus is the son of the Father, then the death of Christ on the cross is the one great act of forgiveness. In his death and abandonment by the Father, the Son absorbs the consequences of humanity's sin into himself. The Trinitarian God is able to forgive in this way and the price of sin is not placed upon the sinner. Nor is the burden of punishment placed upon a third party. The penalty is borne by the One who is sinned against.

The work of Christ on the cross is referred to in a number of ways in the New Testament. A wide range of words is used to describe and interpret the action. The event can be described in terms of redemption, sacrifice, atonement, justification and reconciliation. Some of these describe the mechanism, and some the outcome. Through a sacrifice, atonement is made. People's lives are redeemed. Those who trust in the sacrifice provided are given a right relationship with God. Peace is made between God and those who rebelled against his majesty. God and sinners are reconciled. The new relationship may be drawn in this way.

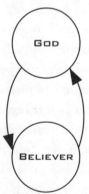

The restoration of sinners starts with the eternal and steadfast love of God. This love is finally and uniquely demonstrated in the death of Christ. God proves his love for humans in that while they were sinners Christ died for them (Romans 5:8). The preaching of the gospel—the news of Christ's death and resurrection—is the power by which God brings about a new creation. Through the power of the Holy Spirit, the evidence of God's love found in the forgiveness of sin brings a change of attitude. People are saved through the washing of rebirth and renewal by the Holy Spirit (Titus 3:5). Those who were rebels die to sin and commit themselves to the service of God (Romans 6). The apostle John puts the matter another way. He declares that we love God because he first loved us, a love that is displayed in the cross (1 John 4:7–21). The cross brings about mutual love relationships between humans and God.

The transformation of the believer that comes with salvation has an effect on horizontal relationships. The cleansing force of the spiritual washing by the Spirit is pictured in terms of a baptism (Romans 6:1–7). Going down under the water signifies death to sin. Coming up out of the water, as it were, is being raised to new life. The change of attitude experienced by being found by the grace and love of God in Christ has its consequences. The believer is to put off the old self (Colossians 3:1–17). A list of the vices to be discarded is provided for that purpose. But rather than remain naked the believer is to put on the virtues displayed by Christ. A list of virtues is included. Above all these virtues, they are to put on love (Colossians 3:14). Christian love is to imitate God's love in Christ. That is, the believer is consigned to do good to all people, especially to the household of faith (Galatians 6:10). Moreover, they are to be patient and kind (1 Corinthians 13:4) as well as humble (Matthew 18:1–4). Within the Christian community, where all have been transformed, love is to be mutual (Romans 12:10). One can infer that the Kingdom of God is to be a community of mutual love relationships. Given the nature of the vertical and horizontal relationships the Kingdom of God may be schematized as follows.

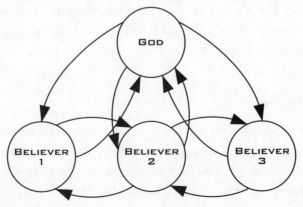

In the overlap of the ages between the advent of Christ and his Second Coming, believers experience the tension of the 'now but not yet'. Habituated in sin they continue to do wrong, but their right relationship with God is not broken. It is kept, because they are in Christ, through the process of repentance and forgiveness. As the new nature in Christ expresses itself, there is a growth in virtuous behaviour and the need for repentance becomes less frequent. This is the process called sanctification. Christian engagement with non-Christians will prove to be frustrating. While non-Christians will be able to love on occasions, the total commitment to the good of their neighbours, at great cost to themselves, will be missing. Relationships will be a shadow of what they should be.

Consummation

When the Lord Jesus returns with the clouds of heaven, the final judgment will take place and his Kingdom will be completed. The sorting of the righteous from the unrighteous that began with the ministry of Jesus (Luke 3:15–18) will be completed. The Bible says that those who have received the gift of righteousness by the grace of God and the work of Christ will gather around the throne of the Father in the New Jerusalem. In other words, the Kingdom of God will have been fully realized. The unrighteous, those who rejected the majesty of God, will suffer the broken relationships that they spawned and encouraged. In the Kingdom, right relationships will have been restored. Everyone will delight in God, delight in their neighbour, and delight in the new creation. God will be present with his people. Rest and peace will be the eternal marks of this new heavenly community.

Conclusion

In the previous chapter we saw that the good is determined by the nature God has given to a thing, and the goal God assigned to that nature. In this chapter we have examined the nature and purpose of humanity. We have found that people have the capacity to think, to feel, to chose and to act. They have the ability to do good for others. Love is defined in terms of good. Love, essentially, is a commitment to the good of others. At the personal and relational level, God's goal for human beings is mutual love relationships. The goal for all humans is mutual love relationships with God and their neighbours.

From the aspect of personal relationships the biblical ethic is 'love God and love your neighbour as yourself'. Behind this command is the goal of mutual love relationships. Love towards God is expressed in obedience. Maintaining God's order is pleasing to God. It is part of God's plan and purpose that people should count others greater than themselves, and commit themselves to securing the good of others. Love towards God is expressed in love towards our neighbours.

The commitment to the good of others fashions the nature of proper relationships, and distinguishes biblical ethics from modern individualistic theories that proclaim self-fulfilment and self-achievement as fundamental moral obligations. While it is true that individual people have to sustain themselves in order to be able to serve others, the recognition that humans are personal and relational beings lifts Christian ethics above legitimate self-service. There is also a personal dimension to morality that cannot be secured by doing that which brings about the greatest amount of good for the greatest number. Knowing that someone is personally committed to your good in an unconditional way brings a joy that is greater than all other goods. Because the goal of personal action is mutual love relationships, love is not an end in itself. Love binds others to the self and forms community. At the same time being loving is all that one can do in the attempt to create and maintain mutual love relationships. We cannot create mutual love relationships by ourselves. In one sense, the most loving thing a person can do is proclaim the gospel for it is by the power of the gospel that people have a new found ability to love God and their neighbours.

Mutual love relationships are not something that humans can generate by themselves. Sin has distorted the human capacity and limited the possibilities inherent in its nature. Redemption and renewal through the work of Christ and the power of the Holy

Spirit is the only way that mutual love relationships can become a reality. Moreover, the tensions inherent in the overlap of the ages mean that mutual love relationships are often damaged through sin. They can only be sustained through the practice of repentance and forgiveness.

In all this, the nature of biblical and Christian ethics is now becoming clear. We have seen that biblical ethics operates at a number of different levels. Firstly, it operates in regard to nature and purpose. This enables us to determine what is good. However it also operates on the personal level. This is the level of love. Before we formalise our ethical theory there is another level that needs to be examined. This is the level of community, to which we now turn.

CHAPTER SEVEN

The Ethics of Community

Two Perspectives

The narrative of salvation history in the Bible oscillates between several perspectives. Attention can be focused on either the activity and destiny of individuals, or the activity and destiny of the group. For example, in the Former Prophets, the text can focus on the activity of King David as an individual, or the fortunes of Israel as a nation. The two perspectives can be illustrated by an example from war. (The illustration should not imply that war should set our way and standard of thinking. The example is merely an illustration of collectivist thinking.) Enemy soldiers looking at one another across a battlefield do not think in individualistic terms. The fight is not between two individuals *per se*. The soldiers see themselves as part of a greater whole. The soldier in the enemy uniform has done nothing as an individual to his counterpart across the battle line. He has not stolen his car or insulted his wife. The soldiers' relationship to each other is not based on any knowledge about the individuals involved. The soldiers are members of two different nations and the nations are at war. This being so, the soldiers think holistically. Each enemy soldier is a member of a hostile community, and is thus viewed as part of a whole. In this case, the wholes are nations and the nations are at war. Were members from both sides of the conflict to meet before the war when there was an amicable relationship between the nations, they would probably think differently. They might see each other as foreigners, but they would treat each other on an individual basis. Both perspectives are legitimate depending on the context. In the context of war the holistic perspective is the relevant one.

Social theorists, while accepting the legitimacy of both perspectives, have debated the question of which perspective is primary. What is the fundamental unit of social reality? Is it the individual or society, the part or the whole? Is society explained in terms of individuals or are individuals shaped and defined by society?

On one side of this debate, there are social theorists who argue that society and its structures are to be explained in terms of the individuals who make it up. The shape and structure of society is determined by the nature of the individual members, and their desires and needs. According to these theorists, the whole is to be explained and understood in terms of the parts. The nature and operation of society can only, in the last resort, be explained by reference to the nature of the members who make it up. This explanation of society is called 'methodological individualism'. Theoretically it is as though humans existed as individuals prior to coming together into society. Living in a state of nature prior to the foundations of society, the individual is seen to have fixed and invariant human psychological features such as instincts, the capacity to think, desires, needs, and so on. Social arrangements are seen as a means of fulfilling these independently-given individual objectives. All forms of social life are seen as the creation of the collection of individual persons. The individual appears not as a *result* of history but as the *starting point*. This 'abstract individual' is not a product of history, but of nature.

Opponents of methodological individualism have usually argued for methodological holism or collectivism. This is the view that society is the fundamental and basic unit. It is argued that the whole is more than the sum of the parts. On this view, the whole is destroyed if it is broken into the parts. We might say that society is like an animal. Animals have individual organs such as hearts, lungs and brains. But if you dissect an animal into its parts you no longer have a living animal. The parts are only truly understood as they operate in the whole animal. According to this theory, society is best seen as the basic unit, and the individual members explained in the light of the whole. Society has properties that the individual members do not have. Some theorists in this school of thought have even suggested that societies can be studied independently of the individual members whose actions they determine.

The relevance of these theories to Christian ethics must be explained. Ethics must operate on a basic unit. If the individual is the primary unit, then it will follow that the good of the individual must be secured. According to this approach, the good of the individual cannot be overridden by the good of the whole society. On the other hand, if society as a whole is the basic unit, then the good of individuals can be overridden by the good of the whole. An example will illustrate the point of difference between the two approaches. On the collectivist view, it would be morally justifiable for individual members of a society to be sacrificed or eliminated for the good of the whole society. The individualist account would view such action as morally reprehensible. It is clear that the determination of a basic unit is extremely significant from a moral point of view.

Choosing Between the Two Perspectives

How are we to choose between these two accounts? Consideration of their strengths and weaknesses would be the normal starting point. In this regard there is much in favour of the collectivist perspective. Or, to put it another way, there is much in favour of rejecting the individualistic account of society. The revolutionary thinker, Karl Marx, promoted a form of collectivism. He subjected the notion of 'the abstract individual' to its most piercing critique. According to Marx, the notion of the abstract individual was "as great an absurdity as the idea of the development of language without living together and talking to one another" (Lukes, 1973, p. 76). Nevertheless Marx did not dispense with the notion of the individual. He goes on to declare that "Man is…not only a social animal, but an animal which can develop into an individual only in society". Other writers like De Bonald declared, "Not only does man not constitute society, but it is society that constitutes man, that is, it forms him by social education" (Lukes, 1973, p. 78). Even the conservative English ethicist, F. H. Bradley, recognized man as a social being and that "the abstract individual" as "a theoretical attempt to isolate what cannot be isolated" (Bradley, 1927, p. 171).

However the weaknesses are not all on the side of methodological individualism. Carter (1990) has shown that there is some ambiguity in relation to collectivist arguments. Collectivists continually contrast the individual member of society to the society as a whole, in order to make their case. Yet if their case is true then the two things cannot be contrasted in such a way. The individual member of society is part of society. It is not as though the individual member is a separate thing that can be held up against another thing called society. The individual is a part of the whole; the society. He or she cannot stand outside it. Collectivist talk is, then, at the very least, misleading. It promotes the idea that the society has a life independent of the individuals that make it up.

Out of the ambiguity and confusion emerges the claim that society is an independent entity. That is, society has its own existence. A simple illustration will make the point clear. Imagine for a moment that you have taken a car to pieces. Every part that can be separated off from other parts has been separated off. You place all the parts in a huge box. An interesting question now arises. Is there a car in the box? There is no doubt that all the parts of a car are in the box, but that does not seem to be the same as having a car in the box. This point is clear from the fact that all the parts collected in the box do not have the same properties as a car. With all the parts disconnected and collected in a chaotic state, the motor will not run, the car will not move, and the brakes will not work. It seems that the parts have to be connected in the right order or set in the correct relationship before we get the properties that we associate with a car. If society is like a machine or biological entity, then the parts are not separate entities that can stand over against the whole of which they are parts. The whole will then be incomplete and non-functional in some way.

Western societies, on the whole, have operated on the individualist view. On this view, the individual is the basic unit of reality and value. Individuals are complete in themselves. Theoretically, at least, they can function adequately by themselves. The adoption of the philosophy of individualism leads to a liberal democratic approach to government and social order. Governments have certain powers to structure society, but the structures and patterns set up should not override the rights of the individual. By way of contrast, Marxist states have adopted the holistic view. On this view the state is the basic unit. Individuals are not complete in themselves. They are merely parts of a greater whole. Moreover the parts are shaped by the whole. On the collectivist view the rights of the individual are subordinate to the power of the state. Individual rights can be overridden in the interest of the whole society. Lenin and others used this view to morally justify the extermination of people who were seen to hinder the good of society.

A Third Option

As Christians we may not be forced to choose either of these two views. The fact that God is a personal and relational being combined with the fact that humans are personal and relational entities provides us with a third conceivable account. In the previous chapter, we saw that the Bible frequently focused on relationship between individuals. An example of this is Jesus' teaching in the Sermon on the Mount. In the sermon, Jesus speaks about what individuals are to do when they encounter another individual. That is, he addresses what should happen in bi-polar relationships (relationships between two entities). Jesus' teaching was thoroughly consistent with the teaching of the Old Testament. Jewish scholars, as well as Jesus, summarized the Law and the Prophets in terms of loving both God and neighbour. The social structures promulgated by the laws given to the nation of Israel could be summarized in terms of mutual love relationships. For the biblical writers, bi-polar relationships seem to be the basic units of social reality. Neither the individual nor society as a whole seems to be the foundational unit. A completely different account of society is adopted.

This new account would be similar to the collectivist position in that it would recognize the reality of relationships. On the other hand, it would not recognize that the 'something more' detected by some holists transforms society into an independent entity. In contrast to individualistic theories, this new theory would recognize that society could not be reduced to a mere collection of individuals. Rather, society would be explained in terms of the individuals who composed the society and the relationships between those individuals. In a large complex modern industrialized society the complicated nature of relationships might make it seem as though the society had developed a nature and mind of its own. But in reality it would not be so. Rather, society would be explained in terms of relationships between individuals that lead to the formation of groups and relationships between groups and so on.

Alan Carter has put forward a theory that coincides with the biblical account of bi-polar relationships (Carter, 1990). He has labelled this approach interrelationism. For the sake of convenience we shall adopt his terminology. However it must be recognized that the terms 'individualism', 'collectivism' and 'interrelationism' can be used for a broad range of philosophical theories, and they cannot be limited to explaining the nature of society. Carter provides an outline of the positions that cluster around these terms. The outline will be appended at the end of the chapter.

It is clear that the account of social reality adopted will affect ethics dramatically. The basic unit of social reality tends to become the basic unit of value. If the basic unit of value is bi-polar relationships, then the consequent ethic will not allow either the good of the individual or the good of society to dominate ethical decisions. Rather the value of personal relationships will determine moral issues. An examination of the biblical material will, I believe, endorse the third option of interrelationism. But before we turn to the examination of the biblical material we need to explore the nature of social structures.

Social Structures

A society is a collection of people living together. Any collection of people can be organized to live together in many different ways. In modern western societies, a basic social structure is the nuclear family. This is a structure made up of a man and a woman, usually husband and wife, and a number of children. In other countries the basic unit is the extended family or the clan. Family units can vary considerably from one society to another. When a system of organization is relatively permanent it is called an institution. The family is an institution in this sense.

There are a number of basic social institutions present in every society. The basic institutions have to do with education, the family, religion, economics and government. Each of these areas will generate further structures. Education, for example, might take place on an individual basis at home, or collectively at a school. Economic order might be based on agriculture and include a system of bartering, or it might be based on manufacturing and cash trading.

Social structures set up patterns or regular ways of doing things within society. People occupying a set place within the pattern are expected to behave in a certain way. That it to say, structures incorporate roles. Within the structure of education that is known as schooling, for example, we find the roles of teacher and pupil. The structures of government include roles like administrators, police officers and judges. In all this it is clear that a society is a complex arrangement of structures, institutions and roles that are interrelated.

The nature of these social structures is disputed. Those who have postulated that society is like an independent organism tend to see them as relatively fixed and difficult to change. Given the rapid change of social structures in the last five decades this view seems totally implausible. At the other end of the spectrum, those adopting an individualistic perspective comprehend them to be fluid and easily changed. Perhaps a weakness of the individualistic perspective is that it suggests that individuals can change structures. The fact is that only individuals in relationship can change social structures for these structures are the patterns of relating adopted by members of a society. It takes a dominant group or a majority to impose change.

The interrelationist account suggests a moderate view of social structures. The British sociologist, Anthony Giddens, in describing what he calls the duality of structure, puts it in the following way: "Social structures are both constituted by human agency and yet at the same time are the very medium of this constitution" (Giddens, 1976, p. 121). Evans brings out the recursive nature of the structure/individual relationship clearly. The human being

> is not only formed by these social relationships; he acts and by acting helps to form these roles in turn. He is not only constituted by these relationships; he himself constitutes them. He plays a role in continuing them, modifying them for better or worse, enhancing or degrading their quality and character (Evans, 1977, p. 145).

The purpose of social structures will vary according to the different accounts. Given the three types of accounts, the purpose will either be (1) the good of the individual members, (2) the good of the whole society, or (3) the good of bi-polar relationships.

Structures and Institutions in the Bible

We are now in a position to examine the nature and type of social structures in the Bible. We shall continue to use the stages of salvation history established earlier. We are asking the question, what kind of structures should we have in society? Does the Bible push us to be collectivist, individualist or interrelationist?

The Kingdom Pattern Established (Eden)

Some very fundamental structures were set up at creation. Marriage and work were instituted. Although the establishment of religion was not explicitly mentioned, it was a fundamental assumption built into the whole arrangement. These structures are not arrangements developed or fabricated, intentionally or unintentionally, by humans. They are built into the fabric of creation itself. The rigidity of these structures will later be loosened by sin, allowing some restructuring.

In the garden, it is Adam and Eve's relationship with God that sustains them. They are united to each other by virtue of their relationship with God the Creator. It is God who creates a help-mate for Adam and binds her to him. Adam and Eve, in relationship with each other, sin against God. We may refer to the God/humanity relationship as a vertical relationship and the human/human relationship as a horizontal relationship. Later Israelite society will be defined in terms of these vertical and horizontal relationships.

The Fall

The created order was hurt by the Fall. Sin assaulted and violated the structures of religion, marriage and work. Whatever the structure of religion was to be in the immediate future it would not follow the pattern of the garden. Humankind was excluded from the presence of God; humans would no longer live and move in the very presence of God. The relationship of husband and wife was also altered. The husband would now dominate his wife in a way not envisaged before the Fall. Even the ground became hostile and work turned to toil.

The rupture of family life displayed itself in the relationship between Cain and Abel. You will recall that Cain slew Abel. As time went by, the various family lines effected the development of nations (Genesis 10). Eventually people gathered together into cities to find a unity and power based on self-interest (see Goldsworthy, 1991, pp. 148–149). The story of the Tower of Babel characterizes sinful humanity's desire to displace God from his rightful place. Human self-interest refused to give the glory to God. It desired a name for itself. The judgment of God dissipated this unity, dissolving much of the power. Given the nature of things, self-interest will always lead away from unity. The question of how God's good structures will be recovered finds a central place in the on-going story of salvation history.

The Kingdom Promised (Abraham)

Abraham was a semi-nomad. Like the later patriarchs, Isaac and Jacob, he wandered around Palestine searching for pasture for his flocks. At this time, families and clans were organized around a head or chief. Abraham was the head of a sizeable clan. The extent of Abraham's power as head of the clan is not explicitly discussed though it seems to have been fairly extensive. By the end of a period of captivity in Egypt Abraham's clan had grown into a great nation.

After the exodus from Egypt, Israel's tribes were "arranged in battle order around the tabernacle, the symbol of Israel's leadership by God and his kingship" (Dumbrell, 1988, p. 49; see Numbers 2). The tribes were united by the Covenant with God on Mount Sinai, which constructed Israel's society and glued it together. At that time the nation was ruled by God through his servant the prophet/priest Moses. For the first two hundred years Israel's structure remained tribal.

> She had no statehood, no central government, no capital city, no administrative machinery. The various tribes enjoyed complete independence of central authority. Tribal society was patriarchal in organization, and without the stratification characteristic of the feudal pattern of Canaan. Though elders of the clans, by virtue of their position, adjudicated disputes in accordance with traditional procedure and were looked up to for the wisdom of their counsel, anything resembling organized government was lacking. The confederation had its focal point at the shrine which housed the Ark of the Covenant, through most of the early period located at Shiloh (Bright, 1960, pp. 143–4).

The horizontal fetters that held the family and clan together were natural bonds. The biological relationship of kinship created obligations and responsibilities as well as the attachments of natural affection. Kinship also bound the clans together into tribes, and these tribes were bound together by the vertical relationship with God established by Israel's history and confirmed by covenant. This vertical bond strengthened and reinforced the natural bonds of kinship.

Our reflection on individualism and collectivism now becomes relevant. You will remember that in that discussion, the issue was the relationship of the individual to society. Some Old Testament scholars have argued that the modern concept of individualism was not discovered until the time of Jeremiah and Ezekiel. Prior to that time, they argue, the nation was the basic unit of understanding.

Hebrew thought reinforced the idea of the solidarity of the whole. The standard example of this Hebraic type of thinking was the story of Achan found in Joshua 7.

You will recall that Achan took of the things devoted to destruction (Joshua 6:17–18) during the conquest of Jericho. The whole community suffered until Achan and his family were destroyed. Some scholars argue that this story illustrates the point that the group as a whole is the basic unit as far as Hebrew understanding was concerned. The whole community suffered for Achan's sin. Achan was part of the unit, the nation of Israel, and as a consequence that unit suffered. Moreover, Achan was part of a sub-group, the family, and the sub-group shared in the punishment.

Certainly the story does not lend itself to an individualistic interpretation. But this does not mean that we are forced to accept a holistic understanding. Surely the whole story could be interpreted along the lines of the epigram quoted by Paul in 1 Corinthians 15:33: "Bad company ruins good morals". That is to say, the story could be interpreted in terms of personal relationships and sets of personal relationships. The family and the clan could be thought of as collections of individuals-in-relationship. The tribes could be seen as a collection of clans-in-relationship and the nation could be viewed as a collection of tribes-in-relationship. In this way the existence of the clans, tribes, and nation are dependent on the existence of individuals-in-relationship.

In reflecting on the claim that individualism played no real part in early Hebraic understanding, H. H. Rowley draws attention to the line of individuals who find themselves the focus of attention in the biblical narrative from the earliest of times. Attention is drawn to Enoch, Noah, Abraham, Moses, Samuel and David. His conclusion is a valid one.

> But in no period of the life of Israel do we find extreme collectivism or extreme individualism, but a combination of both. Some writers or some passages emphasize the one side of this dual nature of man more than the other, but both sides belong to the wholeness of biblical thought in all periods (Rowley, 1956, p. 100).

Individualism and collectivism provide us with two ways of looking at the same reality. We can conceive of situations where the two perspectives can be applied in the same context. When a soldier goes to war, he can be considered from an individual point of view. His family and friends will remember his personal history. If he is killed, his family and friends will claim that he did not deserve to die. On the other hand, his enemies cannot view the soldier from an individualistic perspective. The soldier is part of a group. The war is between national groups and the enemy will not stop to consider whether the soldier is a faithful husband and father and generally a good person. The soldier is part of the enemy, and no consideration is given to his personal intentions. The national intentions disclosed in the declaration of war are all that count. Given the nature of war, the collectivist perspective is the appropriate one to be adopted. The basic units are nations.

In the early part of Israel's history, the biblical writers switch their focus back and forth. Attention focused on the individual switches to the group or nation and back again. Since there cannot be two basic units, this very fact suggests that another explanation or account of the relationship of the individual to society is required. Later in the story of salvation history, Jesus gives us a clue as to the nature of this account. He epitomized the thrust of the Law and the Prophets in terms of personal relationship. Jesus implied that God's purposes revealed in the Old Testament could be understood in terms of personal relationships; that is, God's Kingdom could be understood in terms of love towards God and love towards neighbour (Matthew 22:34–40).

The two great commandments seem to have been a common way of presenting a summary of the Law and the Prophets in Jesus' day. In Luke 10, an expert in the Old Testament Law takes up the same two verses (Deuteronomy 6:5 and Leviticus 19:18) from the Old Testament as a summary of the way to eternal life. Perhaps it was a widespread understanding that the Kingdom of God was made up of two types of personal relationship. Regardless of whether this understanding was widespread or not, Jesus' endorsement of the summary encourages us to move towards interrelationism. On this view both individual and group action can be understood in terms of individuals-in-relationship rather than in terms of individuals alone or the group as a whole.

The rule of the judges certainly lends itself to an interrelationist understanding of how Israelite society operated. Individuals functioned within the traditional structures of the family and clan. When a dispute arose between individuals or families the matter was taken to a judge. The duty of the judge was to approve what was good and to punish wrong-doing. On a broader front, Israel's contact with her neighbours exposed the need for national unity in matters of defence. There was mounting pressure at this time for the appointment of a king. After the warrior Gideon rescued the nation from the hands of the Midianites the people of Israel wanted to proclaim him king (Judges 8:22–28). Gideon rejected the people's demand on the grounds that the Lord God alone was king. Gideon endorsed the traditional understanding that God was the one true Ruler of his people.

The Deuteronomic Covenant predicted and endorsed the appointment of a king (Deuteronomy 17:14-20). However when the elders of Israel came to the prophet Samuel and demanded that he appoint a king, Samuel was very reticent to accede to their demand. Two reasons lay behind this reticence. The first had to do with the motives behind the demand. The demand was motivated by the rejection of the Lord God as king. The second reason had to do with the type of king they desired. They wanted a king like the other nations. They wanted a king who would establish his own power and glory. They did not want a king who would be faithful to the Covenant with the Lord. The Lord God did allow the appointment of a king. By his grace and mercy God was able to bring about his purposes despite the evil desires of a sinful people.

The Kingdom Foreshadowed (David, Solomon)

The first king, Saul, proves to be a failure. He was not obedient to the word of the Lord. He took upon himself the office of priest (1 Samuel 13) and then kept some of the Amalekite livestock that was subject to the ban (1 Samuel 15). The prophet Samuel informed Saul that his Kingdom would not continue and that the Lord had already sought out a man 'after his own heart' to be king. Unlike Saul this new king would keep the Covenant and obey the word of the Lord.

Once again God took the initiative and sent Samuel to anoint David the son of Jesse as king (1 Samuel 16). David displayed his trust in God and his word when he, as the faithful one, represented the whole nation as he stood before the Philistines and their champion Goliath (1 Samuel 17). God worked through David's faithfulness and eventually David took possession of the whole of the Promised Land. At this point the Lord God made a covenant with David. He promised that his son would build a temple in Jerusalem and that he would establish the throne of his Kingdom forever (2 Samuel 7).

Both David and his son, Solomon, "mediate God's rule in God's land" (Goldsworthy, 1991, p. 220). They demonstrated the pattern of the rule of God's anointed saviour-king. Yet their own personal sins showed that neither of them was the promised One. After a succession of unfaithful kings in Israel and Judah the prophets projected the coming of this messianic King into the future. An examination of the pattern will show that God's kingly order is partnered by a priestly order. The people of God related to God on a personal level through the agency of the priests and the temple. But the people of God were related to one another in God's way through the office of the king and the directives of Covenant Law. Again it is the vertical relationship that shapes and holds together the horizontal or social relationships. The failure of Israel and her kings does not discredit God's plan and pattern. The implementation and realization of both the plan and the pattern merely await the coming of God's anointed One.

The Kingdom at Hand (Jesus)

Jesus began his ministry with a startling declaration: "The time is fulfilled, and the Kingdom of God is at hand" (Mark 1:15). The implications of the first phrase of this utterance are clear. The promises of God are about to be fulfilled. God's plans and purposes are about to be implemented. The second phrase fills out the content of those promises and plans. God is restoring his rule. Indeed, it is clear that the Kingdom of God has come near because the King is present. Among the many Old Testament roles and expectations that Jesus fulfilled was the role of Messiah, the Son of David, the anointed King.

The declaration went on to specify the only appropriate response to this wonderful work of God: "Repent, and believe in the gospel" (Mark 1:15). At the centre of each believer's confession of faith in the New Testament was the assertion that Jesus was Lord (Romans 10:9). After his ascension believers assembled together each week to worship him as the risen Lord in obedience and faith.

The *unity* of the local assembly was found in having the one Spirit, one hope, one baptism, and one Lord (Ephesians 4:1–5). Identifying Jesus as Lord and committing oneself to him meant that one had died to sin and been made alive to God (Romans 6). In this sense the believer was a new creature (2 Corinthians 5:17) who lived by the Spirit of God (Galatians 5:16–26). An essential element of being a new creature in Christ was that the new life was to be marked by love. Love was the fruit of the Spirit (Galatians 5:22) and made all the gifts of the Spirit effective in building up the body of Christ (1 Corinthians 13).

The concept of the individual believers being built into the body of Christ is applied to members of the local congregations (1 Corinthians 12:27), to believers spread across different congregations (Romans 12:4–5), and to all believers (1 Corinthians 12:12–13). The horizontal unity experienced both within and across local congregations is based on the vertical relationship with Christ. The body has but one Lord and one Spirit; the Spirit poured out by the risen Lord (Ephesians 4:4). The body grows as its members are properly related to Christ the head, and to one another (Ephesians 4:15–16; Colossians 2:19). The whole body does not find an expression here on earth. It is heavenly reality in which the believer participates by faith.

As the church is devoted to Jesus as Lord, it must, by its very

nature, separate itself off from those who do not recognize that lordship (e.g. 2 Corinthians 6:14–7:1). Hence the church will always be
a sub-community within the wider society. And this separation is
not because Jesus is not Lord of all. He *is* lord of the unbeliever. His
lordship over the church is internally motivated by love but his lordship over unbelievers is by external constraint and final judgment.
Moreover his lordship over the church is direct and explicit. His
lordship over the church is exercised through his Word. Whereas his
lordship over society as a whole, is indirect and concealed.

We must never blur this distinction between God's indirect and
concealed rule, and his direct and explicit rule. The only time that
these two aspects of God's rule will come together will be on the last
day when Jesus comes to judge the world (Matthew 13:1–43). Up
until that time there will always be those who oppose his rule. God's
adversary Satan leads them (Matthew 12:22–37). Being in the
world cannot be equated with being in God's Kingdom. The
Kingdom is something that has to be entered. In the present evil age
it is only entered by faith (Matthew 18:1–4). The temptation to
move from the fact that God rules over all to the conclusion that the
world is the Kingdom of God, is not one that the biblical writers
entertain. However those who adopt a holistic perspective of the
world often entertain the idea. The danger of adopting a holistic
perspective of the world is that it leads down the path of the social
gospel. According to the social gospel, the mission of the church is
to engage in social engineering and change the structures of society.

If we maintain the distinction between God's indirect and
concealed rule and his direct and explicit rule, and, conjoin this with
an interrelationist account of society, one can do justice to all the
threads of biblical theology. Social structures will not be independent
entities that shape and determine the nature of the individual.
Rather, as the patterning of relationships, social structures will not
only influence the development of individuals but be influenced by
those individuals acting in relationship. The complexities of social
change may be daunting but we will not have created and admitted
an independent entity that reeks uncontrollable and irresistible havoc
on the individual members of society. Social ethics and social change

will continue to be realistic possibilities.

The note of fulfilment in Jesus' declaration of the Kingdom introduces us to a biblical perspective that divides history up into two ages. The first age is the present evil age where the forces of evil and death are active and effective. The evil age is followed by the age-to-come where God has vanquished evil and death. The age-to-come is inaugurated by the coming of Jesus, while the present evil age ends with the Christ's return. Christians are seen to live in the overlap between the two ages where both the power of God and the power of the evil one are active. God's promised victory over sin and death has been fulfilled by Christ through his work on the cross. The resurrection is the guarantee of this victory. Yet this fulfilment awaits its consummation. Ours is the age of the now but not yet.

We need to note that the study of the end of the present evil age is called eschatology. The English word 'eschatology' is derived from the Greek word for 'end'—*eschatos*. Eschatology is literally the study of 'the last things' and it covers the events that lead to the end or closure of the first age. Eschatology has to do with the establishment of God's reign. Scholars have adopted different views on the nature of the last things. Some take a futuristic approach. According to these people, God's rule is completely in the future. No account is taken of the fact that Christ rules as Lord in the hearts of millions of believers. Others adopt a realized account of the matter. According to this view, God's rule is present and complete. No account is taken of the different natures of his rule in this present age. The view most compatible with the Scriptures is the account call 'inaugurated eschatology'. This is the view that God's reign has begun in Christ and it will be completed at his return.

The dual nature of God's rule (that is, his direct and explicit rule over against his indirect and concealed rule) and the overlap of the two ages have allowed Christians to take a range of perspectives on the nature of the presence of the Kingdom. Those who operate on an individualistic perspective tend to emphasize the future-ness of the Kingdom of God. For it is only in the future that all people will come under God's direct and explicit rule. Those adopting such a *futuristic* eschatology are open to the charge of relegating the

transformation of society to the future. It is as if they are not concerned about the present. On the other hand those who see the
church universal as the body of Christ in a holistic way tend to
emphasize the fact that God's reign has been realized and that his
Kingdom is a present, not a future, reality. Holding a *realized*
eschatology these people seem to dismiss or trivialize the element of
future hope so prominent in the Scriptures.

One way the holistic perspective has been developed is by
equating the church universal with the body of Christ and drawing
on the imagery of incarnation. This is a very dangerous approach.
The Bible only uses the language of incarnation in relation to the
divine Son of God taking on human flesh. If not used carefully the
imagery could imply that the church was divine in nature. Taking up
this implication, some see the church as the divine incarnation in the
world. In a sense the church is God's hands and feet. As the divine
agent in the world, its task is seen to be the restructuring of the world
through the establishment of just social structures. Justice is seen to
be brought about by political persuasion and pressure. Social
engineering through political activity becomes the way of salvation.
However without the gospel, social justice will be a short-term thing.
It will fail to address the problem of sinful human nature that lies
behind the establishment and maintenance of wrong structures.

It is precisely the dual nature of God's rule that allows the
biblical writers to maintain both a realized and futuristic aspect in
relation to the Kingdom of God. This approach is known as
inaugurated eschatology. God's direct and explicit rule has been
realized in those who respond to the gospel in repentance and faith.
But God's indirect and concealed rule will not be manifested to the
unbeliever until the Day of Judgment. In this sense God's rule is yet
to come. On the Day of Judgment God will make the
consequences of people's conduct match up with their actions.
Those who express their faith in Christ through love will be
rewarded. Those who deny Christ's rule will be treated as rebels.
Inaugurated eschatology has the advantage of generating concern
for the present and hope for the future.

The Kingdom Consummated (The Return of Jesus)

The end of the present evil age will come with the return of Jesus. At this time the subjective regeneration of the believer will be matched by the regeneration of the whole created order. There will be a new heaven and a new earth. The resurrected and transformed believers will enjoy the presence of God as Adam and Eve did in Eden. The community will find its perfection and completion in the presence of God. Those who refused the grace of God offered in the gospel will receive their just reward. They will suffer the final judgment.

Conclusion

The nature of morality is such that it invades every area of life. But morality is no mere intruder. Morality is integral to every aspect of life because it is a facet of reality. However morality has often been broken into two domains. These are the areas of personal and social ethics. The two areas can be separated because they address two different questions. Personal ethics asks 'What should I do?'. Social ethics asks 'What structures should we have in our society?'. While a legitimate distinction can be made between the areas of personal and social ethics, the distinction does not imply that the two areas are unrelated. Social structures frequently set the parameters for personal matters. One cannot ask the question 'Should I go to school?' without the educational structure of schooling. Personal moral dilemmas are sometimes generated by immoral social structures. A woman with four little children in a country where the economic and political structures allow one percent of the population to control ninety percent of the wealth, may well be morally justified in stealing from the rich to keep her children from starving to death. The immorality may be found with the few hoarding all the resources, and causing poverty and death. As a consequence, an ethic that does not cover both areas is an inadequate ethic.

The question of the nature of personal and social reality is of vital importance to any ethical theory. If the individual is taken to be the fundamental unit of personal and social reality, then the individual will become the basic unit of value. If the collective is taken to be the fundamental unit then it will provide the basic unit of value. Whatever the case, the fundamental unit of personal and social reality becomes the primary unit of value, and consequently plays a crucial role in the development and shaping of ethical theory. The argument of this chapter has been that while the Bible does not expressly delineate a theory of society, the implications are such that it appears to tacitly adopt an interrelationist position. One advantage of the interrelationist position is that it leaves social structures as flexible entities that can be changed by the people in society. Another is that it avoids the evils of communism and western liberalism. Neither the individual nor the collective is over-valued. Unlike collectivism, interrelationism allows for a mixed society as the world awaits the Second Coming. The mixed nature of society is consistent with the inaugurated eschatology presented in the New Testament. Believers are aliens and exiles in this fallen world.

The social aspect of morality cannot be ignored. An examination of nature and purpose might lead us to an ethic that is totally individualistic. Such an individualistic ethic would be totally unbiblical. An analysis of the personal aspect of morality revealed in the Bible leads to the goal of mutual love relationships. But the nature of love will not allow us to stop with isolated bi-polar relationships. Love creates community. A loving person seeks the good of any other human that he or she might have contact with. From the social perspective, the goal of Christian ethics is a community—the Kingdom of God.

Table 1

		Individualism	Interrelationism	Collectivism
A	**Dignity**	The individual human being is considered to possess supreme and intrinsic value or dignity.	Individual human beings are considered to possess value or dignity in their relations with other human beings.	The collective is considered to possess supreme and intrinsic value or dignity.
B	**Autonomy**	The individual is autonomous; he or she is self-directed.	Individuals are self-directed, though influenced by others.	The individual is subject to the totality of social forces; he or she is directed by the collective.
C	**Privacy**	The individual ought to be left a private sphere of thought and/or action immune from the incursions of others or a wider 'public'.	The individual ought to think and act, not only with regard to himself or herself, but also with others in mind.	The individual ought to think and act solely with the collective in mind. The thoughts and actions of the collective are of ultimate value.
D	**Self-Development**	The individual can and ought to experience self-development and can do so alone.	Individuals can and ought to develop together, and not at each other's expense.	The collective ought to experience self-development, irrespective of individual members.
E	**Abstract Concept**	The individual is pictured as possessing interests, wants, purposes and needs, etc., independently of any social context.	The individual's interests, wants, purposes and needs, etc. are affected by his or her relations with others and so cannot be abstracted from those relations.	The individual's interests, wants, purposes and needs, etc. are the result of his or her relation to the collective and so cannot be abstracted from it.
F	**Political**	Only the individual can be the source of political authority.	Only the relations between individuals can be the source of political authority.	Only the collective can be the source of political authority.
G	**Economic**	The individual should produce in order to satisfy his or her desires in his or her own way without regard for others.	The individual should produce in a way which takes into consideration not only his or her own desires but also those of others.	The individual should produce in order to satisfy the desire of the collective and in accordance with a plan which has been dictated by the collective.

		Individualism	Interrelationism	Collectivism
H	**Religious or Humanistic Destiny**	The individual is responsible for his or her own destiny.	Individuals are responsible for both their own and others' destinies.	The collective is responsible for everyone's destiny.
I	**Ethical**	The source of moral principles is the individual.	The source of moral principles is interpersonal relations.	The source of moral principles is the collective.
J	**Epistemo-logical**	The individual is the only source and depository of knowledge.	Related individuals are the source of knowledge, and it is dispersed.	The collective is the only source and depository of knowledge.
K	**Methodo-logical**	The individual is the basis of all explanations of social phenomena.	Related individuals are the basis of all explanations of social phenomena.	The collective, with its own laws, is the basis of all explanations of social phenomena.
L	**Ontological**	Only individuals really exist.	Individuals exist in relations with others.	Only collectives really exist.

With some slight modification this appendix is taken from Alan Carter, 'On Individualism, Collectivism and Interrelationalism', *Heythrop Journal*, XXXI (1990), p. 25.

CHAPTER EIGHT

Sketching a Biblically Based Theory of Christian Ethics

The Shape of Christian Ethics

We are now in a position to summarize the general shape of a Christian ethic based on the Bible as the Word of God. Drawing the threads of the last seven chapters together we can list the basic characteristics of this ethic. The following characteristics will be essential if the ethic is to be truly biblical.

Christian Ethics is Theological

As moral agents, humans perform in a moral field or domain. The dimensions of this domain are part and parcel of the creation order. As the Creator of this domain God has a vital interest in its ordering. He has a commitment to good order which is defined in terms of nature and purpose. Everything is meant to move towards the goal set according to its kind. When humans violate God's general order they reject his majesty. Their violation of God's order reflects an attitude that denies his right to rule. Since creation is God's domain, upheld by the word of his power, the way humans treat creation is an expression of the way they treat God. Consequently morality not only has to do with the way individual things are treated but the way humans treat God. To take advantage of an individual because they are poor and helpless is to deny their humanity and to reject the general purpose that God has for all humans. Consequently such actions offend the living God.

Christian Ethics is Creation Based

Moral values are not found in the world in the same way as trees, flowers and animals. They are not objects with spatial dimensions. Yet they are objectively based because they are embedded in the order of reality. They are founded on the relationship between nature and purpose. Philosophers would say that moral values are based on the generic and telic order of creation. The good for any individual thing is found in the goal that God has set (telic order) for the kind of thing that it is. The similarities that we observe between individuals of the same kind (generic order) indicate that God has the same general purpose for all members of the kind. To treat some individuals of the same kind differently is to deny the similarity and discard God's general purpose. Those who are treated differently feel the injustice of their treatment, and so does God.

It is easy to see how a creation or nature-based ethic can be secularized. Secular ethics simply takes God out of the picture. The goals that God has set because of his purposes merely become the goals found in nature. Radical humanists can go even further by denying that there are kinds and purposes in creation. Such a radical approach to ethics leaves it open to individuals to decide what something is and what purpose it can fulfil. While Christian ethicists will not distort the biblical picture in these ways they can twist it out of shape by ignoring the progressive stages of biblical revelation. There are two major distortions found in the literature. The first distortion comes from focusing solely on creation, and the second from focusing exclusively on the consummation.

The approach that focuses solely on creation is called 'Creation Ethics'. Creation ethics formally highlights the nature of things at creation, and for all practical purposes it denies the relevance of the subsequent stages of biblical revelation. Neither the Law nor the final consummation of all things in Christ is given a role in determining the shape of biblical morality. The full contours of God's purposes, it is argued, are to be found in the creation accounts. Often later biblical material is smuggled surreptitiously back into the creation accounts. Sometimes the moral insights of the creationist approach are sound, but the faulty method frequently leads in the wrong direction.

The second approach, that focuses on the consummation, is called 'Kingdom ethics'. The final and completed Kingdom of God is taken as the source of all moral values. The weakness of the Kingdom ethic approach is that it ignores nature and focuses solely on purpose. It can make morality depend on what appears to be the arbitrary will of God. Stress on the telic order can theoretically allow new divine purposes, and this new act of will can overrule the divine commitment made at creation.

The theory being presented in this book emphasizes that both the generic and the telic order are aspects of the will of God. Once creation has taken place, morality cannot be solely based on some arbitrary divine whim. The creation order that God himself upholds will not allow this. For example, God can turn stones into bread, but this action of God would not mean that stones are meant to be food for humans. Without a miraculous transformation of nature as a whole, stones will not biologically sustain human life. Of course, if God were to recreate everything, or to change the order of creation by changing some elements within creation, we would have to operate on a new morality. However the Bible underscores the fact that God is faithful to his original purposes. Both nature and purpose are essential to biblical ethics.

Christian Ethics is Teleological

The link between nature and purpose is not evident until the end is known. The full nature of the Kingdom of God is not apparent until the coming of Christ. Consequently a true and complete understanding of morality cannot be comprehended until the vision of the Kingdom is clear. The earlier stages of the biblical revelation model many aspects of the final vision. In a sense these elements are caught up in the final vision. But it is only the final vision of the Kingdom of God revealed in Christ that enables us to see the picture that governs the whole of the moral life. Biblical Christianity is not only historically teleological but also entails natural teleology. History is seen to be moving towards the ends presumed in the nature of creation. It is in terms of those ends, which are God's purposes, that we understand the order of creation and evaluate whether things are morally right or wrong.

Christian Ethics is Christological

Christ is the goal of all things. He is the one true *telos*. In Christ we understand how things fit together. But Christ is more than just an embodiment of knowledge. He is the agent who brings about the goal. He embodies it in his own person. This means that biblical ethics is profoundly christological. The person and work of Christ is the key to understanding how God has achieved his purposes. That the mechanism of establishing right relationships or atonement is through the death and resurrection of Jesus also means that biblical ethics is grounded in the gospel. The gospel, simply put, is the declaration of Christ crucified. The New Testament writers consistently tie ethical injunctions to the death and resurrection of Christ. Believers who participate in the death and resurrection of esus by faith share a right relationship with God the Father and are exhorted to live worthily of this new relationship.

Christian Ethics is Eschatological

The fact that God has revealed his purposes in a number of stages that find their finalization in Christ means that the moral bits and pieces in the Bible cannot be collected together and used without consideration of their place in the unfolding drama. If God's character and purposes were all unpacked and revealed at the point of creation, then we could read off a complete list of moral values at that point. But that is not the case. Partial insights are exposed in the creation accounts. These insights are supplemented by the later stages of biblical revelation. As a consequence, we are not able to develop a purely deontological ethic using just creation and do justice to the whole biblical revelation even if we supplement it with the Torah. A true and complete understanding of God and his purposes is not made known until the disclosure of Christ, who is the goal of all creation. Morality must embrace not only creation but also its goal or purpose. Only then will all things be given their true ethical significance.

Christian Ethics is Trinitarian

The God of the Bible is a triune God: three persons but one God. The Godhead constitutes a set of bipolar relationships between the Father, Son, and Holy Spirit. As we observed, the notion of humans made in the image of God is not capable of allowing us to transfer the idea of personal and relational beings from the Godhead to human nature directly. The concept of image in Genesis refers to humans being vice-regents, keeping order on the earth on behalf of God. Nevertheless the notion of a trinitarian God opens up the possibility of humans being relational entities. The inter-relational aspect of human nature is revealed in the creation of male and female and the consequent human history.

It is not until the latter stages of biblical revelation that we get a fuller picture of God as Trinity. In John's Gospel the Trinity is painted as a series of mutual love relationships. The Father loves the Son and the Son loves and obeys the Father. The Holy Spirit gives himself in loving service to both. Christian doctrine has come to portray this relationship as mutual indwelling. The use of the notion of mutual indwelling is an attempt to capture the intimate unity experienced in the relationships. It should be no surprise to us that the purposes of God match up with his character. God is constituted by a set of mutual love relationships. His purpose, as revealed in Scripture, is to create a community of mutual love relationships. In his love God desires that others should share the blessing which he himself enjoys.

Christian Ethics is Interrelational

People familiar with the Bible as a whole, and John's Gospel in particular, will not be surprised at the Bible's endorsement of interrelationalism. It follows from the doctrine of the trinity. By way of contrast, one of the dominant ethics in the western world has been utilitarianism. According to classical utilitarian theory, the basic unit of moral reality is the individual agent. The individual's needs and desires determine the good. A consequence of the individual being the basic unit of morality is that the moral rights of the individual cannot be overruled. Marxist theories of ethics, on the other hand, see society as a whole as the basic unit of moral reality. Individual rights may be nullified if they conflict with the good of the whole society. Dissidents may be purged from the group if this will bring good for the whole.

By way of contrast, biblical ethics recognizes individuals-in-relationship or bipolar relationships as the essential component of moral reality. The Kingdom of God will be a place where believers enjoy a right relationship with God and right relationships with neighbours. The Kingdom of God is a set of bipolar relationships. The character of these bipolar relationships is mutual love.

As we have observed, some ethical questions require societies to be considered as wholes. For example, in the case of war between nations we do not consider that each individual has made a commitment to war. The government makes a declaration on behalf of the whole society. There is no great problem here. Just as we can consider a car as a whole and yet reduce it to many parts so we can consider a society as a whole and still reduce it, by analysis, to a set of individuals-in-relationship. In our analysis we must be careful to recognize the pattern of relationships or social structures to be real—a part of the whole.

Christian Ethics is Covenantal

Biblical ethics is covenantal in that it involves parties who are personal agents. God unilaterally created an order that allows certain relationships. Human beings, as represented by people like Adam, Abraham, and finally Christ, can confirm these relationships and commit themselves to uphold and maintain them. All covenants indicate a commitment to uphold and maintain established relationships. Under the New Covenant Christians can participate in a right relationship with God through Christ which, by the power of the Spirit, leads to obedience. Because the Kingdom of God has not been consummated, the Covenant has to be maintained, on occasions, through repentance and forgiveness in this fallen world. Knowledge of right behaviour, and motivation for right behaviour, are found in Christ. Those outside Christ will not correctly or fully understand the moral domain and will not have the power or the will to do what is required on all occasions. This fact reminds us that because biblical morality is covenantal, it generates a responsive ethic. People are exhorted to respond in the right way and keep the commitments they have made in Christ.

Christian Ethics is Inclusive

In Chapter Two we examined the various approaches to ethics. We discovered that theories differed in several ways. Firstly they differed in relation to whether they focused on the action (duty) or the agent (virtue). Secondly, amongst those theories that focused on actions there were differences in relation to how the actions were morally evaluated. Some theories evaluated actions in terms of a feature of the action. This approach was known as the deontological approach. Other theories assessed actions in terms of the ends or goals. This method of evaluation was labelled the teleological approach. Still others evaluated actions in terms of the consequences. This approach was called consequentialism.

William Frankena provided us with good reasons to treat action and agent as complimentary aspects of the same reality. Evidence in favour of this complementary approach is found also in the Bible. Moral evaluations in the Bible are made of both actions and agents. The biblical view of human nature both underlines and explains this two dimensional approach. Human nature is seen to have two aspects. The inner nature is where the direction and character of the self is determined while the outer nature of the body is the instrument that expresses the actions and intentions of the self. Habitual forms of behaviour expose the settled beliefs of the mind and the will. The Bible commits us to both the ethics of duty and the ethics of virtue. We do not have to choose between these two approaches. Furthermore, the choice between the deontological, consequentialist, and teleological approaches to duty has been resolved in favour of teleology.

The advantages of having bipolar personal relationships as the basic unit of morality are now obvious. The Bible provides many examples of the three different aspects of moral action. Motive, the nature of the act, and consequences are all considered to be relevant factors as far as morality is concerned. These are all aspects of personal relationships. All three aspects are evaluated in terms of the goal or purpose of the kinds of things involved. The standard of moral evaluation is set teleologically.

Moreover, a teleological theory that has personal relationships as the *telos* can account for the fact that many moral imperatives appear to be deontological. Once a commitment has been made to creating mutual love relationships, then elements of this type of relationship, such as truth-telling and kindness, for example, appear necessary. After making the basic teleological commitment, many types of actions seem deontological in nature. It is a bit like playing a recognized game such as baseball. Once you make a commitment and start playing the game, the rules take on a necessity and authority not obvious until after the commitment to play. Further, some of the apparently deontological moral elements found in Scripture can be explained in terms of lack of knowledge of the *telos*. Sometimes God just told people what to do because their position in salvation history left them blind to God's goal. The situation is analogous to parents giving guidance to their children before they reach an age of knowledge and discretion. A biblically-based teleological theory of ethics may be said to be inclusive, not just because it incorporates duty and virtue, but because it can explain and include deontological and consequential elements.

Christian Ethics is Complex

The complexity of biblical ethics is found in that it operates from three perspectives. From the initial perspective the goal is located in terms of nature and purpose. Moral good is achieved by matching nature to purpose, and allowing the design to find its God-intended goal. From this first perspective, then, a Christian ethic is simply *to do good*. We do good by promoting the God-intended goal of something. This is the most basic way in which we understand ethics: doing good, which means seeking God's purposes.

Within the context of personal relationships, the ethic is more specifically *to love*. The goal is to achieve mutual love relationships. This second aspect is dependent on the first, for love is a gracious and unconditional commitment to the good. In the Bible love incorporates all the other moral virtues (see 1 Corinthians 13 and Galatians 5).

Finally, from the corporate perspective, the goal is a community of mutual love relationships, and our ethic is *to promote these relationships*. These mutual love relationships extend in two directions. There is a vertical relationship between God and the members of the community, and a horizontal relationship between members of the community. The two-way binding is an essential characteristic of the Kingdom of God. The Kingdom of God is the final goal and as such it is corporate in nature. It includes all the other goals and purposes from the two levels below it.

The use of the word 'complex' to describe a biblically-based ethic is not meant to suggest that the ethic is difficult or complicated. The word is used to indicate that it is made up of several elements. The ethic is not simple, consisting of a single strand. It is composed of three elements operating at different levels: the level of creation, of personal relationships, and of community. It is complex in the sense that it is composite. The logic of the ethic is simple. It flows from the good, to love, and then on to a community of mutual love relationships.

A Suggested Theory of Ethics

With all these characteristics firmly in place we are in a position to state our ethic. As we have observed, the overall thrust of biblical theology lends itself to a teleological approach to Christian ethics. We will approach our task by comparing our ethic to another attempt at stating a biblical ethic. C. Stephen Layman (1991, chapter 5) has suggested a Christian teleological ethic along the following lines. Like us, Layman is convinced that the goal of God's activity in history is clearly the Kingdom of God. His Christian teleological (CT) ethic is presented in the following form.

CT = An act is right if and only if it promotes the Kingdom of God.

Layman's understanding of the Kingdom of God is spelt out in terms of relationships. He claims that the flow of salvation history as it is described in Scripture leads to the view that God has created people for harmonious relationships. According to Layman, God's Kingdom is made up of a number of harmonious relationships. These relationships are between:

(a) God and humans
(b) individual humans
(c) groups of humans
(d) humans and the created order.

As well as the four areas of harmony listed above God desires,
(e) inner harmony within each human.

Layman recognizes that the capacity for deep personal relationships is limited. One can know few people intimately. Relationships, by their very nature, require reciprocity. Both parties to a relationship have to give and receive. People do not have unlimited capacities to give themselves in service to others. Despite this fact, the capacity for relationships with significant reciprocity is significant. The Kingdom of God, then, is a Kingdom of right relationships. All this is well and good, but until we know the nature of harmonious relationships our fundamental principle will be of no practical value. It will not provide guidance.

The biblical material outlined above, and examined in Chapters Four to Seven, suggests that the Kingdom of God is constituted by the type of harmonious relationships we call mutual love relationships. These relationships are harmonious because each of the agents sharing in the relationship are to be lovingly other-person-centred. Mutual love relationships are congenial because each person is committed to the other's good. In the light of this, I would now like to modify Layman's account. Since the approach adopted here is a particular expression of a Christian teleological ethic (CT), we will specify our particular ethic as a mutual love ethic (ML).

> ML = *An act is right if and only if it promotes (creates or maintains) mutual love relationships with God and humans.*

Immediately we specify our ethic in this way a difference between CT and ML becomes obvious. Layman envisaged five different types of relationships within the Kingdom of God. Our new ethic only refers to two. The reason for this change has to do with the interrelationalism of the Bible. Remember that Layman envisages that the Kingdom of God is made up of harmonious relationships between:

(a) God and humans
(b) individual humans
(c) groups of humans
(d) humans and the created order
(e) inner harmony within each human

Our examination of the biblical material suggests that (d) be considered as an aspect of (a). Moreover interrelationalism implies that (c) can be explained in terms of (b). The inner harmony within each human mentioned in (e) must surely be, as Calvin suggested, a function of right relationships with God and others.

In the light of the inclusive nature of the biblical material discussed above, a further revision is warranted. Biblical morality can shift its focus from action to agent. Sometimes moral injunctions concentrate attention on actions, while on other occasions, lists of virtues and vices emphasize the moral character of the agent. In the light of these factors ML should be amended as follows.

> ML = *An action or trait of character is right if and only if it promotes (creates or maintains) mutual love relationships between (a) God and humans, and, (b) humans and humans.*

Given a knowledge of the content of the Bible, and an understanding of mutual love relationships as spelt out in Chapter Seven, this theory now provides us with a general picture or vision of the moral life. The theory gives us a sense of the general direction we ought to be heading. This sense can give us rough moral guidance and set the parameters of our moral deliberations.

A Retrieval Ethic

Because Christians live in the overlap of the ages they will experience several kinds of tension. One is the tension of the 'now' but 'not yet'. Although believers recognize the lordship of Christ, sin is an habitual part of their natures that has to be fought by repentance and faith. Another tension is the moral tension of living in relationship with people who have rejected the majesty of God and continually violate his right order. This is the tension of living in a community that is a mixture of believers and unbelievers. It is not that non-Christians cannot be other-person-centred and loving. They can taste the glorious fruit of mutual love relationships at many points in life, including marriage. But they cannot sustain love in the way required by the gospel. A renewed heart is necessary to do this. On occasions, because of these tensions, it will be impossible to achieve the goal set by our theory of ethics.

For example, imagine a spouse married to a person who wants to leave the marriage and establish a relationship with another partner. No matter what the spouse does, the partner is determined to leave and establish a new relationship. Nothing the spouse can do will stop the fracturing of the marriage. Separation or divorce is not in accordance with the oneness that is the purpose of marriage. In the context where hardness of heart prevents the accomplishment of the goal of mutual love, love would seem to necessitate the retrieval of as much good as possible, or, at least, the reduction of harm. The justification for canvassing a retrieval approach is found in passages like 1 Corinthians 7:10-16. In the latter part of this passage Paul allows that an unbelieving partner might leave the marriage, if that is her wish, so that hostility might be avoided. Paul's words are "God has called you to peace" (verse 15). These words stand in stark contrast to his earlier command to Christian couples that they not separate (verses 10–11). Passages such as this one and the logic of the overlap of the ages drives one to the conclusion that Christians have to operate on both the mutual love ethic, and a retrieval ethic, while they wait for the consummation of all things. Where Christians cannot bring the perspectives of the Kingdom and mutual love relationships into play, the ethic seems just to be 'do good'. The goal will be to retrieve as much good as one can in the situation, and limit as much harm as is possible.

The relationship between what has been called a 'retrieval ethic' and the Kingdom ethic of mutual love needs to be clarified carefully. Referring to a Kingdom ethic of mutual love, and a retrieval ethic, can appear to indicate that there are two different ethics operating. However there are not two different ethics but the same value system operating in two different ways. In both cases the good is determined by the nature and purpose that God has willed. Where sin has not marred the occasion, people can express the values of the Kingdom in full. Where sin has spoiled the scene and limited the possibilities, then some goods might have to be abandoned and others taken up. For example, the oneness of marriage might have to be forsaken for a cessation of hostility.

Two alternatives to a retrieval ethic have been promoted in the past. The first alternative to a retrieval ethic is the doctrine that one has to do the lesser of two evils. To the biblical mind, the idea that God would wish his servants to do evil is abhorrent. The merit of a retrieval ethic is that it is based on love. Biblical love seeks what is good. Given the context of hardness of heart and sin, on occasions the good will be constituted by a reduction of harm. A second alternative to the proposed retrieval ethic is that proposed by what we have called a Kingdom Ethic. Focusing on the consummated Kingdom of God, this ethic requires believers to act as if the consummation had already come. Ignoring the fact that we live in both the present evil age as well as the age to come, this approach adopts the same set of Kingdom values as the ethic put forward in this book, but implements the values in a flat one-dimensional way. The consequences of sin are ignored. Not only is this ethic unfaithful to the shape of salvation history, but it can generate false expectations in relation to many complex situations. Such false expectations have, and will, cause considerable harm.

Doubtless, talk of a retrieval ethic will generate many fears. It may be thought that evil will be smuggled into the Christian value system. In fact, all that this retrieval ethic does is declare that some goods will not be achievable in certain contexts. The shape of this retrieval ethic will be clarified as we discuss particular issues in the later chapters of the book. Nevertheless an illustration might be helpful at this point. Some contemporary ethicists have argued for a position of compromise in relation to homosexual acts. It has been maintained that homosexual acts between people who are permanently committed to each other should be morally condoned. The reasoning is that since these acts contribute to a unity or oneness between the couples, the actions are in line with the purposes of God for human sexuality. A retrieval ethic based on the ethic of mutual love, however, will not condone homosexual acts. The compromise argument is based solely on purpose, and not on nature and purpose. The Bible consistently condemns homosexual acts; they are never considered good. The biblical ethic outlined above makes it clear that homosexual acts are condemned on the grounds that it was God's purpose for male and female to be united as one in marriage. They cannot achieve oneness between male and female. We shall see later that the nature of the biblical union is such that it is the basis for procreation and nurture. Homosexual unions lack this capacity. The nature of the parties involved cannot be ignored. Both nature and purpose have a role in the main ethic and the retrieval ethic.

Conclusion

Armed with a theory, we are now in a position to examine moral issues that confront us today. These issues will fall into two groups. One group of issues like murder, adultery, and divorce are addressed explicitly in Scripture. This group of issues can be approached directly from Scripture giving due deference to the stages of salvation history. Another group of issues like euthanasia, abortion, and genetic engineering are not specifically broached in the Scriptures. We shall have to draw out the implications from the overall picture presented in the Bible. Two different methods will need to be employed. We will demonstrate each method and indicate when and where it is to be used as we deal with particular topics.

Section Three

MORAL ISSUES

Using the theory and insights developed in
the previous section, this section takes up and
examines some contemporary issues.

CHAPTER NINE

Sex and Marriage

IN RECENT YEARS marriage has taken a bit of a battering. It has been assessed in harsh and negative terms. A radical feminist put forward one of the most negative assessments of marriage in the 1970's. Her basic argument was that all men are rapists and that the institution of marriage came about by way of a compromise. Since men were physically stronger than women, ancient women decided that it was better to be raped by one man than be subject to the whims of many—so they attached themselves to one man who would protect them from the others. This was her account of how the institution of marriage evolved.

Not all contemporary views of marriage are negative. Some are very positive even to the point of being unrealistic. The romantic view of marriage has always been popular, and is so today, even though it cannot stand up to the rugged tests of reality. The romantic view imagines that marriage will put all things right. This view may be characterized by the notion of the hero sweeping in on his charger and rescuing the pretty damsel. It is the view that feeds on and grows out of fantasy. 'If only I could get married all my problems would disappear'. The close exchanges of married life soon put paid to these illusions.

The biblical view of marriage is a positive one but it is not based on fantasy. A proper view of sex and marriage can only be derived from working through the material found in the various stages of God's revelation. We shall begin by tracing the morality of sex and marriage through the course of salvation history in an effort to locate the moral values that apply today.

Sex and Marriage throughout Salvation-history

In our modern world people tend to separate out the issues of sex and marriage. There are a number of reasons for this separation. One of these undoubtedly has to do with the fact that modern contraception allows the separation of sexual intercourse and the procreation of children. When the risk of having unwanted children was higher, people felt it was irresponsible to have sex outside of marriage. It was conceded that marriage was necessary for the nurture of children. Now that contraception is reliable, people no longer feel the same way. But the issue of sex and marriage are not readily separated in the Scriptures. They appear as two threads of the same reality. Marriage is a sexual relationship between a male and a female. It is important to remember that each of the partners is a person who has two aspects to his or her being—the inner being that formulates commitments, and the outer being that engages in action. The importance of these two aspects of human nature for an understanding of Christian marriage cannot be overstated.

The Kingdom Pattern Established (Eden)

Genesis 1–3 provides us with a glimpse of reality before the Fall. Genesis 2:4-25 assists us with a paradigm of what marriage was meant to be. Both Jesus and Paul refer back to Genesis 2 as establishing the nature and standard of marriage. The passage finds its culmination in verses 24 and 25.

> Therefore a man shall leave his father and his mother and hold fast to his wife, and they shall become one flesh. And the man and his wife were both naked and were not ashamed.

The context is important for a proper understanding of these verses. The nature of man led to the observation that it was not good for the man to be alone (2:18). After looking for a partner amongst the other animals, God creates a woman from one of Adam's ribs. The use of the notion of "bone of my bones and flesh of my flesh" (2:23) appears to be emphatic. Adam is saying that Eve is the same kind of creature as he is. Eve is a personal and relational being, just like Adam. Verse 23 leads logically on to verse 24. It is because 'woman' is of the same kind, and therefore a fit helper, that a man will leave, cleave, and be one flesh. The origin of the woman indicates the nature of the woman. She is like man. Because she is like man she is able to enter or make covenants and swear oaths of loyalty and solidarity (see Numbers 30). She has the potential to be a true companion and share fully in the task of keeping the garden.

The structure of the marriage relationship is explicitly revealed in verse 24. The Hebrew word used for leaving is a strong word usually indicating a blameworthy act of desertion. In Genesis 2:24 it indicates a breaking of obligation to the parents. However in this instant, because the break is made in order to establish another family, the act of leaving is not seen as morally blameworthy. Leaving is a discrete act occurring at a point in time.

'Cleaving' (or 'holding fast'), on the other hand, is a word that always has a durative sense. It refers to something that goes on and on continually and without interruption. It cannot refer to sexual inter-course in the context of the creation accounts. The Hebrew word for 'cleaving' speaks of bonding, and can refer to an incurable disease. Incurable diseases 'cleave' to a person. One cannot get rid of them. In the context in Genesis 2, the word refers to the permanence of the relationship set up by the act of leaving and cleaving. While the notion of cleaving cannot refer to a sexual relationship, the idea of becoming *one flesh* may have sexual connotations. Most probably, however, it refers to the broader idea of the establishment of one new social unit, a family, under a new head. The basis of this new unit would be the marriage, and consequent unity, of the male and female.

In this context, verse 25 takes on great significance. "The man and his wife were both naked and were not ashamed." The fact that both were naked and not ashamed seems to be related to the sort of relationship that Adam and Eve had entered into. Nakedness con-veys a sense of exposure. Adam and Eve at this point in time model what marriage is meant to be. In a marriage, a man and his wife expose themselves to each other. Where there is love and trust on both sides, partners can expose themselves physically, emotionally, psychologically and spiritually, and not feel threatened. For Adam and Eve this exposure is perfectly appropriate and they feel no sense of threat or inadequacy.

In Genesis 4:1 we read that Adam knew his wife and she conceived and bore a child. While the use of the verb 'to know' to describe sexual intercourse may not be frequent,[2] its use in this context is extremely appropriate. It suggests that the physical intimacy of sex is a symbol of a greater intimacy. By the use of this word, sexual intercourse is portrayed as an activity that involves the whole person. The whole person, not just the body, is exposed to the other. Each knows the thoughts and feelings of the other, and each gives themselves to the other through the act of sexual intercourse. Sexual intercourse does not merely fulfil a biological function. As the evidence unfolds we discover that sexual intercourse is a way of one person offering themselves to another through the body. It is an instrument of indwelling.

The oneness of the husband and wife seems to be the chief purpose of marriage. The begetting of children is not mentioned in Genesis 2, but it is presumed. Prior to this in Genesis 1:28 the male and female humans are blessed and instructed to multiply. The focus on the unitive purpose in marriage in the more detailed account in chapter 2 seems to put the procreative aspect back into second place. The idea that procreation is in second place is confirmed by the notion of 'one flesh'. This notion reinforces the idea of union, and suggests that the new unit is the basic unit of humanity. Marriage is the basis of a new social unit, a new family. If one were to take the early chapters of Genesis as determinative of the nature of sex and marriage, then one would conclude that it had two purposes. The first and most important purpose is unitive: the creation of one entity out of two. The second purpose is the begetting of children. The personal union of husband and wife is the appropriate basis for the begetting and nurturing of children for the simple reason that children are personal and relational beings.

The Fall

Adam and Eve's lack of faith in God and their consequent disobedience had clear ramifications for their sexual relationship.

They realized that they were naked (Genesis 3:7). They did not enjoy being exposed. After rebelling against God's rule their exposure appears to have made them feel vulnerable, and they were afraid (Genesis 3:10). While the text of Genesis does not make the psychology of this new state explicit, the doctrine of sin developed within the Scriptures makes it probable that their lack of trust in God enabled them to see that others could be against them, just as they were against God. They realized that it was possible for God and others to be against them. As is appropriate to this new state of affairs, God makes them garments of skin, and Adam and Eve are clothed (Genesis 3:21). The defensive role played by the garments suggests that sexual desire can now be warped. It may be used towards objects and goals that were not part of God's plan. Subsequent biblical history will show the perversion of sexual desire as a reality. Frequently the pattern of self-giving will be inverted. Sexual activity, from this point on, frequently will involve taking for oneself rather than giving oneself to the other.

The Kingdom Promised (Abraham)

While Abraham is a man of faith who responds to the word of God (Genesis 12:1–9), he is also a slave to sin and inflicted with the fear that sin engenders. On his trip to Egypt he attempts to deceive Pharaoh in order to protect himself (Genesis 12:10–20). Embedded in this narrative is the notion of the sanctity of the marriage union. The account of Abraham and Abimelech in chapter 20 also reinforces the ideal that the unity of marriage is sacred. The incident recorded in Genesis 16 where the barren Sarah gives her slave-girl Hagar to Abraham so that she may obtain a child runs contrary to the ideal established in the garden. The text does not explicitly condemn this act as an act of unfaithfulness, although the way Abraham 'listens to the voice' of Sarai (verse 2) suggests that he is about to make a mistake, as Adam did by 'listening to the voice' of Eve (Genesis 3:17)). The report of the antagonism between Sarah and Hagar may indicate some of the dangers of multiple wives.

In Genesis 19, we encounter the story of Lot in Sodom and

Gomorrah. Despite Sherwin Bailey's statistical analysis of the verb 'to know' the incident has a clear sexual connotation. This much is clear from the fact that Lot has two virgin daughters "who have not known any man" (19:8) whom he offers to the men of the city. Nevertheless it does appear that the homosexual element in the story is secondary to a more primary point. Webb is surely correct when he asserts that "the sexual sin of the Sodomites is part of a more general state of disorder, including inhospitality, xenophobia and violence" (Webb, 1994, p. 77). The men of the city were probably fundamentally heterosexual. As Webb observes the "object was to humiliate the foreigners by subjecting them to homosexual rape, as was often done to prisoners of war in the ancient world"—in which case the moral objection to the actions of the men of Sodom and Gomorrah must be linked to the notion of violent sexual imposition. Such sexual imposition is wrong at two points. It pays no regard to the dignity of human beings, and denies the God-given nature of human sexuality by transposing an offering of the self into an imposition upon another.

It may be suggested that Abraham's polygamy contravenes the marriage pattern. Strictly speaking, Abraham did not practice polygamy, as Hagar was a concubine, not a wife, but this does little to save the Edenic ideal of one man and one woman.[3] Other patriarchs and kings of Israel did practice polygamy. A comment by Wright is helpful at this point.

> Some customs and practices common in the ancient world were tolerated within Israel, without explicit divine command or sanction, but with a developing theological critique which regarded them as falling short of God's highest standards. The customs in question were then regulated by legal safeguards in such a way as to soften or eliminate their worst effects. In this category one could place polygamy, divorce and slavery (Wright, 1983, pp. 175–176).

God's people were slaves to sin, as Paul would say, and their sinful actions did not provide a model of morality. Even though God's people did not adopt and apply God's ideals, these ideals shaped the nature of the protective regulations.

The Kingdom Foreshadowed (David, Solomon)

The exodus from Egypt and the giving of the Law on Sinai are central to the establishment of Israel as a nation. Founded on the Torah, Israel prospered and became a great nation under David and Solomon. It is significant that both the seventh and tenth commandments delivered at Sinai endorse the exclusive nature of marriage. The prohibition on adultery continues to confine sexual activity to marriage. The injunction against coveting your neighbour's wife cannot be limited to sexual desire. One might covet another's wife for a variety of reasons. However the forbidding of coveting is an injunction addressed to the heart and covers areas that would prevent the fracturing of the unity of marriage.

When we turn to the book of Leviticus, we find it is built on the idea that God has separated Israel out from other nations to be his own people. For this reason Israel is to be holy for the Lord is holy (Leviticus 20:26). God's holiness is displayed in his wholeness and completeness. God is separated from human beings by his holiness. Israel is to be separate from the other nations and to express this separation by following God's ways. Wholeness and completeness can only be found in total devotion to the Lord. The so-called Holiness Code (Leviticus 17–26) contains explicit instructions in relation to sexual behaviour (see especially chapters 18 and 20). The restrictions and limitations found there indicate that a person's wholeness and completeness in regards to their sexual nature is found in their devotion to their marriage partner. Adultery and sex outside of marriage are forbidden, as are inappropriate marriage relationships. Furthermore a person is not to have sexual relations with (Hebrew = uncover the nakedness of) certain relatives. No reason is given for these prohibitions except the fact of kinship. Some scholars argue that it is because such relationships result in barrenness or unhealthy offspring. The argument is based on some clues found in Leviticus 20:20–21. The facts of experience can be seen to support this idea. In any case, it seems that marriage, the relationship by which kinship is established, is threatened if entered by kin.

Devotion is essential to the type of relationship that God

desires. Adultery by its very nature destroys marriage relationships. Hence death appears not only to be an appropriate penalty, but a symbol of what is taking place. The life found in the joy of union is destroyed by adultery. In Deuteronomy 22:22 the penalty for a man lying with the wife of another man is death. Both the man and the woman were to die. To modern readers this command sounds brutal and primitive. How often this penalty was actually inflicted we do not know. But the command does indicate the seriousness of sexual and marital fidelity. If sexual intercourse creates a personal and on-going bond then an act of infidelity strikes at the very nature of marriage and at the very basis of family and community life. The institution of the death penalty for adultery acts as a megaphone, and amplifies God's message of where life and goodness is found.

Despite the commandments exhorting marital fidelity, Moses concedes that men will divorce their wives (Deuteronomy 24:1). He sets up the machinery to handle the situation and to limit the damage. Jesus tells us that Moses did this not to establish a new ideal for marriage. Rather Moses permitted divorce because of hardness of heart (Matthew 19:8). In their inner being people had fixed and unchangeable intentions that flouted the will of God. It has been suggested a particular practice provoked Moses to issue this edict. It may be that Moses wanted to stop the practice of men putting away their wives in order to have affairs with other women through short-term marriage and then take their wives back again. If this were so then it is clear that such a practice would be an abomination in the Lord's sight because it treated the bond of marriage so lightly.

The unitive function of sexual intercourse undergirds many of the laws in Deuteronomy 22. If a man rapes a virgin and they are discovered, then the man has to pay the bride price to the woman's father and marry her. He is not allowed to divorce her (Deuteronomy 22:28–29). Such a law, from our cultural and historical perspective, seems very unfair on the woman, but it does follow logically from the unitive nature of sexual intercourse. A unity is created by the act of sexual intercourse and the Law ratifies this unity. The harshness of this law may not have been felt in a culture where woman did not generally choose their marriage partners. The individualism and voluntarism of the modern western mind makes the law seem particularly brutish. However it is arguable that the individualism and voluntarism of modern times have caused far greater harm than this law might have.

There are many indicators that marriage was established by covenant in the Old Testament. Remember that the Hebrew word for covenant (*berit*) has the root meaning of bond or fetter. As we have seen, it signifies a relationship based on a commitment that expresses itself in promises and obligations. The word refers to a relationship that has the property of reliability and durability. The relationship between God and Israel is likened to a covenanted marriage (Hosea 1–3, Jeremiah 3:1–5). This analogy of God as the husband and Israel as the bride reinforces the ideal of marriage as monogamous, and confirms the use of the singular for man and woman in Genesis 2:24. Just as Israel is to have only one God, so a man is to have only one wife. Mutual fidelity is expected.

The covenant of marriage is made with the heart. The dual aspects of human nature explain the unity of sex and marriage. There is an inner and an outer aspect to the union of marriage; it entails understanding and commitment. The mind and the will combine with the emotions, to formulate an intention to be the faithful partner of another. The commitment expressed in the covenant of marriage is the undertaking of the inner being. But the inner being is integrated with the outer being—the body. The partners in marriage give and receive each other as persons through the act of sexual intercourse. Sexual intercourse is an aspect of knowing each other. By its very nature it is an act of commitment. That is why the act of adultery is seen as an act of betrayal. The elements of commitment and knowing, so essential to the purpose of sexual intercourse, also explains why casual or indiscriminate sex is morally abhorrent in the Scriptures. To tear the act of sexual intercourse away from its basis in the committed personal relationship of marriage is to destroy its fundamental nature. Outside of the commitment of marriage, the sex act is trivialized.

It is reduced from a grand act of personal knowing to something much more mundane.

The Song of Songs provides us with a meditation upon human love (Dumbrell, 1988, pp. 234–239). It has as its goal a description of the completeness that human love can provide. The book shows us the way in which two become one. Human love is seen to be stronger than death (8:6–7). The common themes of garden, flowers, trees, blossoms and fruit, found in the book of Songs, take us back to the Garden of Eden. Erotic images are frequently employed, presenting the subject of human love with freshness and an absence of inhibition. In this garden of love, one encounters a fountain of life (4:15) and as an experience it is the summit of human joy (2:3, 13; 4:3, 13–14; 6:7; 7:2, 8). But such love is only possible within the limits that the Garden of Eden stipulates. It is only found within the confines of complete commitment and mutual trust.

The Kingdom at Hand (Jesus)

No detailed treatment of marriage is found in the Gospels. However Jesus viewed it positively (John 2:1–12) and strenuously insisted on the maintenance of the monogamous ideal of Genesis 2:24. His discussion of divorce (Matthew 5:32; 19:1–12; Luke 16:18) reveals that he viewed the marriage vows as unconditional. The obligations generated by the covenant of marriage could not morally be set aside. Paul draws upon the unitive nature of sexual intercourse found in Genesis 2:24 to argue that a Christian should not have sexual intercourse with a prostitute (1 Corinthians 6:12–20). He argues that a Christian is bound to Christ as Lord (v. 15). Sexual intercourse with a prostitute would bind the Christian to the prostitute. Such an action would bind the member of Christ to the prostitute (v. 15) and this is no way to honour God (v. 20).

In 1 Corinthians 7, Paul appears to put forward a low view of marriage. This passage stands in stark contrast to the very high view of marriage sustained in Scripture up to this point. Paul's argument seems to be that marriage is good in so far as it is an antidote to sexual immorality. But for Paul, celibacy seems preferable. However the rest of the chapter makes it clear that Paul was not lowering the value of marriage, but holding it in contrast with one's relationship with God. Paul's argument is that a person's relationship with God takes priority over marriage, even if marriage is the richest and most intimate of human relationships. In terms of salvation history the end-time had come. God was bringing history to completion through the work of Christ and the preaching of the gospel. Time was short (v. 29). This world was passing away (v. 31) and the need for gospel proclamation was great indeed. Celibates were able to give their full attention and time to gospel proclamation. Nevertheless, not everyone was called to celibacy. Sexual desire, and the control of these desires, was a gift from God (v. 7). If one had the gift of celibacy then one should use it to give more time to the Lord's affairs (v. 32).

The fact that marriage is a mutual love relationship comes out in 1 Corinthians 7:3–7. Two aspects of this relationship are drawn out. In marriage, a person's body is not one's own. One's body belongs to the other as well as themselves. Marriage partners have given themselves to each other. As a consequence each person has to give himself or herself to serving the sexual needs and desires of the other. Spouses are to be other-person-centred. Partners can deny the other's sexual needs for a while, but it must be with their agreement and then only for a short time lest Satan tempt them (7:5).

Paul's advice to the married (7:11–12), which he received from the Lord, fits the pattern of mutual love relationships. A husband cannot divorce his wife, and a wife should not separate from her husband. But if she does separate, she is to remain unmarried or be reconciled to her husband. Each is to be committed to the other, and where difficulties are encountered forgiveness and repentance are to operate. If repentance and forgiveness cannot be brought into play, then separation is possible. Remarriage to another is not possible, for the moral obligations generated by the marriage vows are still binding. These are the only two options available for believers. It is separation or reconciliation. Commitment to the marriage partner is never to be withdrawn.

In the Epistle to the Ephesians, Paul draws a parallel between Christ's devotion to his body, the church, and a husband's devotion to his wife (Ephesians 5:29–33). Calling on Genesis 2:24, he elicits an analogy between Christ's unity with the church and the unity between a husband and wife. By using this analogy, Paul implies that the true nature of marriage can only be fully understood through the Christ event. Marriage is patterned on the love of God, and the love of God is only truly and fully seen in Christ's sacrificial death on the cross. Marriage is thus seen to be a relationship of exclusive devotion and service to the good of the other.

Moreover, just as there is only one leader in the church so there is only to be one leader in the family. The unity of any group is fractured if there is more than one leader. The concept of headship in marriage has become repugnant to the modern world because of its abuse. Husbands have dominated their wives and turned them into servants. But the biblical concept of headship finds its place within the framework of mutual love relationships. Christ, the head of the church, is the model. He gives himself in loving service to the church even at the price of his own life. Headship in marriage operates within the dialogue of mutual concerns and understanding, and on the basis of mutual service. It is no wonder that when the qualifications for those who would be overseers or leaders within the congregation are mentioned and listed in the New Testament, that fidelity in marriage is a high priority (1 Timothy 3:2). The Kingdom of God is a Kingdom of mutual love relationships and a leader in the Kingdom must adhere to the model of love or else he will lead his congregation away from God's pattern of relationships.

The Kingdom Consummated (The Return of Jesus)

The Sadducees questioned Jesus about a hypothetical case where a woman had been married to seven brothers (Luke 20:27–40; Matthew 22:23–33; Mark 12:18–27). The question was straightforward and simple. "In the resurrection, whose wife will the woman be?" Jesus' reply contrasted the present age with the age-to-come. Those considered worthy to participate in the age-to-come "neither marry nor are given in marriage". The reason why they neither marry nor are given in marriage apparently has to do with the fact that they are like angels and can no longer die. The relationships of the eternal age are apparently different to this present age. Marriage is not part of the final state of affairs. While marriage as a mutual love relationship may point to the type of relationships in the Kingdom, it is not part of the ultimate reality. Nevertheless it prefigures and anticipates the complete mutual love relationships of the consummated Kingdom.

Given the flow of salvation history, the only way that I can give significance to this revelation is by taking up a clue from 1 Corinthians 13:12. There the apostle informs us that we will know as we have been known. In this present age, sex and marriage is the most intimate knowledge that humans can have of one another. By way of contrast, God has a direct and totally intimate knowledge of every person. We are utterly and completely known by him in a direct and non-physical way. My suggestion is that in the age-to-come humans will have a way of knowing and a form of intimacy in relationships, that is direct and does not involve human sexuality. We will know all our neighbours, including our earthly marriage partners, in a completely intimate and direct way. While this suggestion is speculative it does accord with the notion that the Kingdom of God is to reflect the very character of God. The Triune God enjoys the intimacy of direct knowledge.

Conclusions

We have recounted the main passages in the Bible in relation to the nature and purpose of both sex and marriage. The flow of salvation history suggests that we must give primary attention to the material in the creation accounts. Here the unspoiled image of the nature of things is revealed. Marriage has to do with leaving, cleaving, becoming one flesh, nakedness, knowing and procreation. With the Fall the nature of things is distorted and the purpose of both sex and marriage is subjected to futility. The purpose of sex and marriage is clearly revealed in Christ. The goal is mutual love and the true nature of love is disclosed on the cross. It is a sacrificial self-giving to the good of the other. When we use our imagination and intuition to integrate the clues provided by the evidence we come up with an ideal that may be summarized in the following way. The ideal has two aspects that accord with the two aspects of human nature. The first aspect is covenantal and encompasses the inner being. We will symbolize this aspect using the letter I.

(I) Marriage is basically a covenant or agreement between a man and a woman based on mutual love. Love is the unqualified commitment of one person to the good of another through every circumstance of life. The purpose and goal of this type of personal relationship is a unique form of unity. As such it provides the basis of a new social unit into which it is appropriate for children to be born and nurtured. The marriage relationship is to bear all the marks and virtues of a mutual love relationship. Breaks in commitment are to be healed through repentance and forgiveness.

The second aspect of marriage incorporates the outer being. The commitment of the inner being finds a unique expression in the bodily act of love. The indications given in Scripture about the nature of sexuality and its God-intended purposes also confirm the traditional Christian insight into the nature of human sexuality expressed by the following normative standard represented by the letter O.

(O) The nature of human sexuality is such that the goal and purpose of sexual intercourse is mutual indwelling and unity. Sexual intercourse is primarily an activity by which one person gives themselves as a person to another person through the body within the framework of covenantal commitment. It is an act which should incorporate and symbolize the giving of the self, and the reception and acceptance of the other. Secondly, sexual intercourse may be an act of procreation. The social unit arising out of the unitive nature of sexual intercourse is the appropriate context for the nurturing of children. Personal and relational beings ought to be nurtured in the framework of the personal relationship of marriage.

Sex and marriage are two aspects of the one reality. They

correspond to the outer and inner aspects of human nature. Marriage incorporates the two moral standards expressed by I and O. In addition, the biblical description of sex and marriage stated above incorporates all three elements of biblical morality— creation, personal relationships, and community. The sexual mode of human nature finds its goal in sexual intercourse. At the personal level of the relationship the goal is a unique unity expressed in mutual indwelling. The bi-polar unit created by the marriage is the basis for procreation and the development of community.

The Greek philosopher Plato categorized sexual desire as part of nature that humans shared with the animal world. This animalistic aspect of human nature did not rate highly with Plato, when compared with the realm of pure ideas and the activity of the mind. Eventually a stream of thought emerged that saw human sexual activity as something to be rejected, and even despised. A tradition that viewed human sexuality as shameful developed and found its way through the medieval period into the modern world. In the English speaking world it found some expression in the Victorian period. The Bible knows nothing of this negative attitude towards human sexuality. Certainly the wrong use of sex is condemned, but the proper expression of human sexuality is regarded as a spiritual thing. The Song of Songs rightly sees sexual love as a source of delight. As we have observed, it is meant to be an expression of a much wider personal relationship where a man and a woman open up their minds and hearts to share with each other. It is an act of mutual love and indwelling that defies adequate description.

Given the biblical understanding of sex and marriage one can understand why the themes of sex and marriage are inseparable in the Scriptures. The nature of sexual activity is such that marriage is the only truly appropriate framework for sexual activity. In locating the biblical ideal in relation to sex and marriage we have just begun our task. We have located an ideal that will act as a standard by which we can evaluate the morality of various sexual activities. In the light of this ideal it is not surprising that the biblical writers consistently condemn fornication (sex between unmarried people), adultery, rape and homosexual acts.

However, we have to realize that we live in a fallen world where there are practical difficulties to be faced. Locating the ideal is only the beginning. Putting the ideal into practice may be more difficult than anticipated. The fallen world has corrupted human nature and erected barriers in the way of God's good purposes. We shall turn our attention to these difficulties in the next chapter.

CHAPTER TEN

Divorce and Remarriage

Some Practical Difficulties

Having a clear notion of the biblical ideal of marriage is not enough to secure a good marriage. We live in a fallen world, and in this fallen world people have learnt habits and traits of character which are not only sinful, but also damaging to personal relationships. People who are spoilt in early childhood often develop into self-centred individuals who cannot give themselves in service to others. Other people are so repressed by dominating and overbearing parents that they do not learn to express their emotions. Often these people lack the skill of bringing their feelings to the surface of their consciousness. These people find it difficult to express their feelings to their partner. Other people are able to bring their feelings to the surface but lack the skill of identifying their emotions. The assorted range of psychological incapacities that one could list indicates that the causes of marriage breakdown are varied and complex. However, this is not the place to go through the ways people are psychologically damaged and the type of injury they suffer. All we need to note here is that people living in a sinful world are frequently not able to give themselves in loving service to others. Consequently they are not easily able to maintain a happy marriage. Some find it impossible to maintain a marriage at all.

Sometimes people's lack of ability to give themselves is not a matter of psychological or emotional incapacity. It may be a matter of philosophy or ideology. One of the most devastating popular philosophies of modern life is called 'individualism'. You will remember that back in Chapter Six we examined the notion of methodological individualism. Steven Lukes (1973) in his classical

study of this philosophy located seven different types of individualism. The popular philosophy that we are concerned with contains
a cluster of different ideas. It is based on the notion of 'the abstract
individual'. The notion of 'the abstract individual' maintains that
the individual existed prior to social and political life and had fixed
and unvarying human features such as instincts, reason, desires,
needs and purposes. Social structures are the creation of individuals and merely allow individuals to fulfil their goals. Clustered
around this 'abstract' individualism are other brands of individualism, specifically epistemological, ethical, political and economic
individualism. A brief outline of these doctrines will be helpful in
understanding one modern line of thought.

Epistemology is that branch of philosophical inquiry that
endeavours to provide a theory of knowledge. It is fundamentally
concerned with the question of how people know what they know.
So epistemological individualism is the doctrine that asserts that the
source of knowledge is the individual. The popular individualism
referred to above blends epistemological individualism with ethical
individualism. According to the doctrine of ethical individualism,
the source of morality is the individual. The individual knows what
is best in regard to their life and is therefore in a position to set the
goals that determine the moral standards of their life. Taking the
notion of autonomy to its logical conclusion, the individual is seen
to be the creator of moral values. On this view morality is merely
subjective. Each person has his or her own moral standards and it is
considered immoral for anyone else to try and impose other
standards upon an individual. As such, ethical individualism is
subjective and stands in contrast to objectively based ethics where
"the criteria governing moral judgments are not open to choice but
are given" (Lukes, 1973, p. 106).

Added to the beliefs of epistemological and ethical
individualism is the creed of political individualism. Trading on the
notion of 'the abstract individual', citizens are seen as independent
centres of consciousness who generate their own wants and
preferences. Governments get their authority only by the consent
of the citizens. On the basis of this notion, seventeenth and

eighteenth century political theorists developed 'social contract' theories. According to these theories political representation is representation of individual interests and not the interests of groups or classes. The purpose of government is seen to be enabling individuals to secure their interests. A key role of government is the protection of individual rights. The final ingredient in popular individualism is economic individualism. This is the doctrine that "sees in the individual and his psychological aptitudes the necessary basis of society's economic organization" (Lukes, 1973, p. 89). It is thought that "the actions of individuals will suffice to provide the principles of society's economic organizations" (Lukes, 1973, p. 89). On this view, governments seek

> to realize social progress through the individual by allowing him all the scope for his free self-development which is possible.
>
> It believes that, for this, two institutions are necessary: economic freedom (that is, freedom of enterprise) and private property (Lukes, 1973, p. 89).

It is interesting to note that some versions of individualism see care of others as the best way to secure individual interests. Yet this care of others cannot be identified as what the Bible calls love, because self-interest is the dominant motive. There is no other-person-centredness, and no real grace. The lack of these two elements in individualism work against the formation of mutual love relationships. The best mutual self-interest can establish is an exchange relationship. It is important to recognize the difference between theories of individualism and the theory of mutual love relationships. The theory of mutual love relationships embraces interrelationism not individualism.

We could persist with more examples and illustrations but the point is that there are many psychological and philosophical forces alive in this world that militate against the development of good marriages. Becoming a Christian does not make one immune to these forces. Conversion brings a new power and a new will into people's lives, but this new power does not immediately cancel past history. Being 'in Christ' secures a right relationship with God, but life 'in Christ' has to be lived out through repentance and faith. When a believer falls away from the image of Christ through doing wrong, then by the power of the cross he or she is restored through repentance and faith. While the victory in Christ has been won, the struggle to live 'in Christ' can be both fierce and prolonged. It is a sad fact of life that, just as many non-Christians do not have the capacity to live together in marriage, so many Christians lack the capacity to live happily together in wedlock. Hopefully these Christians might receive and accept counselling not to marry. But such counselling is usually rejected. The truth is that there are many troubled and painful marriages in the world today both inside and outside the church.

In the western world in previous times social attitudes and legal constraints would discourage separation and divorce. Perhaps the doctrine of individual autonomy did not pervade society as it does today. People would press on in unhappy and painful marriages. But this is not the case today. For better or for worse, people will not tolerate dissatisfaction or unhappiness in marriage. Divorce and remarriage has become commonplace. The issue before us in this chapter has to do with how evangelical Christians should respond to the present situation.

Before we begin an examination of the biblical material specifically related to divorce, we need to remind ourselves of the nature of marriage. From our overview of the biblical material in the previous chapter we can see that marriage is one of the most intimate and important of human mutual love relationships. As such it is meant to reflect the unity that is to be found between Christ and the church. It is based on steadfast love and consummated by each partner giving themselves to the other through the body. In marriage a wonderful unity can be found. It is a unity that reflects the unity of the Trinity since it is founded on the same gracious and unqualified love. It is a source of joy. Joy comes from the knowledge that someone is totally and unconditionally committed to one's good. One can see why God might hate divorce. It frustrates his ultimate purpose, destroying mutual love relationships and bringing pain and misery in place of peace and joy.

Divorce and Remarriage in the Bible

The Kingdom Pattern Established (Eden)

Neither divorce nor remarriage are mentioned in the creation accounts. The paradigm established in the garden did not include separation or remarriage.

The Fall

The entry of sin into the world fractured Adam and Eve's relationship with God. The fracturing of this vertical relationship had its consequences upon the horizontal relationships between Adam and Eve. In clothing themselves Adam and Eve not only hid their outer natures but also indicate a new inner attitude of distrust. The consequence of a wrong relationship with God is the same throughout salvation history. The fracturing of people's relationship with God has consequences upon people's relationships with one another. A person who cannot serve God will find it difficult to truly serve anyone else.

The Kingdom Promised (Abraham)

Although Abraham was chosen by God, he was not immune to sin. On two occasions he put his wife and marriage at risk in order to protect his own life (Genesis 12:11–20; 20:1–18). It is hard to tell whether Abraham's attitude to marriage was typical of the period. But both incidents confirm the sanctity of marriage in God's eyes. God will not allow Abraham or others to treat marriage lightly.

The Kingdom Foreshadowed (David, Solomon)

Later, when the details of God's covenantal relationships with his people were spelt out, Moses conceded that men could divorce their wives (Deuteronomy 24:1). In the last chapter we noted that he sets up the machinery to handle the situation and to limit the damage. Jesus confirmed that Moses did this not to establish a new ideal of marriage. Rather Moses permitted divorce because of hardness of heart (Matthew 19:8). People refused to go God's way and some remedial action needed to be taken so the situation did not become chaotic. Even if this particular law was an attempt to stop the practice of wife swapping by means of short-term marriage, the Law still reveals the value God placed on the bond of marriage.

Divorce seems to have been practiced widely enough in the days of Moses for it is mentioned in several statutes. In Leviticus 21:14, Moses conveyed the Lord's command that a priest was not to marry a divorced woman. Only the priest and his immediate family could eat of the sacrifices offered at the tabernacle. Yet the divorced daughter of a priest who had returned to her father's house was still eligible to partake of the offering (Leviticus 22:13). In Numbers 30 the vows of widows and divorced women are viewed differently to those of married women. A husband could nullify his wife's vows under certain conditions but the vow of widows and divorced women could not be nullified and were binding.

The prophet Malachi used the imagery of marriage to cover Judah's covenantal relationship with God. Delivering a word of judgment, Malachi condemned the faithlessness of the people of Judah in their relationship with him. In this condemnation God forbids faithlessness in marriage and declares that he hates divorce (Malachi 2:10–17).[4]

The Kingdom at Hand (Jesus)

The New Testament addresses the question of divorce in the context of the 'now but not yet' tension found in the overlap of the ages. It is extremely significant that Jesus attacked the withdrawal of commitment to a marriage partner in a most vigorous manner. Withdrawal of commitment was equated with adultery. It is the withdrawal of a person's commitment to his or her marriage partner that leads to adultery, and may be seen as the cause of adultery. Withdrawal of commitment brings about the collapse of all the wonderful possibilities of joy that are found in mutual love relationships. The destruction of such a relationship is a form of spiritual death. The Old Testament penalty, whether it was ever practised or not, was thoroughly appropriate. The penalty mimicked the outcome. The nature of the act was synonymous with the consequences.

In Matthew 5:32 Jesus proclaimed that any man who divorced his wife caused her to commit sexual infidelity and made her an adulteress. Furthermore he added that any man who married the divorced woman committed adultery. What is the logic here? Firstly, it seems clear that this injunction does not cover the woman who has already been involved in sexual infidelity. (An exception clause was included in Jesus' utterance. If the wife had already committed adultery then the husband could not be the cause of her becoming an adulteress.) In divorcing his wife, Jesus declared, the husband caused her to become an adulteress. In a patriarchal society, a woman needed a husband to find any kind of security and life. Jesus' argument seems to be consequentialist in nature. The husband's action is immoral because it caused the woman to break the marriage bond she vowed to keep. The woman adulterates the marriage relationship by giving herself to another in the act of sexual intercourse even if it were in a legal marriage. The exception clause indicates that whatever the husband's motives in putting his wife away, he is not putting away his wife on the grounds that she has been sexually unfaithful. He may have found some fault in her, or he may just desire another woman. Clearly the husband is the one who is withdrawing his commitment. However in this passage the focus is not on the immorality of the husband's action of withdrawal, but on the immoral and unacceptable consequences.

The context in which Jesus makes his declaration is significant. It is made against the background of Deuteronomy 24:1. This was a passage used by some Jews to justify divorce on a variety of grounds. Apparently many Jews felt that having a certificate issued by the husband was enough to free the woman from her marriage covenant. The point of Jesus' proclamation is that the woman is not free. In putting her off, the husband makes the woman deny her vows. According to Jesus' logic any man who married her would commit adultery because her vows still held. The point of the assertion was that marriage vows were unconditional. The obligations created by the marriage vows continued despite the actions of the husband.

In Matthew 19:9, the context is slightly different. Again the background is the Mosaic decree on divorce, but the proclamation is directed to those husbands who divorce their wives and remarry. Jesus declares that if a husband breaks or withdraws his commitment to his wife in order to marry another then he is guilty of adultery. Again there is an exception. If the woman had already been sexually unfaithful, then the husband does not cause her to commit adultery. The reasoning behind this exception, as we have seen, has to do with the fact that sexual intercourse is a way of giving oneself to another through the body. In the case where the wife had been unfaithful she had already broken the covenant by giving herself to another. But the focus of attention is not on the exception in this passage. The focus of attention is on the intention of the husband to withdraw his commitment. In this passage it is the withdrawal of commitment, and not the consequences of the withdrawal of commitment, that is under attack. In focusing on the moral implications of the marriage vow, Jesus is highlighting the reality found in the inner nature. He is drawing attention to the state of the man's heart. The man's thoughts and values have led him to formulate an intention that is the inner equivalent of the bodily action of adultery. The man's heart is evil. It does not match up to the will and purpose of God.

The careful reader will have noted the significance given above to the exception clauses in both the passages in Matthew. There is a longstanding and popular interpretation of these statements of Jesus that see them as justifying divorce in the case of adultery. Several things suggest that this interpretation may not be warranted. The first has to do with the notion of steadfast love. In a later section of the Sermon on the Mount (Matthew 5:43–48), Jesus expounds upon the gracious nature of love. Love is to be showered upon the righteous and the unrighteous. It does not operate on the principle of exchange. "For if you love those who love you, what reward do you have?" (Matthew 5:46). Love finds a place for forgiveness. Secondly, in Matthew 19:8 Jesus explicitly states that Moses only allowed divorce because of hardness of heart. Thirdly, the context of each passage is the defence of the biblical ideal of marriage. In the latter passage Jesus explicitly quotes from Genesis 2. Fourthly, as was observed above, the logic of the passages does not demand the justification of divorce on the grounds of adultery. The focus is on the act of breaking the marriage through adultery.

The nature of marriage as a bipolar relationship always allows that the other partner could dissolve or diminish the marriage through adultery or desertion. The point that Jesus is making, by implication, is that the godly person will operate on the basis of love and will not want to deny or nullify the marriage vows made. If the faithful spouse can stop the break-up of the marriage then godly love demands that he or she do so. If the faithful spouse cannot stop the sundering of the relationship then justification is not the issue. In terms of the ideal of marriage as a mutual love relationship, divorce is never endorsed. It only ever comes about because of a lack of genuine love on one side or the other. The burning issue when a marriage is broken is whether or not the faithful partner is bound to the unfaithful spouse and to the marriage commitments made. Clearly the moral obligations of the marriage covenant are still morally binding, but sin has destroyed the good that God intended. The important question is whether or not a retrieval ethic might be brought into play. Jesus does not address this question. The apostle Paul, however, does address the particular case of the unbelieving partner leaving the believer. To use Paul's words "the brother or sister is not enslaved" to the marriage (1 Corinthians 7:15). We will return to this matter a little later. For now we need to note that *to think in terms of justification is to change the logic of love.* Luke reminds us in the Parable of the Good Samaritan that it is inappropriate to use the Law to justify oneself. Christians need to be careful that they do not use the teaching of Jesus in the same loveless way.

Some scholars would argue that I have misinterpreted the Matthean passages in regard to this matter. They argue that Jesus was not talking about relationships that *should* not be broken but about a state of affairs that *could* not be broken. These scholars argue that marriage creates a bond like the bond of kinship. Kinship is a familial relationship and it is biological in nature. Kin includes parents, children, cousins, aunts, uncles, and so on. Kinship relationships are established biologically and cannot be changed. No verbal utterance or disavowal can undo the biological links. My father will always be my father no matter what happens. A little thought will reveal that the marriage relationship is not constituted by biological links. Although consummated by a biological act, it is constituted by the giving and receiving of vows. The weight and strength of the obligations generated by these vows are such that they *should* never be denied or broken. The exclusive nature of the marriage relationship is defined by the devotion of one person to another. Devotion excludes all others. The fact that it is devotion to a person means that it is ongoing and not temporary commitment. Persons are ongoing agents and a commitment to a person, as against a commitment to do something for a person, is an ongoing thing. The nature of the marriage relationship demands that it be for life. Death is the only thing that should break the bonds of commitment. The commitment can be ignored, dismissed or denied—but it is immoral to do so.

Following the teaching of Jesus, Paul in his letter to the Corinthians does not allow Christians to divorce (1 Corinthians 7:10–11). If things become too difficult Paul allows that the couple may separate for a time and then be reconciled to each other. Divorce and re-marriage are excluded by these instructions. The thinking behind the instructions is not difficult to follow. The attitude necessary to establish a marriage is steadfast love. Such love counts the other greater than oneself and gives preference to the needs and desires of the other over one's own needs and desires. Being other-person-centred this love is gracious and unconditional. This commitment of love cannot be conditional or the unity and trust of marriage would not be generated. Conditional love is self-defeating if the goal is a mutual love relationship. Placing self-interest above the interests of the other destroys the unity and oneness that is part of God's plan and blessing. Both partners must keep the commitment to the other if any of God's possibilities are to be realized in their lives. The principle of mutual love is embedded in Paul's instruction on sexual relations in marriage in 1 Corinthians 7:3. Paul declares: "the husband should give to his wife her conjugal rights, and likewise the wife to her husband".

Paul's advice appears to differ in the case of an unbelieving spouse (1 Corinthians 7:12–16). This passage is the source of the so-called Pauline Privilege, a doctrine that declares that the believer is free to remarry if the unbelieving spouse leaves his or her partner. However a thorough study of the text reveals that Paul has the same concerns as before. His concern is that divorce should not take place (vv. 12–13). Mutual love relationships require the commitment of both parties. In the case where both are Christians, and members of the Kingdom of God, commitment is the order of the day. To give up loving would be to leave the Kingdom. A non-believer is not motivated to keep his or her commitment in the same way. They may want to leave. If so, the believing brother or sister is not bound to restrain them from leaving. The unbelieving partner should be allowed to leave in an amicable fashion. Keeping peaceful relations at this point might permit certain possibilities in the future; namely, winning the partner by evangelizing them through word or deed. The obligations that love places upon the Christian spouse are clear from the injunctions in verses 12 and 13. If the unbelieving spouse consents to live with the believer then there should be no divorce. The believer should lovingly serve the other, seeking his or her good, with the added bonus that the unbelieving partner might be saved through the believer's witness. But if the unbelieving partner does want to leave then the believer is to let them go peacefully.

There is very considerable scholarly debate over what Paul means when he declares that "the brother or sister is not enslaved (or bound)" in verse 15 of 1 Corinthians 7. The notion of being fettered or bound occurs twice in 1 Corinthians 7. In giving advice to the unmarried Paul recommends the status quo (1 Corinthians 7:27). "Are you bound to a wife? Do not seek to be free. Are you free from a wife? Do not seek a wife." Later in verse 39 he proclaims that "A wife is bound to her husband as long as he lives". He goes on to affirm, "But if her husband dies, she is free to be married to whom she wishes, only in the Lord". Some scholars note that the Greek word used in verse 15 is different to the word used in verses 27 and 39. Since both the Greek words can be used of the binding of marriage, I do not think that this fact is overly significant. What is significant is that in both verses 27 and 39 there is an antithesis between the notions of 'being bound' and 'being free'. If one is free, then one is not bound, and if one is bound then one is not free. Given the covenantal nature of marriage, we must conclude that verse 15 means that the believing partner is not bound to keep his or her marriage commitment because the unbelieving partner has broken the marriage and left. It is the commitment that binds one spouse to another, and when a spouse is freed from the partner they are freed from the commitment. In such cases the goal of a mutual love relationship cannot be achieved.

The differences in interpretation at this point seem to be based on one's general understanding of Paul's approach to moral issues. Some people understand Paul to have a deontological approach to morality. According to these people, Paul's understanding of the moral 'ought' is such that it is binding because of the nature of the injunction. It is probably thought that in regard to Paul the feature of the act that makes it binding is that God commanded it. Correspondingly it is argued that verse 39 supports this interpretation. A spouse is bound to a partner until death. The idea is that the commitment of marriage is morally binding until death and that is the end of the issue. But if one thinks that Paul had a teleological view of ethics then one can argue that it is the goal of the commitment that determines when it is binding.[5] Certainly the ideal is that the commitment should only be broken by death. The point Paul is making in verse 39 is that the marriage vow is broken by death not that it is only broken by death.

It is clear that death makes the marriage vow empty and void. The partner is no longer present to be the object of loving faithful service. The object of the commitment has been removed by death. While Paul insists that the moral commitment made in marriage should not be broken he appears to recognize eschatological factors that make the commitment void. The commitment of the believing spouse is made void if the unbelieving partner leaves. The goal of a mutual love relationship cannot be achieved. The object of the believing partner's love has withdrawn. While it must be agreed that Paul is not raising or addressing the question of remarriage in this passage, the logic of his thinking does help us address this contentious issue. Understanding 1 Corinthians 7:15 in a deontological fashion means that the marriage commitment of the believing partner is still valid and effective after the unbelieving partner has permanently withdrawn from the marriage. If this were so, then the commitment would have no other purpose than stopping the believing partner from making another commitment to someone else. The commitment would be a negative commitment. It would be a commitment not to be committed to anyone else in marriage. On the other hand, understanding this passage in a teleological way would mean that the believing partner is not free to negate any marriage vow, but that in some circumstances the marriage vow is made null and void. The difficulty is found in the fact that while the moral obligation of the marriage commitment is still binding, being unconditional, it is ineffective. The commitment does not and cannot generate the goal it was meant to achieve. Hence there is room for a retrieval ethic.

While Paul does not explicitly state that the believer whose unbelieving partner leaves is free to remarry, it is more than reasonable to draw this conclusion. The unbelieving partner's leaving breaks the bipolar relationship of marriage. The believer's commitment to the unbelieving partner is incapable of operating and finding expression. It is as though the partner were dead. If the believer is freed from the marriage commitment to the unbeliever then logic requires that he or she is free to marry. The believer/unbeliever situation is totally unlike the believer/believer situation addressed in verses 10 and 11. The believers have good reason to remain committed to God's purposes and, especially his purpose for them in marriage. The believer whose unbelieving partner has left might have good reason to get married again. Having had a regular sex life the abandoned believer might not be able to exercise self-control in this regard. Paul's earlier advice might be relevant. If one is not able to exercise self-control and is in danger of falling into the practice of fornication, then "it is better to marry than to be aflame" (1 Corinthians 7:9).

The Kingdom Consummated (The Return of Jesus)

The problems of divorce and remarriage will not exist in a perfect Kingdom where people are not given and received in marriage. However the consummated Kingdom holds out the hope of a new way of knowing each other. This new way of knowing promises a depth of joy not knowable in this age. It is a joy that comes from complete mutual indwelling. People in the present evil age can taste this joy at the human level through the experience of a godly marriage. At a spiritual level they can experience it in their relationship with God through Christ.

Conclusions about marriage and divorce in the Bible

The biblical texts that deal with the matter of divorce are consistent with the ideals of marriage found in Scripture when consideration is given to the progression of salvation history. Both Jesus and Paul indicate that marriage is a bipolar relationship and, as such, requires the commitment of both partners to make the marriage work. Jesus' pronouncements tacitly recognize that sexual intercourse with someone outside the marriage is an act of commitment that violates the marriage vow. Paul perceives that the eschatological dimension of salvation history impinges upon the ethical perspective in relation to marriage break up. The overlap of the ages means that believers and unbelievers do enter into relationships. The motives and understanding of marriage adopted by unbelievers will not always sustain a marriage. But if a believer is married to an unbeliever who is willing to maintain the marriage, the believer is to pursue his or her marriage vows faithfully. The great concern is that Christians are not to break or withdraw the unconditional vows made in matrimony. They are to be faithful as their heavenly Father is faithful.

Contemporary Situations and Concerns

In the last chapter we saw that the Bible gives us two clear ideals. These are the ideal of covenant (I) and the ideal of sexual relationships (O). In addition to this the Bible leaves us with the implications of the eschatological movement of salvation history. Marriages are meant to be mutual love relationships. An unconditional commitment to the good of the other is necessary on both sides. Love ought to be mutual, but what should happen when it is not? The ideals of marriage and sexual relationships, combined with the implications of biblical eschatology, suggest that three different policies are relevant. The first policy applies in cases where both spouses are Christians. The second policy is to be employed where one partner is not a believer. And the third policy has to do with the social policy adopted in relation to unbelievers.

Policy One: Marriage between Believers

Both the character and action of believers are to be marked by love. They are to reflect the love of their King. A believer should never withdraw a commitment to love his or her spouse. In a moment of sin or weakness a believer might fail to be committed to the good of his or her marriage partner in a particular situation or for a period of time. In these situations the believer is called upon to repent. The relationship is to be restored by re-commitment and forgiveness. Even if the period of pain and hurt is prolonged and the partners cannot bear to live together, neither the Bible nor our ethic allows unconditional commitment to be reduced to conditional commitment. Nor does the Bible allow that other-person-centredness be turned into self-centredness. The partners may separate but the only acceptable future action is reconciliation. While a marriage may go through difficult times, the believer has the motivation and the resources to maintain it. With renewed hearts, prayer, the power of the Holy Spirit, and the support of fellow believers, hard times can be traversed. Pastoral and personal experience suggests that the difficult times can be times of real growth in the marriage relationship. Love is tested in hard times, but when a spouse sees that his or her partner will pay a great price to keep his or her commitment of love then the marriage is strengthened. Recognition of the depth of the love of a spouse is a source of true joy and these times can bring great riches to a marriage.

All of this presumes that Christians will be obedient to the revealed Word of God in relation to marriage. But what if, for example, a believer turns from his or her believing partner and goes off to a far country, divorces and remarries. The possibilities of reconciliation are virtually non-existent. In the meantime the deserted partner lacks the gift of celibacy (1 Corinthians 7:1–9). Is he or she free to remarry? On the grounds of the fact that it is better to marry than to be aflame (1 Corinthians 7:9) it could be argued that remarriage was not just an option but a command. Certainly given the argument in 1 Corinthians 7 the partner ought to pray for the gift of self-control so that he or she might give themselves more fully to the Lord's concerns (v. 32). But if the gift is not forthcoming, what then?

The logic of the Kingdom of God, which is the logic of the Kingdom of mutual love relationships, suggests that a believer who leaves his or her spouse and refuses to repent would no longer qualify as a member of the Kingdom. Jesus endorsed this logic when he declared that such people should be treated as gentiles and tax collectors (Matthew 18:15–20). Interestingly Jesus keeps the balance required by mutual love relationships in presenting the other side of the coin. In the following passage he proclaims that those who refuse to continue to forgive others will not find the forgiveness of God (Matthew 18:21–35). The unforgiving will find no place in the Kingdom of the forgiving God. To live in God's Kingdom in the overlap of the ages demands a heart that exercises itself in repentance and forgiveness. There is some scriptural warrant, then, for treating the deserting spouse as a non-believer. And if this is so, the command of Paul to the believer with an unbelieving spouse would be applicable to the believer whose Christian partner leaves and will not return. In this case the believer would not be bound by his or her marriage vows and would be free to remarry. The unrepentant partner has made the vow null and void.

Marriage breakdowns between believers seem to divide into two kinds. Firstly there are those marriages where each partner desires to be obedient to the Word of God. Difficulties might lead to separation but, in theory, with good counselling, good teaching, and congregational support the possibility of restoration through reconciliation remains open. Frequently, however, Christian married couples hide their problems and by the time they surface the path to reconciliation requires an extraordinary effort. In the meantime difficult relations have disposed the partners against making such an effort. Christian morality necessitates that local congregations provide an environment that encourages openness between marriage partners as well as sound teaching and good counselling resources.

The second kind of marriage breakdown between Christians is where one partner has fixed intentions about leaving the marriage. In these cases, any call to repentance, forgiveness, or reconciliation is met by hard-hearted indifference. It has been suggested above that this type of case be treated like the case of the Christian with a non-believing partner. While the two types of marriage breakdown between Christians is logically fairly clear, the great difficulty is found in applying the categories. A real problem is often found in determining when the first type has deteriorated into the second. Locating the point of no return may be a very difficult task.

Policy Two: Believers with Non-Christian Partners

The difference between Christians and non-Christians is highlighted in the New Testament. Christians follow the Lord Jesus. Non-Christians willingly or unwittingly serve Belial, the one who opposes Christ. The contrast is between light and darkness, righteousness and lawlessness. The Christian is warned not to be associated with those who inhabit the world of darkness (2 Corinthians 6:14–7:1; Ephesians 5:3–21). Paul specifically cautions the Corinthians that "bad company ruins good morals" (1 Corinthians 15:33). While these are general warnings, they may legitimately be applied to marriage. Of all the associations Christians can have with non-Christians, marriage is the most intimate.

A little reflection will disclose the reason behind the warnings. Christians and non-Christians have two different masters, and these masters commend two different sets of values. People are not indifferent to values. People with different sets of values tend to clash. Paul makes this clear when he asks the rhetorical question, "What accord has Christ with Belial?" (2 Corinthians 6:15). Since marriage is about union, the two becoming one, then it would be absurd to imagine that two people with two opposing sets of values might be welded together. If there were some overlapping values, common to both, then there might be some chance of a partial welding. But the Bible reminds us that in the end the difference is like that between light and darkness.

While it would be unwise, not to say sinful, for a Christian to knowingly marry a non-Christian, it does happen. But many 'mixed' marriages are spawned by the conversion of one of the marriage partners after the marriage. Given the material discussed above, the dimensions of Paul's advice in 1 Corinthians 7:12-14 can now be mapped out. The marriage of a believer to a non-believer will undoubtedly create tensions. If the unbelieving partner is willing to live with the believer and put up with these tensions then there should be no separation. If the unbeliever leaves then the believer is not bound because God has called them to live in peace (1 Corinthians 7:15). But if the unbelieving partner does not leave then there will be a new dimension to the relationship. The believing partner has a right relationship with God through faith in the work of Christ. As a consequence the unbelieving partner will have an indirect relationship with God through the believer. He or she may see a reflection of the love of God in their partner. The Word of God may be explained to the unbeliever. Through this indirect connection the unbeliever may be saved (1 Corinthians 7:16).

The Christian married to a non-believer, who is willing to maintain the marriage, will have to exercise all the gifts of the Spirit (Galatians 5:22). There will be a special need for love, patience, kindness, goodness, faithfulness, gentleness and self-control. Even with the exercise of these virtues the non-believing spouse may grow weary of the differences and the tensions they create, and want to leave the marriage. The non-Christian partner's permanent withdrawal from the marriage means that the believer is no longer able to exercise the commitment made at the wedding. The logic of being freed from this commitment is that he or she is free to remarry. It must be noted that while the logic of mutual love relationships allow this possibility it does not encourage it. The steadfast love of the Christian spouse would encourage and work for the maintenance of the marriage.

Policy Three: Social Policy

It is one thing to discuss marriage relationships between those that recognize the lordship of Christ and are members of the Kingdom of God; it is another thing to set up social policies for those who are not Christians and are not committed to Kingdom values. Yet biblical moral values are relevant for society at large. Non-Christians refuse to recognize God's telic order, and because of their sinful natures they are unable to do what God requires. Nevertheless non-Christians are part of the generic order of creation, and, as such, are designed in a way that means their fulfilment and completion is found in the moral order revealed in Scripture. It follows that Christians ought to press for the acceptance of the biblical moral order as the basis for social structures.

However, it has to be realized that in this fallen world it may not be possible to secure a Christian moral base for every structure. Because settling the nature of social structures is a political activity, it may be practically impossible to exert enough social influence. In fact, if the number of Christians in society diminishes this task will become more and more difficult. The ethic of mutual love relationships always gives us a second option at this point. Using biblical values to evaluate the circumstances, Christians can work to secure structures that maximize good or minimize possible harm.

In relation to marriage, Christians should exert effort to have the biblical ideals of sex and marriage embedded in the law of the land. At the same time Christians should press for structures that retrieve the situation and minimize harm when marriages fail. In practical terms this would mean encouraging the state to provide marriage-counselling and periods of trial separation, giving time for reconciliation. After these avenues have been exhausted then divorce would need to be allowed.

The issue of de facto marriage is a difficult one. The biblical view of sexuality entices one to think that de facto marriage should be recognized by the state. The sexual and psychological bonding that can come from living together may lead to some form of union. It is tempting to think that this union might be the very stuff of marriage. Yet the biblical doctrine of marriage is clearly covenantal, involving a total and explicit commitment of each partner to the other. This covenantal element is the essence of marriage, and if it is not found in a relationship then that relationship could not be called a marriage. Marriage involves both the inner and outer being. Conceivably a couple may make a total and explicit commitment to each other in private, in which case the relationship would qualify as a marriage. Yet the fact that de facto couples refrain from making a public commitment to each other must be significant. One can only presume that, despite denial to the contrary, there is no unconditional commitment in de facto marriages. If there was a sense of total commitment, why wouldn't de facto couples make it public—since, presumably, they want to be recognized as a social unit by the society at large. If they do not want to be recognized as a social unit then such couples clearly do not want the status of marriage.

In the light of this discussion, is state recognition of de facto marriages something that Christians operating on a biblical ethic should encourage and endorse? An affirmative answer to this question might, imaginably, be mounted on the basis of a retrieval ethic. Arguably, state recognition might bring these relationships under some regulation and this regulation might prevent some injury or harm. On the other hand, recognition of de facto relationships could imply the recognition of some form of serial marriage. The tacit recognition of serial marriage would do grievous harm to the biblical concept of marriage. On the other hand failure to recognize de facto relationships as marriage might bring great harm to de facto families in that they might be excluded from certain government benefits. Women and children might suffer greatly if they were deserted and no government benefits were available. Making a decision about this issue is not easy. The answer to the question depends upon a study of the harm done. My view in regard to the contemporary local scene (Australia) is that less harm and more good will be done if de facto relationships are legally recognized. But the recognition of de facto relationships would need to be balanced by the requirement that Christians make every effort to explain and model the Christian view of marriage.

CHAPTER ELEVEN

Homosexuality

A Brief History

The history of the treatment of homosexuals in the western world makes for horrifying reading (see for example Spencer, 1995). Homosexuals have been ostracized, mentally and physically abused, vilified and even killed. Such victimization encouraged homosexuals to provide mutual support for each other in the formation of a counter-culture. A homosexual culture sprang up in Europe, centring in Germany, in the latter part of the 19th century. As a consequence sexual acts between consenting adult males were decriminalized by the end of the 19th century in France, Spain and Italy. Hitler decimated the movement before the beginning of the Second World War.

The persecution of homosexuals seems to have been caused, in the main, by a psychological condition found amongst heterosexuals, called homophobia. Homophobia is the name given to heterosexuals' fear of homosexuality that precipitates the rejection of homosexual people. Some psychologists suggest that it may be a defence mechanism instituted by the homophobe's own dormant homosexual desires. Whatever the cause of this hostility towards homosexuals, it meant that most homosexuals felt alienated from society and, as a consequence, kept the fact of their homosexual orientation hidden from family and friends.

An incident in a New York bar in 1969 between the police and homosexual patrons saw the dawning of the Gay Liberation Movement. Violently rebelling against the passive acquiescence of abuse by homosexuals in the past, this movement rejected the label 'homosexual' in favour of the notion of being 'gay'. The new gay movement was anything but acquiescent. It was angry, open, visible and political. Gays declared that they were proud of their sexual orientation and became very active in a program to get homosexual orientation and behaviour accepted in society at large. A number of elements in the gay program came together to make their agenda particularly effective. Drawing on their history of victimization, they were able to elicit a strong sense of sympathy towards the need for change. The post-war philosophy of deconstructionism also provided an instrument to argue for a shift in social attitudes.

Deconstructionism may be understood using the categories of nature and purpose. The biblical account of human sexuality understood sexuality in terms of the male and female. It also located the purpose of human sexuality as a unity that can sustain the issue and nurture of children. Decontructionists declared that there is no given nature, and no fixed purpose for humans. Rather, humans are beings with free will who can create their own natures and decide upon their own purposes. They argued that powerful groups like the church who had dominated society had vested interests, and in order to protect their interests they had structured society in a certain way. It was maintained that the interests of these groups were secured by controlling the expression of human sexuality. Control was exercised by the social structure called marriage. In particular it was thought that the church had imposed a monogamous and heterosexual structure upon human sexuality. It was argued that alternate doctrines of sexuality from the east had shown that the purpose of sex was relative to the particular culture from which it came. Now that it was clear that this structure was merely a construct, one among many, it was seen to be the time for deconstruction. The influence of the church was in decline. The time had come for people to recognize their true nature as free individuals and restructure society accordingly. The time had come for people to be liberated from sexually oppressive structures.

In the post-war democratic west, political activity had become the popular means of social change. Political activists gathered groups of like-minded people and publicly demonstrated for the desired change. This favoured method of change did not focus on evidence, argument or logic. Using numbers, political agitation and moral indignation, the favoured method proved to be extremely effective. The Gay Liberation Front adopted this political methodology and pursued social change with frantic intensity. A homosexual block within the prestigious American Psychiatric Association (APA) decided in 1970 that it would systematically disrupt the meetings of the APA (Bayer, 1981). The goal of this political campaign was not the mere social tolerance of homosexuals and homosexual behaviour, but complete social acceptance. Homosexuals made themselves out to be just another legitimate minority group, akin to being left-handed.

As a result of the disruption and threats of disorder, in 1973 the APA removed homosexuality from their Diagnostic and Statistical Manual. The Manual contained a list of recognized psychiatric disorders. This concession of the APA that homosexual orientation was not a psychiatric disorder opened the door for political pressure to be applied to other professional groups such as psychologists and medical practitioners. The capitulation of these groups meant that by the beginning of the 1990's the popular press widely proclaimed that homosexual behaviour was as normal as heterosexual behaviour.

It is important to understand that at the centre of the whole gay political program was the idea that the goal or purpose of sexuality was not given or fixed. According to this deconstructionist understanding, the goal of one's sexual nature had to be individually discovered. The evidence, it was suggested, indicated that individual human sexual natures varied. Different natures would have different and appropriate goals. Consequently, it was argued, toleration was not enough. Morality demanded that homosexuals and homosexual behaviour be accepted and endorsed, just like heterosexuals and heterosexual behaviour. Because it was seen as 'natural' any effort to change homosexual orientation was seen as morally repugnant. The program was aggressively executed. From a logical point of view, if it is accepted that there is no objective goal for human sexuality built into the very order of creation, then the 'gay argument' is both logical and powerful.

What Are We Talking About?

Once again the distinction between character (being) and action (doing) is relevant. The word 'homosexuality' can be used in several ways. The term can be used to refer to an act (or class of actions), or to a disposition to act in a certain way. Dwyer's definition is helpful at this point for it covers both character and action. He defines homosexuality as a "*preference*, on the part of *adults*, for *sexual behaviour* with members of their own sex" (Dwyer, 1987, p. 64). Consequently a homosexual will be an adult person with a preference for sexual behaviour with members of his or her own sex. This definition will allow that someone may have a homosexual orientation, and not engage in homosexual acts nor be willing to engage in homosexual acts. Such a person will be a homosexual because of his or her disposition. It will also allow that someone in prison might engage in homosexual acts, and prefer heterosexual relationships outside of prison. These prisoners would not be homosexual because their preference was not for sexual behaviour with the same sex. According to this definition some sexual conduct during adolescence would not be counted as truly homosexual since that is the period when people are still developing a mature or settled disposition in relation to their sexuality. A few homosexual encounters may just be a phase of development. The important ethical issues that will be the centre of our attention concern the life-style that surrounds a settled homosexual disposition. So that the definition will be perfectly clear we must note that the term 'sexual behaviour' refers to those actions or infatuations which lead to physical fulfilment or orgasm.

The distinction between male homosexuals, or gays, and female homosexuals, or lesbians, is an important one and cannot be ignored. The lesbian population is clearly smaller than the male counterpart. The cause of same-sex orientation appears to be different for males and females. The orientation is traced to genetic, biological, social or psychological factors in males. In females it appears to have more to do with sexual abuse by males and the philosophical perspective adopted.

The adoption of our definition will help prevent misleading claims. For example, some time ago on one of the morning television shows in Sydney it was claimed that thirty-seven percent of the male population was homosexual. An advocate of the homophile movement based this claim on the evidence adduced in the Kinsey Report (Kinsey, 1948). Kinsey had observed that thirty-seven percent of males have at least one experience of homosexual arousal to orgasm. Using Kinsey's evidence to draw such a conclusion ignores the fact that people might go through various experiments or thoughts in their psychosexual development, without being habituated to them. Besides this fact, Kinsey's figures have been attacked, and, to a degree discredited, because he included the population of a large male prison in his sample population causing some distortion to the figures.

Two further terms must intrude at this point. These are the terms 'inversion' and 'perversion'. 'Inversion' refers to an exclusive, habituated and apparently involuntary sexual orientation towards others of the same sex. 'Perversion' indicates sexual attraction or involvement with members of the same sex by a person who is naturally heterosexual in orientation. It is the apparent exclusive and involuntary nature of the invert's disposition that has generated much of the moral discussion and is the focus of attention in this chapter.

Homosexuality and the Bible

Proponents of gay liberation have developed a number of strategies in dealing with the biblical material. Two of these strategies are fundamental to the defence of the gay life-style. The first is in relation to particular passages that appear to condemn homosexual acts. Proponents argue that the context of these passages, when examined in detail, reveal that the Scripture is not addressing the life-style and practices of people with a fixed homosexual disposition. Rather it is argued that the texts are addressing the occasional homosexual practices of heterosexuals. These practices include homosexual rape and homosexual intercourse where there is no mutual consent. The claim is that the biblical writers were not familiar with the condition of true homosexual orientation and did not confront it as a moral issue. The second strategy appeals to broad biblical themes like love, and highlights the implications of these themes in relation to the moral evaluation of homosexuals and homosexual activity. Comments on these and other strategies will be made as we move through the biblical material.

The Kingdom Pattern Established (Eden)

The place given to the creation accounts in the establishment of sexual values was discussed in Chapter Nine. You will remember that the schema instituted in the creation accounts was not just a statement of fact. The account of creation was meant to say more than just 'this is the way it was'. We saw that both Jesus and Paul drew on these accounts to say 'this is the way it ought to be'. In other words, the accounts acted as a paradigm, setting the standard. The account could do this because it incorporated both generic and telic order. Janzen (1994) showed that such paradigms were dotted throughout the Old Testament and that they were not designed just to state facts but to delineate and disseminate moral values. When the creation accounts are given their proper role, the details included become highly significant. The picture presented is the creation of Adam and Eve not (to quote the old joke) Adam and Steve. Heterosexuality is clearly the norm.

We need to note that no suitable partner was found among the animals that God had created (Genesis 2:20). God created a woman and Adam declared that she was suitable because she was his type. She was 'bone of my bones and flesh of my flesh'. A distinct implication of this passage is that bestiality, or sex with animals, is not a moral option. Here the Bible explicitly denies what the deconstructionists, by logic, must allow. Sexual orientation is not a matter of personal preference. The object of sexual desire and affection is limited by the nature of the object as far as the biblical writers are concerned.

The Hebrew words *ish* (male) and *ishah* (female) indicate a complementarity in nature between men and women that fits them for marriage. Anatomically this complementarity finds its expression at a very basic level in different genitalia. The penis fits the vagina. Because of these differences, sexual intercourse is capable of providing a sense of being complete, a sense of oneness, thus fulfilling the goal of unity. Biologically, men are capable of impregnating women, and women have a nature that can carry and nurture children. In this way a couple can fulfil the command to be fruitful and multiply. While human nature has many aspects, the biblical writers saw these various elements to be integrated in a holistic way. This being so one would expect these physical and biological differences to issue in variations at other levels. For example, it may explain why men and women display subtle differences in the way they think about aspects of reality. However, granted that men and women are both human, these variations will tend to be subtle in nature. Moreover, it would be expected that these differences would lead to different sex roles. The fact that sex roles change from culture to culture and over time does not defeat the claim that this complementarity exists. The variation in sex roles could be explained by this complementarity taking on different forms in different contexts. The fact that it expresses itself differently in different contexts is no argument against its existence.

Not all advocates of gay liberation reject the notion of complementarity. Some argue that homosexual couples display a form of complementarity. However this complementarity is not based on differences of a physical and biological nature. Rather it is a complementarity of personality. The different partners in same sex relationships express their character in different ways, and these ways are complimentary. The partners' personalities, it is argued, befit and benefit one another. While there is some substance in this claim, this type of complementarity is not the male-female complementarity adduced from the Scriptures. It is the type of complementarity that many friendships might display. It has nothing to do with people's sexual nature. Clearly gays and lesbians cannot experience the oneness of marriage, because they lack the prerequisite basis for complementarity. People of the same sex cannot fulfil the goal of human sexuality. From the aspect of nature and purpose homosexual acts must be seen as immoral.

God creates male and female (Genesis 1:27) and declares this duality, along with the rest of creation, to be very good (Genesis 1:31). God declares these things good because it suits his purposes. The male-female relationship of marriage and the multiplication of humanity in and through the family are explicitly part of God's plan and purposes. In both theory and practice, the gay liberation movement not only denies the generic order of creation—what kinds of things there are—but the telic order as well—what each thing's purpose is. We shall observe the consequences of this denial later. For the moment we need to note that gays and lesbians tacitly reject God's declaration when they participate in homosexual acts. The more radical gay liberationists explicitly attack the institutions of marriage and the family because of the moral values embedded in these structures. They want to be free to structure both sexual relationships and 'family' in whatever way they think fit. In this sense, sections of the gay movement are against both marriage and the family.

The Fall
In Chapter Ten we observed that the Fall involved not only the breaking of a right relationship with God but the rejection of God's order. Sin, the attitude that rejects God's right to rule creation, leads to sins that incorporate the denial of both generic and telic order. Just as Adam's sin set him on a course of disobedience so it is with men and women today. In engaging in homosexual activity people disown the kind of entity they are and the purposes God has for the kind of being they are.

The Kingdom Promised (Abraham)
A key passage of Scripture in relation to homosexuality relates an incident in the life of Lot at the time of Abraham. This is the story of Sodom and Gomorrah discussed earlier in Chapter Nine. Even relatively conservative scholars now adopt a revisionist approach to this passage. Richard Hay comments that "there is nothing in the passage pertinent to a judgment about the morality of consensual homosexual intercourse" (Hays, 1996, p. 381). He goes on to cite an

oracle in the prophet Ezekiel. "This was the guilt of your sister Sodom: she and her daughters had pride, excess of food, and prosperous ease, but did not aid the poor and needy" (Ezekiel 16:49). The implication being that the biblical writer viewed the sin of Sodom as the sin of inhospitality. However the very next verse in the Ezekiel passage, verse 50, goes on to say "they were haughty, and did an abomination before me. So I removed them when I saw it". Schmidt points out that various things are abominable in the Old Testament including same-sex acts. Leviticus 18:22 and 20:13 declare that lying with a male as with a woman is an abomination. Ezekiel's oracle, when taken in full, reinforces the traditional interpretation.

It does appear, however, that the homosexual element in the story is only one aspect of the moral disorder under condemnation. Webb is surely correct when he asserted that "the sexual sin of the Sodomites is part of a more general state of disorder, including inhospitality, xenophobia and violence" (Webb, 1994, p. 77). The men of the city were probably fundamentally heterosexual. Their "object was to humiliate the foreigners by subjecting them to homosexual rape, as was often done to prisoners of war in the ancient world", in which case the moral objection must be linked to the violent sexual imposition of the men of the city upon the foreigners. Such sexual imposition pays no regard to the dignity of human beings and denies the God-given nature of human sexuality by transposing an offering of the self into an imposition upon another. It does appear, however, that same-sex activity is part of this general disorder and comes under the judgment of God. The sequel to the Sodom narrative found in Judges 19 carries the same combination of disorders and must be treated in the same way.

The Kingdom Foreshadowed (David, Solomon)

In the long process of the settlement of the children of Abraham in the Promised Land under a king of God's choice, many things helped to shape Israel's identity as the people of God. Chief among these were the expressions of the covenant setting out God's expectations and Israel's responsibilities. One statement of Israel's covenantal responsibilities is found in the book of Leviticus (Leviticus 27:34). In this book the act of "lying with a male as with a woman" is categorically proscribed on two occasions (Leviticus 18:22; 22:13). Some background material is necessary to understand the import of these two texts and the attempts to revise them.

> The broad concern of Leviticus is with how the covenant relationship between Yahweh and Israel which has been given formal expression in the Sinai Covenant (Exodus 19-24) is to be maintained, given the frailty and sinfulness of Israel (Webb, 1994, p. 81).

Forgiveness, which is extended through the sacrificial system, is crucial to the survival of Israel as a covenant people. After outlining the functions of the sacrificial system (chapters 1–7) and the priesthood (chapters 8–10) the book contains sections on the laws of purity (11–15), the Day of Atonement (16) and the so-called Holiness Code (17–26). The concept of holiness dominates the book. God is holy. The Hebrew word for holiness carries two main ideas. These are the ideas of separation and completeness. God's completeness and purity separate him off from humanity. He is single-minded in his commitment to the good of others. His love is steadfast and untainted. The people of Israel can be holy in so far as they dedicate themselves to the service of God and separate themselves from the sinful disobedience of the world.

If a thing or person was dedicated to God it was set apart for his service and not available for common use. Persons and things not dedicated to God were profane and were available for common use. Profane things were further divided into clean and unclean things in the section on purity (Leviticus 11–15). The distinction between clean and unclean things seems to have been an instrument for teaching the people of Israel about the nature of devotion. Devotion was demonstrated by careful obedience to the injunctions on purity. The clean/unclean distinction seems to have been arbitrary in nature and not intrinsic to the order of nature. The clean/unclean distinction was a symbol of a deeper underlying reality. This was the reality of holiness. In observing the distinction between the clean and unclean, people showed their devotion to God. Jesus in his teaching on the tradition of the elders (Mark 7:1–23; Matthew 15:1–20) indicates that nothing that goes into a person can defile him. Mark understands that by this affirmation Jesus has "declared all foods clean". Later Peter has a dream and an experience that convinced him that gentiles were not unclean. The dream was about preparing unclean creatures for a meal but Peter later understands it to refer to the conversion and acceptance of the gentiles. The dismissal by both Jesus and Peter of the laws on cleanness must be taken as evidence that the clean/unclean distinction is not intrinsic to the created order.

In an attempt to justify homosexual acts between consenting couples some scholars have argued that the injunctions against same-sex acts in Leviticus refer to acts of cultic prostitution in pagan religions. It is argued that these acts are not part of the modern gay lifestyle. Others have argued that the prohibition and denunciation of same-sex acts were aspects of the purity code that was made obsolete by Jesus. Webb (1994) demonstrates that the context of these injunctions in the book of Leviticus does not allow either of the two revisionist interpretations. The injunctions come in a section on general sexual morality and not in the section on ceremonial purity. Homosexuality is included in the passage on sexual relations in general along with incest and adultery.

> In this respect chapters 18-20 in general contrast sharply with chapters 11-15 where the commands and prohibitions relate entirely to matters of ceremonial purity: clean and unclean foods, the ceremonial purification of women after childbirth, the cleansing of lepers, and instructions regarding bodily emissions. Cultic and ceremonial matters come to the fore again in chapters 21 and following, but in chapters 18–20 the focus lies elsewhere (Webb, 1994, p. 80).

A question can be asked that raises the issue of the application of these Levitical injunctions to the Christian life. After all, these commands and prohibitions are part of the Old Covenant, the Sinaitic Covenant, and the Christian is under a New Covenant.

Surely these laws have no place in the Christian life. It is at this point that the importance of biblical theology becomes relevant. Biblical theology recognizes the progressive unfolding of God's plan of salvation. The Old Covenant contained in the Pentateuch, and the New Covenant contained in the New Testament, are two different packages. But the old foreshadows the new. In the total movement of salvation history from creation to re-creation, the generic order of creation does not change nor does God abandon his original purposes. Paul is able to say, when talking about the Law of the Old Covenant as a package, that Christians are not under the Law (Romans and Galatians). Nevertheless he proclaims that the New Covenant based on the love of God in Christ (Romans 5–8) gives birth to a community of love (Romans 12–13). His insistence that love fulfils the commandments (Romans 13:8–10) can only be understood as rational if morality is based on the created order. Moreover he can maintain that love is the fulfilling of the Law. Paul's interest in the fulfilling of the Law while maintaining that Christians are not under the Law only makes sense if there is some continuity between the Old and the New Covenants. This continuity is found in the order of creation and God's purposes for creation, which find their renewing and fulfilment in the New Covenant. True, Christians are not under the old package called the 'Law', but the framework of creation that surrounds both packages provides for some continuity. In the terms of the writer to the Hebrews, the shadow shares the same shape as the reality.

The fact that the Law of the Old Covenant proscribes and condemns same-sex relationships is significant for the Christian. The Levitical texts confirm this conclusion when they supply a reason for the prohibition. Both texts declare it is an abomination. That is to say, it is abhorrent to God. The practice offends God because it denies his order and his purpose.

The Kingdom at Hand (Jesus)

Paul is the only New Testament writer who explicitly discusses the issue of homosexual behaviour. It is highly unlikely that Paul was not familiar with the passages in Leviticus. Nevertheless the Levitical prohibitions did not provide the reasons for Paul's condemnation of homosexual behaviour. Paul condemns it because it does not conform to God's will as it is revealed in the creation accounts. The logic of a key passage in Romans deserves careful attention. The context is determinative for our understanding.

In the letter to the Romans, Paul sets out his understanding of the gospel of Christ. He appears to have a number of reasons for doing this. One of these reasons has to do with the justification of the way God treats humanity. Paul is eager to establish the righteousness of God. The righteousness of God is, for Paul, revealed in the gospel (Romans 1:17). Two aspects of Paul's theology come into play at this point. One has to do with the justice of God in judging sinners. The other has to do with the mercy of God in saving sinners. For Paul the gospel clearly manifests both God's justice and God's mercy.

The discussion of homosexual behaviour is found in chapter 1 in a section concerned to establish the conclusion that "all have sinned and fall short of the glory of God" (Romans 3:23). It is important for Paul's argument to establish that both Gentiles and Jews have sinned. In the first part of his argument he focuses on well-known pagan sins. While the pagans did not have the Word of God, God's power and divinity was obvious in the things that he had made (Romans 1:19–20). The contingent nature of reality pointed to Someone beyond it. The notion of creation implied the existence of a Creator, one who was not subject to creation. Despite the evident existence of God people exchanged the "glory of the immortal God" for idols in the image of created beings (Romans 1:23). The topic of homosexual behaviour enters the discussion at this point and is seen as a consequence of the exchange. Exchanging the truth about God for a lie, people worshipped and served the creature rather than the Creator. As a consequence "God gave them up in the lusts of their hearts to impurity, to the dishonouring of their bodies among themselves" (Romans 1:24–25). The discussion of homosexual behaviour that follows is an illustration of a general lusting after impurity.

> For this reason God gave them up to dishonourable
> passions. For their women exchanged natural relations for
> those that are contrary to nature; and the men likewise gave
> up natural relations with women and were consumed with
> passion for one another, men committing shameless acts
> with men and receiving in themselves the due penalty for
> their error (Romans 1:26–27).

The nature and logic of the exchange is important. Although
creation explicitly hinted at the existence of the Creator, people
wilfully ignored the clues. The consequence of their wilful activity
was that they became ignorant and futile in their thinking (Romans
1:21). Not acknowledging the existence of the Creator, they did
not seek out his will or his way. They were ignorant of creation's
true nature and the objectives and goals embedded therein. This
ignorance allowed humanity to set its own goals, based on its own
desires. Since humanity was responsible for its own ignorance it was
without excuse (Romans 1:20). In his indignation at their denial of
him and the good he offered, God gave them up to their own
desires and passions. God's righteousness, Paul claims, is shown in
his anger against the unrighteousness of humankind.

Paul may have taken any one of a number of sins to illustrate the
depravity that flows from idolatry. However he uses homosexual
behaviour as the illustration. His reason for adopting this particular
sin appears to have been that it was widely recognized among
Gentile writers as being 'against nature'. That chapter 1 has Gentiles
in mind is reinforced by the fact that the focus is on idolatry. For
Paul, this was the cardinal sin of the Gentile world. Interestingly he
includes male and female same-sex relationships in the discussion.
All of humanity is covered in the argument. In chapter 2 he turns
his attention to the Jewish world. The Jews boast in the Law but
dishonour God by breaking the Law (Romans 2:24). The principal
sin of the Jews is their attitude of self-righteousness that expresses
itself in the condemnation of others. Such hypocrisy emphasizes the
fact that Jews also were sinners (Romans 2:1).

We might turn aside for a moment to a topic that is really
incidental to the discussion of the morality of homosexual acts.

This detour is justified by the amount of attention given to the point by commentators. On the basis of Romans 2:1, at least one commentator stresses the point that the "self-righteous judgment of homosexuality is just as sinful as the homosexual behaviour itself" (Hays, 1996, p. 389). The point is undoubtedly true, yet the way it is stated can cause great confusion. The ambiguity of the word 'judgment' is the problem. The word 'judgment' can have a range of meanings, moving from a weak sense to a very strong sense. In the weak sense the word refers to an act of evaluation. In this sense people might evaluate some activities as wrong and other activities as right. In the strongest sense the word refers to the process of declaring someone guilty of some wrongdoing and inflicting a punishment or a penalty. Very often people decide that someone has done something wrong and adopt a hostile or negative attitude towards them. This negative attitude will usually work itself out in ways that are harmful. The harm is justified by the perpetrators on the grounds that it is a penalty or a punishment. Christian love will not allow Christians to be judgmental in this second or stronger sense. Love requires the doing of good to others. Nothing in the early chapters of Romans or the teaching of Jesus prevents the Christian from making a moral evaluation of the homosexual behaviour and concluding that it is morally wrong.

Some proponents of the gay life-style have argued that even moral evaluation of homosexuality is morally wrong. The argument is that evaluation leads to declarations that homosexual acts are morally wrong, and declarations that homosexuality is morally wrong incites and induces people to inflict punishment and harm upon homosexuals. We need to respond to this argument before returning to the text of Romans. In reply it must be stated that the Christian gospel does not lead in the direction of causing harm. Christians are exhorted to leave the punishment of sin to God. Forgiveness and mercy are to be the order of the day (Luke 6:37–42; Matthew 7:1–5). Jesus came to forgive sinners, and the servant is to be like the master. The grace of the believer is to extend even to enemies (Luke 6:27–36; Matthew 5:39–42). Paul will not allow believers to judge one another (Romans 14). Rather he exhorts believers to have sensitive consciences so that they will not cause distress to others. However *evaluations* can legitimately be made. They are made so that each person can give an account of their own actions when they stand before the judgment seat of God (Romans 14:9–12). This would suggest that Christians ought to teach that homosexuality is morally wrong in the Christian community so that believers "by testing may discern what is the will of God—what is good and acceptable and perfect" (Romans 12:2). It also suggests that people ought to refrain from making public evaluations in contexts where such evaluations might incite harm. I presume such declarations should not incite harm amongst a group of right-minded Christians.

Returning to the text of Romans 1, numerous attempts have been made to reinterpret the first chapter so that it does not evaluate homosexual acts between consenting couples negatively. Boswell (1980) argues that the Greek words for the phrase for 'contrary to nature' in verse 26 should be translated as 'beyond nature'. His thesis is that the passage is not about gays with fixed same-sex dispositions, but individual heterosexuals who go beyond their own natures and engage in the occasional homosexual act. A number of exegetical studies have shown that the use of the Greek phrase in this way is highly unlikely (Schmidt, 1995). Moreover the logical flow of Paul's argument forbids this interpretation. His argument is about collective humanity, not isolated individuals. Others like Countryman (1988) argue that all the key terms in the passage can be interpreted in a consistently different way. The sum of his approach is that homosexual activity may offend social custom but it is not a sin against nature. He concedes that it may be unclean in the Levitical sense but denies that it is sinful. His major point is that Jesus has abolished the distinction between clean and unclean and secured sexual liberation. We have already seen that chapters 18-20 of Leviticus is not part of the purity code. This fact alone would be enough to sink Countryman's thesis. Further, Schmidt (1995) has reviewed the exegetical evidence and found that Countryman's position is unsupportable.

In 1 Corinthians 6, Paul makes the point that a person's

standing in Christ is inseparable from his or her behaviour (see Webb, 1994, pp. 91–94). Paul makes a distinction between the saints (believers) and the unrighteous (unbelievers). In the long term, behaviour will reveal those who are truly saints. Reminding his readers that "the unrighteous will not inherit the Kingdom of God" (1 Corinthians 6:9), Paul includes a list of the type of people who will fail to secure eternal salvation. Included in this list are two terms that cover the active and passive roles in male same-sex intercourse. Webb demonstrates that the passage is making a number of pertinent points. One is that homosexual behaviour is characteristic of the unrighteous. Persistence in such behaviour is taken to be a mark of unbelief. But the situation is not hopeless. God's process of renewal "which has now entered the final phase through the work of Christ and the outpouring of the Holy Spirit" offers cleansing, sanctification, and justification (Webb, 1994, p. 94). The effectiveness of the process cannot be doubted. Paul writes: "And such were some of you" (1 Corinthians 6:11).

In 1 Timothy 1:8–10, Paul provides a list of vices that includes sodomites or men who "practice homosexuality". This section of his letter is directed against false teachers who maintain that the Law is the only resource one needs to live a godly life. Paul does not disagree with his opponents about things that the Law labels as immoral. The Law, like all sound doctrine, is "in accordance with the glorious gospel" (1 Timothy 1:11). Rather his disagreement is with those who trust in themselves to find salvation through works of the Law and not in the mercy of God revealed in the gospel.

The Kingdom Consummated (The Return of Jesus)

Some advocates of gay liberation have used the statement of Jesus in Luke 20:27-40, examined in Chapter Nine, to argue for sexual promiscuity. Presuming that sexual activity will continue in the world to come, they contend that Jesus' declaration that there will be no marriage in heaven implies that people will be free to experience sexual intimacy with anyone they please. There are two major problems with this approach. Firstly it relies on an assumption about which the Scriptures are silent. Then, having drawn a picture of the world to come in a very speculative and unwarranted fashion, they adopt this portrait of the world to come as the norm or standard for the period of the overlap of the ages. This way of understanding the text is clearly wrong. The New Testament writers consistently condemn fornication for Christians as they await their Lord. The word 'fornication' in the New Testament clearly refers to sex outside of marriage.

This revisionist argument raises again the issue of methodology. We might take the opportunity to contrast the salvation-history approach of this book with two other approaches to Christian ethics. The first approach that we will consider is often called a 'Creationist ethic'. This ethic focuses on the generic order of creation and argues that the generic order provides us with enough insight to draw up a set of moral values. We have argued that this methodology falsely presupposes that the telic order of creation is contained in the generic order of the fallen world, and that human minds can read that order. The second approach is often labelled 'Kingdom ethics' in that it takes the final picture of the consummated Kingdom and draws it back into the present age ignoring the various stages of salvation history. The 'promiscuity argument' outlined above is a form of Kingdom ethics. It is doubly wrong in that it has drawn a false, or at least highly dubious, picture of the future Kingdom and has then, for good measure, ignored the stages of salvation history. In so doing it has drawn the future back into the present, trampling on the flow of salvation history.

Conclusions

The biblical writers knew nothing of the modern distinction between inverts and perverts. Their focus was always directed towards homosexual behaviour. There is a logic that runs through all the biblical passages on homosexual behaviour. A man should not lie with a man as with a woman because it is 'against nature'. The word 'nature' here is used to describe not what happens in the fallen created order but the plan and purpose of God established at

creation and imbedded in creation. The theological use of the word
'nature' includes both generic and telic order. Creation provides an
ideal in relation to human sexuality. God's plan and purpose was
that male and female should cleave to one another in marriage.
Hence Paul can theologize on the abandonment of God's plan, and
include both gay and lesbian behaviour in his condemnation.

There can be no doubt, given the biblical evidence, that a
Christian who desires to serve the Lord and do the will of his or her
heavenly Father cannot justifiably participate in homosexual
activities or pursue a gay life-style. Those Christians who find
themselves with a homosexual disposition will need the support of
their local congregation. The struggle to live 'in Christ' may be very
hard and very painful. The avenues of repentance, forgiveness and
renewed commitment, are always open to them as they are to every
Christian no matter what the sin. The knowledge that the victory
has been won in Christ will furnish the motivation to persist in the
struggle. Local congregations will need to educate heterosexual
believers to set aside any homophobic attitudes and behaviour and
to display the commitment to the good of others that is to be the
mark of Christian love and fellowship.

Confirmatory Evidence

Picture a butter knife. Its nature is determined by the design and its
nature determines its function or goal. The knife could be used
to open a can of fruit or to cut a bone in a piece of steak. The
probability is that used for either of these purposes the knife could
be damaged. Used as a lever it could bend or break. The metal used
for butter knives is not high tensile steel. It is not designed to bear
the force placed on a lever. Nor is the metal hard enough to take an
edge that could cut through bone. The biblical account of sexuality
parallels our account of the knife. God created male and female
humans with several goals or purposes in mind. He wanted humans
to experience the joy of mutual love relationships in the intimacy
of marriage. Human sexuality was to be contained within this
framework of mutual love and was to be a means of giving oneself

to the other through the body. Out of this mutual indwelling would come the issue of children.

If our understanding of the morality of the Bible is correct then we would expect that homosexuals would have a higher rate of mental and physical disorders. And this is exactly what we find in the scientific and medical evidence. Schmidt (1995, pp. 100–130) and Satinover (1996, pp. 49–70) provide evidence and documentation. Anal intercourse is the basic factor in regard to the physical disorders and diseases. The anatomy of the anus is such that it tears relatively easily and is prone to admit whatever micro-organisms that come along. By way of contrast the vagina has tough flexible walls that generally protect it from abrasion and infection. In regard to mental disorders, there is a much higher rate of alcohol and drug abuse as well as depression and suicide amongst homosexuals. The gay liberation movement argues that a repressive and homophobic society has driven homosexuals to drug and alcohol abuse. It is asserted that "Homosexuals 'internalize' the negative attitudes of society by engaging in self-destructive behaviours" (Schmidt, 1995, p. 115). But it is at least equally plausible to argue that these conditions have more to do with the fact that God's design for personal relationships has been ignored. The fact is the research that has been done reveals that homosexuals find it nearly impossible to sustain exclusive long-term sexual relationships. In so-called gay marriages exclusive fidelity to one's partner is almost nonexistent. The promiscuity rate among homosexual males is phenomenally high in comparison to heterosexuals, suggesting a psychological need for new relationships. Further, the sad reality is that practising male homosexuals have a life expectancy some two decades shorter than their heterosexual counterpart.

Treatment or Abuse?

The biblical material reviewed above suggests that the only moral options for a person with a homosexual disposition are celibacy or change of orientation. Proponents of the gay life-style have reacted aggressively to these suggestions arguing that both options are ethically reprehensible. Their argument in relation to celibacy can be dealt with quickly. Espousing a form of individualism, they claim that people are profoundly sexual beings and that the repression of sexual desires is unhealthy. Morality demands gratification and self-fulfilment. We have seen that biblical morality embraces neither individualism nor self-fulfilment as the basis for ethical judgments. Celibacy is expected of all people outside of a marriage relationship since sexual intercourse is God's instrument for devotion to another and the establishment of a family.

The argument against therapy for a change of orientation is more complex. It is based on two premises. The first premise is that homosexuality is innate or inherited. It is claimed that people are born with the disposition. The second premise appears to depend on the first. It is the premise that homosexuality is irreversible. It is claimed that the disposition cannot be changed. A range of genetic and biological evidence is advanced in support of the first premise and the first premise is used to support the second. Additional support for the second premise is found in the claim that re-orientation therapy is rarely, if ever, successful. Given the establishment of the two premises the argument runs that if homosexuality is natural and innate it is normal. This being the case there is no need for therapy. Moreover, since homosexuality is normal and irreversible, it is morally repugnant to put homosexuals through a painful treatment program. Furthermore, since the treatment program is designed to change a nature that has been given, it is working against nature, and, consequently it will not only be painful but damaging.

Examination of the evidence for both premises will help establish the validity or invalidity of the argument. We shall begin with the first premise claiming that homosexuality is innate. Mitchell (1994) reviewed the medical and psychological literature and found it fairly inconclusive.

At present there is no convincing demonstration of a definite psychological or biological cause of homosexuality. Despite that, there is a growing body of literature, particularly in the field of genetics, which suggests that it is not beyond the realms of possibility that a causative process, for at least some of those with homosexuality, may one day become established fact. However, the current literature would suggest that a single process accounting for all is unlikely and that a multifactorial understanding is most appropriate (p. 118).

Along with this quotation we should include his caution that the fact that a gene is involved does not indicate whether a condition is a disease or an unusual variant of normality. The gene may just set the boundary conditions of the field of possible actions.

Another psychiatrist, Jeffrey Satinover, reviewed all the medical and psychological research in relation to homosexuality and came to a similar conclusion (Satinover, 1996, pp. 71–117). He comments that "science has accomplished almost nothing we did not know from common sense: One's character traits are in part innate but are subject to modification by experience and choice" (p. 117). Focusing on the compulsive and addictive nature of homosexual behaviour, Satinover observes that such behaviour produces alterations in the brain and that these alterations are directed by choices, especially initial choices. The addictive and compulsive behaviour patterns are "reinforced by *the progressive erosion of the ability to choose differently*" (p. 175). As a consequence "the capacity for moral choice is slowly undermined as the compulsion tightens its grip" (pp. 175–6). Schmidt (1995, pp. 131–153) examines the evidence and proposes a multi-variant model of the explanation of homosexuality taking into account such factors as biology, culture, environment, moral values, reinforcing experiences and choice. We must conclude that even though there is evidence that genetic and biological inheritance plays a part in the development of a homosexual disposition, it does not establish that homosexuality is innate in the manner required to vindicate the argument against therapy.

In relation to the second premise of the argument against therapy, there is considerable evidence to defend the reality of changed sexual orientation. Satinover (1996, pp. 168–209) demonstrates that the success rate, while difficult to quantify, of both secular and religious treatments, is about 50% or above. Religious treatments seem to be more successful because they acknowledge the patient's helplessness to change the condition and call on a higher power. Schmidt (1995, pp. 153–159), acknowledging the difficulty of quantification, does not come up with a success rate but reports numerous successful programs. The sceptical proponent of the homosexual lifestyle may always doubt the evidence or argue that those apparently re-orientated are just damaging themselves by repressing their true and natural orientation. Interestingly Schmidt (p. 155) records the words of a former homosexual some ten years out of the lifestyle. "Homosexual activists want to convince not only the public but *themselves* that change never occurs, because *if I exist, each of them must be haunted by the possibility that they, too, might find the power to change.*" The fact is that reorientation for a homosexual is possible. While it may be a difficult and painful struggle at least one former gay who found Christ can testify that "I only know I would rather live one day as I am today than for an eternity the way I was" (Schmidt, 1995, p. 159).

Compromise and Retrieval?

Suppose we concede that change is difficult and that some strongly motivated homosexuals have tried and failed. Do sympathy and love demand that Christian ethics adopt a retrieval strategy? In recent times a number of theologians and ethicists have tried to secure what may be seen as a compromise position. Kimball Jones, following the lead of Helmut Thielicke, is one such writer. He concedes that homosexual acts are contrary to the will of God for human sexuality but argues that our moral judgments must give more importance to the reality of sin within the objective order of this world. Absolute inverts, it is suggested, have a fixed and unchangeable nature. Celibacy and sublimation is not possible. This fixed nature is the result of the effects of sin. Since the absolute invert cannot change his or her nature and is not responsible for being what he or she is, then the only moral requirement placed on them can be that they act responsibly within their given framework. Responsibility, in this case, would mean that they are loving and other-person centred and act in the same type of way that heterosexuals are required to act in their heterosexual relationships. That is, they are to be monogamous.

Charles Curran, a Catholic theologian, also affirms that for the absolute invert "a somewhat permanent homosexual union is the best, and sometimes the only, way for him to achieve some humanity" (Batchelor, 1980, p. 94). But Curran objects to Jones' use of the doctrine of sin. For Curran the structure of human sexuality remains even though the invert cannot live according to it because of the infecting power of sin. Jones' position is best understood if we make a distinction between the objective and subjective orders of reality. He would argue that because of sin the objective order of certain people's (the absolute invert) sexual nature is changed from that of the creation order. Not only is it changed but also it is fixed. The only moral domain of responsibility for the invert is the subjective one. Curran declares that "sin affects this present order but does not do away with all the moral distinctions which are based on both creation and redemption" (Batchelor, 1980, p. 94). Curran refuses to recognize a change in the objective natures of the inverts. He argues that every attempt should be made to overcome the homosexual condition but where these efforts fail some form of permanent homosexual union may be the best moral option.

The 'Compromise Argument' as we shall call it looks very similar in its logic to the retrieval ethic adopted earlier in this book and applied to the issue of divorce and remarriage. But I want to contend that the 'Compromise Argument' is invalid and that a retrieval ethic cannot operate in the case of homosexual activity. The reason for adopting this position is simple. In the case of heterosexual remarriages, the new marriage may retrieve some good and prevent some harm. A complementary mutual love relationship is possible in the case of divorce and remarriage. God's goal for human sexuality, a mutual love relationship between a man and a woman that can produce and nurture children, can be held up to a heterosexual couple. This goal is not possible for a gay couple.

It is not surprising that some evidence suggests that permanent homosexual unions are virtually non-existent. Using only secular medical and social science publications, Schmidt has correlated a lot of the evidence in relation to promiscuity and fidelity. He concludes that "the number of homosexual men who experience anything like lifelong fidelity becomes, statistically speaking, almost meaningless" (Schmidt, 1995, p. 108). He goes on to state that "promiscuity among homosexual men is not a mere stereotype, and it is not merely the majority experience—it is virtually the *only* experience". His concluding remarks on the issue include both male and female homosexual relationships. "In short, there is practically no comparison possible to heterosexual marriage in terms of either fidelity or longevity. Tragically lifelong faithfulness is almost nonexistent in the homosexual experience". Satinover's survey supports this conclusion (Satinover, 1996, pp. 49–70). Less than two percent of homosexuals are monogamous. Given that as few as two in every three hundred people are homosexual there is the possibility that there *might* be one monogamous gay couple in every fifteen thousand adults. Permanent homosexual unions are an illusory goal.

Even if permanent unions were possible, there would still be the issue raised earlier in the section on confirmatory evidence. Homosexual behaviour damages the body, predisposes people to a much higher rate of mental disorders, and severely shortens life expectancy. Such behaviour is not good stewardship of the body and must be proscribed by Christian morality. The sad fact is that the adoption of the compromise position would retrieve no good and avoid no harm. No good would be retrieved in terms of fidelity and longevity in sexual relationships, and no harm would be avoided in terms of disease, mental disorders and lifespan.

Concluding Remarks

The gay liberation movement has adopted the philosophical perspective of deconstructionism to underpin gay rights. This perspective is founded upon the doctrines of individualism and autonomy. The facts, according to this perspective, are that people are particulars. That is, they are unique individuals. Moreover they are unique individuals who have the ability for deciding and choosing their own goals. A key moral value generated by this perspective is the value of self-determination. Self-determination includes the right to accept and shape the particular nature they have. Since nature and purpose are logically linked together, self-determination also includes the right to set whatever goals appeal to the particular individual. In other words each individual has the right to establish their own set of moral values.

The dominant philosophical perspective found in most western societies known as liberalism also adopts the perspective that people are individuals who gain their status as deciding and choosing beings. Allowing that people share certain similarities, liberalism does not deny the reality of kinds. Nevertheless, the status of individuals as autonomous beings affirms the moral right of individual freedom as long as the exercise of this freedom does not harm others. Liberal societies have generally approved homosexual acts between consenting adults. In this regard the gay liberation movement has received general support in the west. However liberal philosophy will not extend support to the radical notion of restructuring society for it would harm those who have a commitment to the traditional notion of family. With this proviso, the gay movement has received qualified support in most western societies.

Trading on the philosophy of deconstructionism, the proponents of gay liberation have pleaded the cause of anti-discrimination. To distinguish between people on the basis of their sexual orientation, and to treat them less favourably in relation to employment, housing, education, goods and services is, they assert, immoral. Christian morality can agree with this assertion as far as it goes. In a fallen world awaiting the consummation in Christ, Christians can adopt a retrieval ethic. The Kingdom cannot be established in a mixed society of believers and unbelievers. Christian love is gracious and requires that Christians do good to all people regardless of race, gender or religion. Sexual orientation can easily be included in this list. Moreover Christians are required not to be judgmental. They cannot feel superior when other people make what they see to be a defective moral choice for they know themselves to be morally defective in so many ways. Nor should they punish people for their defective moral choices. Judgment belongs to God.

Unfortunately the gay and lesbian social agenda goes far beyond securing the right to employment, housing, education and freedom from vilification. Built upon the foundation of the philosophy of deconstructionism, segments of this so-called liberation movement want to dismantle the traditional structure of the family and outlaw traditional moral values in the area of sexuality. They not only want to write their own set of subjective sexual values, but they also want these values imposed upon society at large. Evidence for this disturbing fact in Australia is found in the Report of the Senate Legal and Constitutional Reference Committee of its *Inquiry into Sexuality Discrimination* published in December 1997 by the Senate Printing Unit in Canberra. The Report makes recommendations about changes in relation to the Sexuality Discrimination Bill 1995.

Various homosexual activist groups, individual homosexuals, and groups sympathetic to their cause made the majority of the submissions to this committee. Over 90% of the footnotes in the report refer to evidence given by such groups. The Bill defines sexuality in terms of heterosexuality, homosexuality and bisexuality. The Report wants asexuality added to the definition and insists that bisexuality be retained as a distinct sexuality in the Bill. It recommends an amendment to Clause 6(5)(c) to the effect that harassment of a person on the grounds of bisexuality include a refusal to accept bisexuality as a distinct sexuality. Citizens who refuse to acknowledge the category of bisexual would be charged with discrimination. A distinct deconstructionist tone is clearly evident in the document. The subjective desires of individuals are to take precedence over the objective biological categories of creation.

Perhaps the most dangerous element in the recommended amendments is the proposal that a person or an organization may not claim an exemption from certain provisions of the Bill on the grounds of religious belief. The recommendations include clauses in relation to government funded religious bodies that would open up such bodies to the direct influence of gay and lesbians. A submission by Ms Kristen Walker, Lecturer in International and

Constitutional Law at the University of Melbourne, testifies to the purpose of these clauses:

> In relation to religious bodies and schools, I consider that exemptions should not be available for these institutions. This is particularly so in relation to schools, where lesbian and gay students would then be deprived of important role models and, again, the myth of child abuse and the stigmatization of lesbians and gay men as perverted would be perpetuated.

Another group, the Alternative Lifestyle Organization, went even further than the proposed recommendations advocating that there should be controls over what is said from the pulpit in sermons.

Homophile movements have traded upon the unjust actions of homophobic groups in the past to harvest the sympathy of the present generation. Exploiting this sympathy they have ignored the facts of scientific and medical research to propagate a myth that enables them to challenge the structures of our social organization. Attacking the world-view underpinning our social structures, they have fabricated their own story about reality. It is a story that allows the individual to determine his or her own nature and goals in relation to sexual matters. In so doing they turn the creature into the creator, and deny the plan and purposes of the One True God. Their idolatry serves only their own interests. It is subjectivism at its worst. It denies the objective aspects of reality.

The moral clash over the legitimacy of homosexual acts is fundamentally a collision of perspectives. Given a commitment to the perspective of deconstructionism or liberalism, homosexual acts between consenting adults appear morally right. But given the perspective of the Bible, homosexual acts are clearly morally wrong. Because each group argues from within a different framework of thought, little will be achieved by public debate. People will argue from different frameworks and talk at cross-purposes. In the end, people will need to change the framework of their thinking before they are convinced by the arguments of the opposition. Christians must fall to prayer on this matter and exhort the Spirit of God to work in people's hearts. At the same time, they can argue that the biblical picture fits the experience of reality in a more comprehensive and complete way. In the meantime the encounter will generate animosity. From the gay perspective, Christians, when they declare homosexual acts to be morally wrong, will appear to be hostile and unloving. Homosexuals will feel that a fundamental moral right is being attacked or denied. In pointing out where the good is to be found and harm avoided, Christians will think that they are doing the right thing. They will be surprised at the ferocity of some of the gay responses to their actions.

The pressure of the gay and lesbian agenda makes Christian witness and action exceedingly difficult. On the one hand, strong public pronouncements declaring that homosexual actions are morally wrong may incite some people to immoral and harmful behaviour. Christians committed to the good of all people will not want this to happen. On the other hand, a failure by Christians to make it clear that homosexual activity is morally wrong and harmful may see society restructured in a way that mitigates against God's will and brings about the denigration of the family. Christians must walk a difficult path. They must work to secure good for all, including gays and lesbians, and, at the same time, oppose any structural changes or legislation that might jeopardize the institutions of marriage and the family.

CHAPTER TWELVE

Abortion

ABORTION IS AN ancient practice designed to meet the problem of unwanted pregnancies. The offspring of sexual union is removed from the life-support of the womb before it is fully developed. In recent times the debate over the morality of abortion has polarized. People in favour of abortion have argued that a woman has a right over her own body, and that at the early stages of development the foetus can be considered to be just an extension of the woman's body. Anti-abortionists have argued that the foetus is a unique and separate human being from the moment of conception and therefore has the right to life. Arguments from both sides of the debate have mostly converged at the point concerning the status of the foetus. Some basic questions have emerged from the modern debate. When does human life begin? Is the taking of human life always wrong? Should governments legislate against abortion?

The biblical writers do not explicitly address the issue of abortion. Abortion was practiced in the ancient world and the Jewish people undoubtedly knew about it (Gorman, 1982, Chapter 1). The reason why no biblical writer comments on the practice is unknown. Some scholars argue that abortion was so abhorrent to the Jewish mind that no comment was necessary. Others interpret the silence to mean that the practice was widely accepted and was not considered a moral problem. But silence is no argument. We will have to consider the overall perspective of the Scriptures and draw out any legitimate implications for this topic.

A Biblical Starting Point

From a biblical point of view, the starting point for thinking about this topic must be the concept of marriage. As we have seen from the biblical perspective marriage is the basic social unit. While the primary purpose of marriage is unity, marriage is the unit of procreation. A man and a woman give themselves to each other in loving service, and children issue from the ensuing union. The commitment to each other in marriage is meant to be total and unconditional. The commitment to the other is a function of the inner being. But the commitment to the other includes both aspects of being—the inner and the outer. Each is committed to the other in body and soul. The spouse as an object of commitment is a being whose inner and outer natures are totally integrated. The commitment of the heart is expressed through the giving of the body. Character and actions are intrinsically linked. What one formulates in the heart finds its expression through the activity of the body.

The nature of the marriage commitment has implications for both sexual practice and procreation. The ideal of exclusive mutual indwelling combined with the integration of body and soul will not allow a spouse to use a third party for sexual pleasure or procreation. Biblical injunctions label such action as adultery. In adultery the union forged by mutual indwelling is stained and falsified. The fetters of faithfulness and openness are diminished.

Moreover, the commitment of each to the other in body and soul entails a commitment to any issue from the marriage. The nature of the personal relationship of mutual indwelling is such that it creates a moral bonding between the marriage partners, and any issue that flows from that relationship. The new personal and relational being generated in procreation is an extension of the outer aspects of both partners. Further the inner being of the new child will be nurtured and shaped by the parents. Procreation through marriage yields beings of the same kind at the biological level. At the moral level, the biblical expectation is that it will replicate the same type of relationships. The child will share personal relationships with the parents. And the moral pattern mapped out for these personal relationships is the pattern of mutual love. Parents are to love their children and children are to love and honour their parents.

According to the biblical picture of reality, the good that Christian parents will want for their children is the good found in a right relationship with God and with others. But Christian love does more than just make a commitment to children when they arrive. It desires that others may come into being and share the joy of right relationships. Christian love desires to see the community grow. The number of loving relationships that can be practically sustained in the circumstances sets the limit to the number of children. Too many children for the psychological, economic, and social circumstances will result in neglect and harm. The biblical view of marriage developed in a previous chapter does not demand that every act of sexual intercourse be open to the possibility of procreation. At the same time, this view would recognize that contraception might be done for selfish and immoral reasons. The command to Adam and Eve that they be fruitful and multiply and fill the earth (Genesis 1:28) obviously extends to their seed. The context of the command within the creation accounts makes this clear. The flow of salvation history gives this command an eschatological dimension. There will be a point in history where the command has been fulfilled and the earth is filled. So while people ought to have an attitude that welcomes new members into the human community, the expression of this attitude will be within the boundaries set by the circumstances of history. Contraception may be a legitimate part of the moral life.

Those who take a consequentialist approach to ethics will raise an important question at this point. If contraception is morally permissible, then why not abortion, since both actions have the same outcome? The answer to this question is found in the fact that the biblical writers do not take a consequentialist approach to ethics. As we have seen, the determination of the moral good is based on nature and purpose. On these grounds two basic questions arise. What kind of thing are we dealing with? What purpose does God have for this kind of entity? Prior to conception we are dealing with ova and sperm. Without the unity achieved through syngamy (fusion of nucleii), neither the sperm nor the ova have the possibility of developing into human life. The natural processes see an enormous wastage of both sperm and ova and nobody seems to be greatly troubled by it. However the issue of the nature of the entity after conception has been a topic of much debate. This is because the possibility of life has not yet been realised and a human entity has only begun to emerge.

It will be important to make some general comments about the discussion on the nature of the human embryo and foetus. The first point to be noted is that the discussion has generally been conducted within the framework of the ethics of duty. That is to say, the focus has been on the action of abortion and the status of the foetus rather than the character of the agents involved in the action. Stanley Hauerwas (1981) and others have made serious criticisms about the limits of this approach, and highlighted the weaknesses. Among other things, Hauerwas points out that any pregnancy involves the parents, and that the attitude and character of the parents are key factors in the decision making process. The question is basically decided, for Hauerwas, by the fact that the Bible requires an attitude of love and a character committed to the good of others. The status of the foetus appears to have no great relevance from a biblical perspective. It is the attitude of the parents that is primary.

The ethics of virtue approach to abortion outlined above seems to adopt the right entry point into the discussion in the contemporary context. The issue of abortion is much broader than the discussion of the status of the embryo or foetus. Yet ethics cannot operate just at the level of community and love. While it is true that the Kingdom of God is a community of mutual love relationships and the goal of each member is to create and maintain mutual love relationships, there is more. Love is defined in terms of the *good*. The good is located by consideration of the nature and purpose that God has given to things. The basic shape of things is revealed in the Scriptures and the details worked out using the biblical framework and the empirical knowledge gained by experience and interpreted within the biblical framework. So a place is left for the question—what is the nature and purpose of this zygote, embryo or foetus?

What is it?

In answering this question we must be careful to remain within the biblical framework and to avoid the presuppositions of Western liberalism. Remember that Western liberalism adopts the individual as the basic unit of moral reality. By way of contrast, the biblical writers appear to be committed to bi-polar personal relationships as the basic unit. The goal of procreation is not just the creation of a new individual; it is the creation of a whole new set of mutual love relationships. With the conception of a child, the horizontal mutual love relationships between father and mother is replaced by a set of three bi-polar relationships. This includes the original one between the father and the mother, plus the two new ones between the individual parents and the child. The two vertical relationships between the parents and God are extended to three. The child enjoys God's love and is invited to return that love by treating everything in accordance with its kind. Ethical questions cannot simply be reduced to consideration of the consequences on the individual. The individual is locked into a set of relationships and all these relationships count.

Given the biblical worldview, a reductionist account of human nature must be rejected. The spiritual, sociological and psychological aspects of life cannot be explained solely in terms of biology. Nor can biology be reduced to chemistry and physics. There are aspects of reality that cannot be studied under a microscope. The observation of the senses is not enough to answer the question of identity. Before one can identify what a thing is, one has to understand its nature (design) and its purpose (goal). These two aspects of understanding are related. If one understands the design, then one will understand the goal. Conversely, if one knows the goal, then this will bring insight into the design. It is clear that natural teleology is a part of the framework of understanding.

Moreover, historical teleology is also a necessary element in understanding the identity of a thing. An embryologist encountering an embryo at the eight-cell stage, isolated from the womb of the mother, will not be able to see that the design is human. There will be no arms and legs, no head or torso. The entity cannot be recognized as human until it is placed within its historical sequence. It has come from the mating of two humans, and, given normal circumstances, it will develop into a full human being. The argument that the embryo is just a bundle of cells requires the abstraction of the embryo from the historical processes surrounding it. The abstraction from history allows the denial of the reality that the embryo is human. But the abstraction from history is a denial of the sequential nature of reality. This argument embraces a punctiliar view of reality. A punctiliar view of reality breaks things up into discrete moments. Judgments are made about the embryo at a moment in time. The understanding of the embryo is limited to the empirical properties that can be discovered at a particular point in time. Isolating the embryo from the framework of history, and denying the natural teleology of the created order, allows the embryo to be identified as just a bundle of cells and assigned a low value. The abstraction of the embryo from the realms of generic order and telic order reduces it to a meaningless hunk of matter.

The fault in this approach lies with the perspective adopted. Hume demonstrated that any attempt to make sense of the world merely on the basis of empirical observation was doomed to failure. Modern genetics defeats this argument in another way. It demonstrates that empirical examination can reveal that the embryo is human.

Properties or Essence?

The question of identity is logically linked to another aspect of the abortion debate. This aspect is the discussion of personhood. While the biblical writers do not use the term 'person', the concept lies behind the use of a range of words. A major study of the use of this relatively modern word by the philosopher P. F. Strawson suggests that the term is a basic concept that affirms both a state of consciousness and material characteristics to a single individual. The usage of this word is perfectly consistent with the biblical view of humans, where individuals have both an inner and outer being.

Pro-abortionists have argued that only persons have a right to life, and that the foetus is not a person. According to this argument persons are defined in terms of the properties they possess. The definition of person has varied according to the philosophical perspective adopted. Yet almost all definitions include the idea of rationality. We will not be far from the mark if we summarize the definitions and conclude that generally persons are defined as thinking and choosing beings. Since the foetus does not possess the ability to think and choose, then it is argued that the foetus is not a person. Anti-abortionists have replied by arguing that the foetus is a potential, emerging or actual person.

The debate is complicated by the fact that there are at least two different concepts of personhood in operation. One view has a long history and is found in early Greek and Roman philosophy. The Greek notion of substance is central to this ancient concept. The substance of a thing was what it really is, as opposed to its appearance. The substance was the thing in essence. The essence remained the same whereas the appearance changed through time. If one takes an essentialist view of personhood, it is a something that is there from conception to death. Personhood is carried by the thread of individual existence moving through space-time. The essence is the continuing entity that lies behind all the changes of appearance that are a part of human life. The other concept of personhood is more recent. It goes back to a view that maintains that a thing is nothing but a bundle of properties. This view declares that there is nothing in which the properties reside. According to this view, a person is an entity that is consciously aware, capable of rational reflection, able to formulate preferences and act on intentions. Any entity, be it human or not, is not a person unless it has these capabilities or properties. The essentialist view of personhood would give the foetus the status of a person from the moment of conception. On the other hand, the 'bundle theory' view of personhood would only allow that the foetus is a person when the appropriate properties or capabilities have been acquired.

Both concepts of personhood have their merits. One accounts for the continuing or on-going identity of individuals, while the other accounts for the characteristics that we encounter when we engage a person. The older essentialist view favours the argument that the foetus is an actual person, and most anti-abortion arguments are built on this foundation. The bundle theory is used by the pro-abortionists to argue that the foetus is not a person, and therefore should not be treated with the respect of a person. On this view the foetus, at an early stage, is just a bundle of cells with very few relational or personal properties. However it must be observed that these two views are not incompatible. In fact a combination of the two views is necessary to give an adequate account of our experience of persons. Persons are on-going beings, and not just discrete bundles of properties at distinct moments of time. At the same time, the on-going person acquires new properties and capacities as he or she develops, while losing some properties and capacities at various points along the way. The combination view of personhood would admit that there is an ongoing underlying essence that causally explains the gradual development of the properties that we associate with persons. The word 'person' would then cover the on-going being and the capacities that we normally associate with personhood.

The fusion of the biblical framework of thought and the empirical knowledge gained from genetics moves us in the direction of a type of essentialism. On this view there is a substance that constitutes the person, and causally explains those properties in virtue of which an individual is called a person. The substance is DNA, and the genetic code contained therein organizes the nature and emergence of properties. The genetic code is not determinative of behaviour, but sets the boundary conditions for behaviour. The environment and one's nurture will also shape the choice of behaviours. The fact that the genetic code is not determinative of behaviour explains why identical twins can look alike but have quite different characters and nurture different areas of ability.

The Status of the Foetus

A major source of confusion in the abortion debate can now be addressed. The confusion is the result of different uses of the word 'person'. When an essentialist uses the word, it is referring to the on-going entity that begins at conception and continues through space and time until death. From an essentialist point of view, the abortion debate is about the value of the entity that threads its way through time. The value is found in the kind of thing it is. From the beginning, regardless of the properties the embryo displays, it is 'human' kind. Those who adhere to a 'property' view of reality argue that the developing foetus only has the value of a person when it displays the properties of a person. Personhood is then defined in a certain way. Entities who do not display these properties are not accorded the value of a person. People relying on this type of argument are also depending on the punctiliar view of reality. The argument is that because the embryo or foetus does not possess certain properties at a certain time, then the embryo or foetus is not a person and should not be accorded the value of a person.

It will be no surprise to those who have followed the train of thought in this book to learn that the biblical picture supports the essentialist view. Morality is all about the value of kinds. This is why moral values are universal. R. M. Hare's celebrated doctrine that universalizability is a feature of moral judgments is perfectly correct. Being one of the kind 'human' is enough to secure an intrinsic moral value. Christian love demands that nature be allowed to attain its goal. God's purpose for all entities of this kind is that they are nurtured in such a way that they might enjoy mutual love relationships with God and other humans. From the time an entity becomes human, love obligates people to nurture and secure its prosperity so that it might reach and enjoy its goal. Given that the foetus is human in nature, then humanity is obligated to do everything to see that it can achieve God's purpose.

Before we discuss the question of when an entity becomes human, several observations need to be made. The first has to do with a popular movement against abortion. This movement highlights the right of the unborn to life. Biblical ethics endorses this protest against abortion, but it has a different focus. Biblical ethics focuses upon obligations, not rights. The concern of the

biblical writers is that people give what they owe. Christian ethics
is about determining what is owed to others, and not about
claiming one's rights. Of course, if someone owes you something
then you have a claim upon that person. Rights are a logical
corollary of obligations. The issue of difference is the matter of
focus. A focus on rights can facilitate and encourage selfish and self-
centred behaviour. A community built upon a 'rights' ethic would
be fractured and disharmonious. Love is other-person-centred and
is focused on giving what it owes. A biblically based Christian ethic
aims at creating a community of mutual love relationships.
Harmony is achieved because each member is willing to give to the
other. Ideally, in a community of mutual love, people would not
need to claim their rights. My objection to the 'Right to Life'
movement is not a strong one. Foetuses cannot claim their rights,
so the movement reminds people that they have an obligation in
this regard. I would prefer, nonetheless, that the reminder be
phrased in terms of what people owe to the foetus, and not what
the foetus might hypothetically claim from them.

The other observation has to do with the way some
philosophers approach this debate. I have in mind here people like
Peter Singer, and those who adopt his preferential utilitarian
approach to ethics. For these people, abortion is morally justifiable
because the foetus is not a person and only persons have a right to
life. My first objection is the one listed above. An ethic based on
rights is a self-centred ethic that will encourage and foster
selfishness. Such an ethic can be used to justify the manipulation of
reality in the interests of the individual. My second and major
objection is that these people end up 'defining' human entities out
of existence. Rationality is a key characteristic of persons for Singer.
Since a child does not develop the higher rational processes until
well after birth, both abortion and infanticide is morally justified
on his theory. Different definitions of personhood would result in
divergent decisions. Conducting ethics in this way means that
morality seems to become an arbitrary matter. As we saw in
Chapter One, good explicit definitions are extraordinarily difficult
to sustain. Polanyi (1958) has shown that this is due in part to the

fact that there are always tacit elements in our understanding that cannot be specified. There are great dangers in operating on the basis of philosophical definitions of personhood.

Our biblical approach to ethics operates in a much more straightforward way and in accordance with common sense. A full and explicit definition of human nature is not required. The foetus is an entity that issued forth from other human beings and will, if the circumstances are conducive, develop into a full human being. The issue of properties and capacities is irrelevant. The foetus is a being of a certain kind and acquires the value given to that kind.

Becoming One of a Kind

When does the formation of a separate individual human take place? This is a question that cannot be avoided even if we take an ethic of virtue approach. If people are obligated to love one another and welcome others into the community, then it is necessary to know that the foetus is an emerging person, and when it became an emerging person. We are reminded here that love cannot discriminate. If a being is of the type 'human' then it is to be the object of love. The obligation is universal in that it covers all humans that we might engage or contact in some way.

Wennberg (1985) meticulously describes the range of what he calls "decisive moment theories". Decisive moment theories are those theories about the nature of human life that identify a moment when the life of the foetus ought to be protected. He confirms that there are seven different moments that have been proposed in the literature. The seven moments are: (1) conception, (2) implantation, (3) human form or shape, (4) viability, (5) the beginning of brain function, (6) sentience or having the power of sense perception, (7) birth. Wennberg's conclusion is consistent with a view of personhood that combines the essentialist and property theories. He argues that the foetus should be valued from the time of conception. Moreover he argues that as the foetus grows and acquires more capacities and attributes it should have an increased value. The foetus realizes its full value at birth.

Attractive as Wennberg's position may be, it is inconsistent with an ethic based on kinds. The central question from a biblical perspective has to do with the point at which the genetic material from the parents may be regarded as a human being. When does the genetic material from the parents become human in kind? In the created order, neither the sperm nor the ovum by itself has the capacity to actualize its potential. Both have the potential for human life, but the actualization of this potential requires that the two be united. The gametes are human but they are not human beings. The question is, when does the human being begin?

Many scholars have argued that an individual human being begins with syngamy. Syngamy refers to the union of the male and female genetic material into one new cell containing a new genetic code. These scholars would argue that it is at this point in time that the boundaries of the new human being are established. The process of establishing a new identity by installing boundaries is called 'individuation'. The boundaries give a thing its status as an individual. One can see why people may conclude that individuation is secured at the time of syngamy. While sperm and ova may be human by themselves, they do not establish the boundaries of a new human being. The boundaries are established when the genetic material from both parents is united in one new cell containing a new genetic code.

Perhaps the greatest challenge to the argument that individuation occurs at syngamy has come from Norman Ford (1988). In his book, *When did I begin?: Conception of the Human Individual in History, Philosophy and Science*, he argues that individuation does not take place until fourteen or fifteen days after conception. Ford concedes that genetic identity and human life is established at fertilization. However, he argues that the existence of an individual, the individuated human being, is not secured till the formation of the primitive streak in the fourteenth or fifteenth day. His argument is based on the nature of the new entity up until the point of gastrulation. Gastrulation refers to the process that takes place between the fourteenth and nineteenth days, whereby the embryo takes on a distinctive and recognizable 'body plan' (see Andrew L.

Ford, 2000). For a good part of the time prior to this stage, the cells making up the embryo have the capacity to form any of the cells necessary for human development. These stem cells can become bone, muscle tissue, hair or whatever. In these early stages the cells are totipotent. They have the potential to produce all the different types of cells that make up the human body. During gastrulation, the cells are differentiated into three layers from which, with further differentiation and growth, will develop all the tissues and cells of the foetus proper. The first part of Ford's argument is that up until this stage there is just a collection of undifferentiated cells with no human form.

The second part of Ford's argument relies on Aristotle's distinction between form and matter. According to Aristotle matter without form has no identity. The form or intelligible pattern is what makes things intelligible. Moreover the soul is the form of the human. Since the form of the human is the soul, Ford argues there can be no human identity until the cellular matter is ordered in some recognizably human form. And since the earliest stage of this ordering is found at the time of gastrulation then this must be the time when the human material becomes a human individual. Gastrulation is the beginning of the individual's history.

If, as Norman Ford suggests, there is no new human individual prior to the formation of the primitive streak, then for a period of fourteen days beginning with conception the embryonic cells do not have any great value. They are just a mass of biological tissue having the same value as some skin or kidney cells.

> Thus the destruction, waste, disposal and manipulation of early embryonic material would be ethically unproblematic.
>
> On this basis, many of the objections raised against the use of early abortifacients (e.g. 'Morning after' pill), or some aspects of the IVF methods, or human cloning for research purposes, or even the production and use of embryonic stem cell lines, would all be immaterial (A. L. Ford, 2000, p. 18).

Norman Ford's position provides a convenient justification for research using the embryo at this very early stage.

Andrew Ford has furnished us with a detailed reply to the first part of Norman Ford's argument. We shall only recite the counter-argument relevant to our summary of Norman Ford.

Ford claims that there is no differentiation in the embryonic cells up until at least gastrulation. Although macroscopically this may appear true, a closer examination reveals a much more complex series of events. Molecular and intra-cellular differentiation actually occurs from fertilization. Indeed it has been shown that it commences from the time the sperm penetrates the zona pellucida of the oocyte (A. L. Ford, 2000, p. 21).

Individuation begins when the sperm first penetrates the ova. The membrane covering the ova changes in order to prevent any other sperm from achieving penetration. Significantly, a boundary is drawn at the time of fertilization. Plus, the cell differentiation of the outer and inner surfaces of the blastomeres and the distinct distribution of the intercellular components in the developing morula indicate both differentiation and a functional unified coordination within the morula. Andrew Ford concludes:

If each of these early cells was only a loosely connected, independent cell with no teleological coordination, then these indications of organization, interaction and dependency make little sense.

Moreover,

Their development as a functional whole is teleologically oriented towards the emergence of the human foetus, then the neonate, infant, and then the adult.

The primitive streak stage is neither the beginning nor the end of the process of individuation.

In the second part of his argument, Norman Ford relies on Aristotle's distinction between form and matter. For Aristotle the form of the human is the soul. The soul is the organizing principle that gives human matter its shape and character. This distinction is not biblical. In the Bible the soul is the inner being and it stands in contrast to the outer being, the body. Both the soul and the body have different forms in the Aristotelian sense. The inner being refers to the conscious self that is composed of mind, emotions and will. Given the biblical insight into the nature of the soul and the empirical knowledge gained by modern research, it would make better sense to argue that the soul (consciousness) emerges as the bodily capacities develop according to the genetic program contained in the zygote. Each soul would operate within the biological boundaries established by its genetic code.

Cooper (1989) has demonstrated that while the biblical writers may have viewed the soul and body as different substances, they saw both substances functioning as an integrated unit. Each substance is seen to be dependent upon the other. The scientific evidence suggests that the fertilized ovum is not just another bundle of cells. It is not like a collection of skin or kidney cells. These skin or kidney cells are just part of a human being, and when detached from the individual do not have the capacity in themselves to divide and develop into a new being. The fertilized ovum is not just a collection of cells, it is an individuated being. From the time of fertilization a boundary has been established. The fact that at some time the cells within this boundary are totipotent, or the fact that some of the cells become the placenta and are discarded, is irrelevant. A human being might lose some teeth through natural processes or an arm through an accident, but this does not indicate that he or she has lost his or her identity as an individual. The boundary is established and the genetic code and other chemical codes as principles of organization are in place and operating. Nor would the process of twinning, where the stem cells divide to form two embryos, threaten the status of the original being. Had it not divided, the original embryo would have remained an individuated being with a genetic code operating as a principle of organization. When it divides there are two individuated beings with identical genetic codes operating as a principle of organization. The status of the beings, whether there are one or two, does not change. They are *human* beings.

Given the biblical framework of thought and the evidence of

modern science it would be reasonable to suggest that the soul (consciousness) would emerge when the biological development provided the capacity for it.[6] More importantly, the view that the fertilized ovum is a human being and an emerging person is thoroughly consistent with the biblical revelation. The Psalmist declares that God created his inmost being and knitted him together in the womb (Psalm 139:13). Perhaps the most substantial point to be made here is the claim that this whole process is God's work. It was his plan and purpose that humans come into being in this way. Tampering with God's work at this point would be a monstrous sin. In relation to this last point some will argue that God has given dominion to mankind and that humans are allowed to modify and change creation. It is true that humans are given permission to use plants and animals as food. Destruction is not banned. As we observed in Chapter Five, dominion refers to humankind's role in keeping God's order. Certain things can be used by humans but God demands an account of the use to which creation is put (Genesis 9:1–5). Humans are forbidden to take human life (Genesis 9:6). The Lord gives life and only the Lord has the right to take it away. Humans are God's agents in the world and God will call to account anyone who kills his agent.

A Biblical Approach to Abortion

If the entity formed after the fertilization of the ovum has established its own boundaries and is able to organize its own development, then it must be considered a being and not just a bundle of cells. And if the fertilized ovum is a functional whole, teleologically oriented towards the emergence of the human foetus that will develop into an adult human being, then it must be recognized as a human being and an emerging person. The nature and the purpose of the fertilized ovum confer on it the status of a human being and an emerging person. The Christian response to the establishment of this new entity is to be one of love. Love will want to see the entity flourish and accomplish its purpose. To this end love will want to welcome and nurture the emerging person and surround it with the opportunities that will encourage it to engage in mutual love relationships. The hope will be that through this community of mutual love the emerging person might come to know the forgiveness of God in Christ and enter into his Kingdom.

A New Feminist Challenge

Some of the older arguments in favour of abortion relied on the belief that the foetus was just a bundle of cells and not a human being. The new middle ground occupied by some contemporary feminists does not agree that the foetus is just a bundle of human cells. The foetus is given significant value from the time of conception. Cannold, for example, adopts a gradualist approach to the matter.

> The point is that the development process is a continuum, with fertilization of the egg by the sperm at one end, and the birth at the other. Any attempt to place a wedge somewhere in this gradual process and declare that before the wedge the foetus doesn't matter, while after the wedge it does, is a decision that is as much a part of the sea of subjective values around abortion as any other (Cannold, 1998, p. 37).

Cannold, acknowledging the first premise of the 'pro-life' argument, concedes that abortion is killing. But she rejects the second premise that killing is always wrong. The 'pro-choice' position is moral, she argues, because killing can be justified. A mother must have good reasons to abort, consider everyone's interests and needs, and make the decision thoughtfully and lovingly. Finally she must grieve over the fact that there was a need to make the decision at all.

The debate has been moved, by the new middle, from the issues of the status of foetal life and a woman's right over her body to the topic of motherhood and the woman's responsibility for her child. Attention is focused on the relationship between the mother and her could-be child. The essence of these relationships is identified as commitment. The mother/child relationship is seen to be personal and unique. If the pro-choice mother-to-be considers that "she will be unable to be a good mother to her could-be child—the pro-choice woman believes her foetus would be better off dead" (Cannold, 1998, p. 115). The argument is that if the could-be mother is not committed to the child then the child's life will not be worth living. The misery of being abandoned by one's mother is seen to destroy the value of life. The reason why the could-be mother will not commit herself to the foetus is relatively unimportant. It could be career, finance, or the lack of a partner to help with the parenting. While the needs of everyone who will bear some responsibility for the child should be considered, a woman may choose to abort in order to fulfil her individual aspirations.

There is a perverse moral inversion to this new 'middle of the road' argument. After correctly identifying the need for commitment by the mother to the child, the argument does not go on to conclude that mothers-to-be ought to commit themselves to their could-be child. Rather the necessity of the 'oughtness' is turned around back-to-front. If the mother-to-be for some reason does not *want* to make the commitment to the child, a commitment that she 'ought to make' because of the unique and personal relationship created by motherhood, then she is free to abort the child because the child would be better off dead.

Cannold objects when this approach is called selfish or self-centred. A woman who aborts her child-to-be may still want to make a contribution to others in the world. It is just that she doesn't want to make the contribution of mothering a child. It is assumed that women are entitled to chart their own destiny in this way. After commenting that a certain woman's choice to abort "was consistent with her valuing herself as a journalist", Cannold goes on to comment that the woman in question "would have had to have been a different person, with a different set of values, to have chosen to adopt or keep the child, in the same set of circumstances" (Cannold, 1998, p. 114).

The mother must be true to herself. This is critical if the decision to abort is going to be ethical. Cannold argues that most women who favour abortion on demand do operate on a system of moral values. Ethics, she claims, is central to the 'pro-choice' position. "We use our moral values to define the kind of people we are, and the kind of world we want to live in…acting on our values is as essential to life as food or water, while being unable to act on them cripples our self-respect" (Cannold, 1998, p. xv). There is no doubt an ethic in operation here, but it is not the ethic of the Bible. It is an ethic of individualistic utilitarianism. According to this ethic, each individual person, be it man or woman, is free to shape their own lives in accordance with their own goals. Meaning in life is found in self-achievement and self-fulfilment.

By way of contrast, biblical morality is built upon the nature and purpose of things. Humans are the kind of thing they are because of the nature God has given them and the purposes God has for them. Humans are persons who are able to think, feel, value and choose. Human nature is what it is because of the goal God had in mind for humans. This was the goal of mutual love relationships. Human nature, and hence, to some degree, the goal of human nature, is objectively fixed in the created order. The feminists who occupy the middle of the road in relation to abortion are part of the contemporary deconstruction movement. Not happy with the order of creation and the nature of things as they are, this movement wants everyone to be god in their own lives and set their own goals. Rather than recognising the sinfulness of humanity as the problem with the created order, these feminists find nothing wrong with the human subject and suggest that each individual ought to take control and reorganize the objective created order. The manipulation and reconstruction of reality is seen as the way to true freedom.

There is no doubt that the pro-abortion movement is politically driven. Cannold, like others, recognizes "that without full reproductive rights—and that includes abortion—women's crusade for freedom and equality is beaten before it's begun" (Cannold, 1998, p. xix). Political structures should be such that each individual is free to shape themselves and set their own goals. The motives of the anti-abortion movement are interpreted in the light of this political agenda. "The goal of anti-choice women in supporting a movement which seeks to make abortion illegal is not the preservation of 'innocent' life, but the conscription of all women who have conceived to motherhood" (Cannold, 1998, p. 110). These could-be-mothers do not want to make a choice prior to becoming pregnant, but when pregnancy comes. At this point they want to be free to either commit themselves to having a child and the responsibility of growing, rearing, and parenting that comes with the child, or decide against parenting and have an abortion. "Abortion provides the means for women to consider motherhood not as a destiny, but as choice" (Cannold, 1998, p. 116).

The biblical response to Cannold's argument is that effective contraception would allow women the freedom to choose to be mothers or not. Because the chief goal of sex in marriage is that the two should become one, contraception is a moral option. The Christian woman may or may not want to be a mother, but this is not the essence of Christian freedom. The Christian doctrine of freedom so eloquently advanced in the New Testament is a freedom from sin and rebellion against God. It is the freedom to obey Christ, and find the joy and peace of mutual love relationships. It is the freedom to express one's true nature and to find the goal for which one was created. In true objective freedom the Christian is free to reject the illusionary subjective freedom of all the modern liberation movements, including the feminist movement and its demands for abortion. In the end this new middle ground is committed to an ethic based on individualism and autonomy. It is an ethic that focuses on the individual self and finds meaning in self-achievement. As an ethic it stands a long way from the biblical position.

Difficult Cases

The general shape of a biblical perspective on abortion should now be clear. New human life is to be welcomed and nurtured. But this may not always be possible in a distorted and fallen world. Cases of ectopic pregnancy are clear examples where abortion may be justified. In an ectopic pregnancy the fertilized ovum remains in the fallopian tube and does not descend to the womb. If the pregnancy is allowed to continue, the fallopian tube will rupture and both the mother and foetus will die. Our ethic clearly allows the abortion of the foetus in such cases. At the level of nature and purpose, saving a person's life at the expense of the life of an emerging person would be justified. The good of the foetus cannot be achieved in such cases. From the aspect of personal relationships love demands the maintenance of the existing mutual love relationships that the mother enjoys. The loss of the mother's life together with that of the foetus will destroy existing mutual love relationships. The goal of maintaining mutual love relationships would also justify the abortion.

There may be other cases where abortion would justified. The example of pregnancy due to rape is often cited. But such cases are far from clear. If there was a chance that the pregnancy did not threaten the life of the mother in some way, then the mother may find the joy of a new mutual love relationship a great motivation to keep and nurture the child. Each case would have to be examined in the light of our ethic and a judgment made. It must be remembered that difficult cases do not provide the basis for good policy.

CHAPTER THIRTEEN

Euthanasia

L IKE ALL ISSUES of life and death, the subject of euthanasia is an extremely emotive topic. A passionate commitment to a point of view can often blind us to the strength of opposing views. This is particularly true in regard to a moral assessment of the practice of euthanasia. Opponents often think that the case against the practice is so clear and overwhelming that they cannot understand why anyone would advocate it. Advocates frequently feel that opponents lack compassion and understanding. It is important to identify and comprehend the fears and concerns, and the understanding and arguments of both opponents and advocates. Morality requires that the rejection of arguments come only after fair and reasonable consideration. There is no doubt that the pain and suffering some people are asked to endure is extreme. The question has to be raised why people are forced to endure such suffering.

In Australia the euthanasia debate gained a new impetus with the passing of the *Rights of the Terminally Ill Act* by the Northern Territory legislature in 1996. This Act allowed the killing of a person and/or assisting with the death of a person by a medical practitioner under certain conditions. Although this Bill was invalidated by the subsequent *Euthanasia Laws Act 1997* passed by the Federal Parliament, a number of people were able to take advantage of the provisions of the Northern Territory legislation. The first to die under the provisions of the Bill was a retired carpenter named Bob Dent who had been suffering from prostate cancer for over five years. Mr. Dent dictated a statement the day before he died. In this state- ment he describes the condition that led him to seek euthanasia.

I have no wish for further experimentation by palliative care people in their efforts to control my pain. My current program involves taking 30 tablets a day. For months I have been on a roller coaster of pain made worse by the unwanted side effects of the drugs.

Morphine causes constipation, laxatives taken work erratically, often resulting in loss of bowel control in the middle of the night. I have a rubber sheet on my bed, like a child who is not yet toilet trained....My own pain is made worse by watching my wife suffering as she cares for me; bathing and drying me, cleaning up after my 'accidents' in the middle of the night, and watching my body fade away...I have always been an active, outgoing person, and being unable to live a normal life causes much mental and psychological pain, which can never be relieved by medication. (Cited in *Euthanasia, Death and Dying: An Anglican Resource*, published by the Social Responsibilities Commission, Anglican Church of Australia, 1998, pp. 3–4.)

One cannot but empathize and commiserate with a person in this condition. This is the sort of case that has given rise to voluntary euthanasia societies around the world. These societies have argued for the painless termination of life with the consent of the patient. The groups advocating the practice offer two main arguments for voluntary euthanasia. The first is that compassion demands it in those cases where death is the only way of alleviating extreme pain. The second has to do with the notion of autonomy. That is, the idea that the individual has the freedom and right to decide whether he or she will live or die. If we are to evaluate these arguments we must see what the Bible has to say on the topics. But before we do this we need to consider what the practice of euthanasia involves.

What is Euthanasia?

There has been a lot of confusion about the use of the term 'euthanasia'. As a result, various social surveys report conflicting information about the public's attitude to the practice. Put simply euthanasia is the termination of the life of a patient by a medical practitioner. It involves a doctor giving a lethal injection that kills the patient. As such, euthanasia is not to be confused with the cessation of medical treatment where the treatment has proved to be both useless and burdensome. The withdrawal of intervention that is intended to save and extend life is not to be misconstrued as intervention designed to kill. If we accept the definition of euthanasia as the termination of the life of a patient by the instrument of a fatal injection, then we avoid the debate over active and passive euthanasia. Previously people have used the term 'passive euthanasia' to refer to the withdrawal of treatment which was keeping the patient alive. In such cases the patient would have died without the intervention of the doctor. This being so, passive euthanasia may be seen as letting nature take its course, in which case it is not a form of killing at all. Nor is euthanasia to be confused with the proportionate treatment of pain. There is concern in some cases that in the treatment of some terminally ill patients, the amount and type of medication necessary to relieve extreme pain may also shorten the patient's life. In such treatment the intention is usually to treat the pain, and not to kill the patient.

Voluntary euthanasia refers to the practice where the patient asks for his or her life to be terminated. Non-voluntary euthanasia refers to cases where the patient cannot ask for it (e.g. where the patient is in a coma). Involuntary euthanasia designates the practice of euthanasia contrary to the will of the patient. That is, involuntary euthanasia is the practice of terminating life against the expressed desires of the patient. No responsible social group has come out in support of involuntary euthanasia, so we can put this to one side.

Methodology

Like abortion, euthanasia is one of those issues that is not explicitly mentioned in the Bible. In this sense it is similar to other modern issues like genetic engineering and ecology. Because euthanasia is not explicitly mentioned in Scripture, we will not be able to adopt the method followed in the previous chapters in relation to sex and marriage and homosexuality. No specific details are supplied in the Bible on this topic on which we can draw. How, then, are we to proceed?

Given our understanding of the unity of the Scriptures and their developmental framework, the way forward is not difficult to find. As we have seen, it is possible to build up an accurate integrated picture of God and his purposes, provided, of course, we exegete the parts of Scripture within the framework of salvation supplied by the Scripture itself. In this way we can develop a big picture covering many aspects of life. Some of these aspects will be relevant to the issue of euthanasia. Jochemsen has argued, for example, that the biblical perspective provided by the big picture supplies us with information about personhood, health, death and medicine, and that these matters are directly related to the issue of euthanasia (Jochemsen, 1995). In other words we can use the Bible in an indirect manner to address the issue. In our survey of the biblical material we will focus on those aspects that impinge upon the issue of euthanasia.

A Matter of Perspective

People's perception of reality is shaped by their grid of beliefs, understandings and commitments. People use this grid to interpret their existence and give their lives meaning. The Bible indicates that many people in Jesus' day could not see that Jesus was the Lord of Heaven, even though he did many miracles in their sight. Because people have other 'lords', their commitment and understanding prevented them from seeing the truth about Jesus. Many people today see themselves as lord in their own lives, and this commitment and understanding precludes them from recognizing Jesus as Lord. The truth of this insight about the perception of reality extends well beyond the bounds of religion. It is true of knowledge in general. For example, a person who believes that all is matter, a materialist, will never recognize spiritual entities, because his or her original understanding and commitment to the proposition that only matter exists blinds them to the possibility.

The fact that beliefs, understandings, and commitments shape people's perception of reality is significant in the euthanasia debate. People come to the debate from various perspectives. Because of these different perspectives, people see the pain and suffering of terminal illness in different ways, and so respond to the problem in various ways by suggesting different courses of action. It is not possible to outline all the distinct ways people view the problem of pain and the issues of euthanasia in an introductory text like this one. An outline of the contours of two widely held and fundamental positions will be enough to provide an adequate discussion of the main issues. We will compare two clusters of ideas that form two fundamental perspectives. We will examine a biblical perspective and one we might call 'enlightened individualism'. In both cases we will observe that the perspective drives the conclusions in relation to the question of euthanasia. That fact that some people might adopt the perspective but not hold the complete set of beliefs is irrelevant to our discussion. We only have to assume that such people hold enough of the cluster to drive them to the relevant conclusion.

Enlightened Individualism

The first perspective finds its origins in the eighteenth century. This century saw the development of a cluster of ideas that were regarded as progressive and liberal. The notion of the supernatural and the idea of God's revelation were dismissed. Reality was seen to be limited to the natural world. This was the world known through the five senses. Knowledge of reality was to be gained by observation and experiment. It was concluded that such empirical knowledge demonstrated that everything, including the functioning of the human mind, could be explained in terms of the organization and activity of matter. The natural world was the material world. It was thought that the ignorance and superstition of religion caused much of the human unhappiness of the past. The optimism of this enlightened age believed that when humanity jettisoned the superstitious beliefs and understanding taught by religion it would find true happiness. Once people recognized that they were part of the natural order of things and understood their own natures, they could go about their true goals of self-preservation and self-fulfilment.

Retaining the perspective that humans were self-conscious beings who were able to think, feel and choose, they argued that people had the capacity to evaluate their own actions and the consequences of these actions without the guidance of the Scriptures. The capacity of people to think, evaluate, and choose suggested that people were self-governing or autonomous beings. According to this secular perspective, meaning and purpose in life was thought to be found by setting and achieving one's own goals. This was part of the whole process of self-achievement and self-realization that not only gave one an identity but also made life so valuable. Health was vital to self-achievement and self-realization. Vitality and an ability to function fully and properly were seen to be essential if one was to reach one's goals. The ability to enjoy life was believed to come with the capacity to choose goals pleasing to oneself and the pleasure of self-achievement. Function and enjoyment determined the value of life.

The perspective concentrated on this material earthly life. People were seen as very complicated biological beings analogous to machines. According to this view medicine was the art of repairing the machine. Medicine assisted the individual to function properly and to find enjoyment in life, but when the machine could no longer function efficiently and the burdens of life, specifically pain, outweighed the pleasures, then medicine had a moral obligation to provide a good painless death. Compassion demanded this much. The word 'compassion' maintained its usual sense in this argument. Compassion, or love, encompassed a commitment to the good of others. However the good was defined in terms of pleasure and the avoidance of pain.

Death did not present a problem on this view. People were material beings who came into existence through other material beings. Personal life, that which is uniquely human, came with the emergence of consciousness. People attained consciousness and passed out of consciousness. Death was inevitable. The real issue was about the way it came. Because autonomy is essential to self-creation it is perfectly consistent to argue that people be free to make a decision about the time and circumstances of their demise. Since people 'make' themselves it was argued that they ought to be able to 'unmake' themselves. The logic was faultless. The nature of reality was such that compassion demanded the practice of euthanasia. People had the right to choose when they died and the medical profession had a moral obligation to provide a service of euthanasia.

A Biblical Perspective

The biblical account of salvation history draws a completely different picture to the one given above. The Bible begins with the declaration that Yahweh, the God of Israel, is the Creator of all. The consequence of God being the Creator is that all is his. Consequently he is Lord of all. By God's action, man became a living being (Genesis 2:7). As a consequence, life and death are in God's hand (Deuteronomy 32:39). To take the life of another is to take something that God has given. Moreover, humans, made in the image of God, were delegated the task of maintaining God's order in creation. To shed the blood of one of God's servants is an offence against the Master himself. The judgment of God is that those who kill another human, will, in turn, lose their own life (Genesis 9:6).

After the Fall, Israel has a special place in the plan and purpose of God. Israel is to model God's order to a watching sinful world. Among the powers delegated to humans in their ordering of society is the power of death. Capital punishment is warranted in certain cases where people have offended against God's Law. Killing is also warranted when foreign nations fall under the judgment of God. The Lord is seen to be the Ruler of Israel, and those who attack Israel are seen to be challenging God's rightful sovereignty. As Israel moves into the Promised Land, the nations around about are seen to be in rebellion against the Lord of Heaven because of their commitment to other gods. Hence Israel is seen to be inflicting the judgment of God on these nations. However the commandment to the people of God is that they should not murder (Exodus 20:13).

That is to say, that individuals should not kill on the basis of their own will and desire. Life presents the opportunity of knowing God and enjoying his blessing. Hence it is of supreme value. Consequently, one is not to "stand up against the life of your neighbour" (Leviticus 19:16). If someone is injured or ill every reasonable attempt is to be made to maintain life. People should not profit by allowing another to die. Neither should one allow another to die in order to avoid the burden of serving them.

As we have seen, life, according to the Bible, is the gift of God. It is only fitting that the God who gives life is the One who takes it. Job summarizes this perspective when he declares that the Lord gives and the Lord takes away (Job 1:21). Individuals do not own life—it is God's. Consequently, from the biblical perspective, suicide is an attempt to take oneself out of the hands of God. Euthanasia, which is a form of assisted suicide, would be seen to be morally reprehensible from the biblical perspective. Ironically, those who adopt the doctrine of enlightened individualism will undoubtedly perceive this evaluation of suicide to be morally reprehensible, causing unnecessary pain and suffering. The essence of the problem here is that these people do not have a biblical view of God as Creator. If they have a concept of God at all, they apprehend him to be a supreme being, but as a being like themselves, standing within, and subject to, the logic of the created order. They fail to see God as the One on whom everything depends for its existence and continuation.

Like the humanists, the biblical writers also see persons are thinking, feeling, willing, self-conscious beings. The biblical writers have a view of autonomy, but it is not the view of the enlightened individualist. The strong view of autonomy adopted by the individualists refers to the ability to establish one's own values and goals. The biblical perspective takes on a weaker concept. People are free to choose from a range of possible actions before them. In this sense they are autonomous. But they cannot create their own system of moral values. Moral values have been established by God and built into the very order of creation. People are autonomous in that they can disobey God and ignore his values, but they are not free to create their own set of moral values. Unlike the enlightened individualistic perspective, the biblical writers do not see the meaning and value in life found in self-actualization. Rather the significance of life is found in right relationships with God, others and creation. Thankfully the meaning of life is not totally based on what the individual can achieve. It is the gift of God in Christ.

Illness and disease is not just a fault in the machine of creation, according to the Bible. Rather, as C. S. Lewis has pointed out, the pain and suffering of illness and disease is God's megaphone shouting to the world that all is not right. It screams out that there is a breakdown in mankind's relationship with God. Just as aches and pains in the body can be indications of various medical conditions, so the unhealthiness of the world testifies to creation that humanity's relationship with God has been fractured. Medicine has a holding and restorative role within the biblical perspective. Medicine is to make use of the possibilities present in creation to restore health. Its job is not to control and order life. Fulfilling an aspect of the function of the stewardship of the world given to humankind, medical practitioners are to overcome mental and physical disturbances, restore bodily order, and heal disease. Medicine is given this caretaker role as humanity and creation awaits the Day of Salvation where redemption will find its completion.

For humanists, who reject the notion of the supernatural and the after-life, death is the end of everything. The biblical perspective stands in stark contrast to the humanist picture. "It is appointed for man to die once, and after that comes judgment" (Hebrews 9:27). These two different outlooks on death lead to very different accounts of life. For the humanist, life is everything. For the Christian, life provides a taste of both the goodness of God and the pain of sin and disorder. Death is a passage to eternity and a new heavenly order.

When pain and suffering become unbearable, the humanist has nothing else to hope for but the relief found in death. For the Christian, life is immeasurably more complex than simply balancing out pleasure and pain. Life finds its meaning in good and loving relationships with God and one's fellows. In the midst of pain and suffering the Christian can know the joy of giving and receiving love. The Christian can know the hope of an eternal life filled with the joy and the delight that comes with right relationships. Indeed the suffering of pain can strengthen Christian faith for it amplifies the meaning of Jesus' suffering and death. The pain that Jesus underwent to restore right relationships with God takes on a new significance. Jesus suffered more pain and anguish in his death on the cross than any human can ever know. The agony of having his Father turn his face away from him after an eternity of feeling the radiance of his love is a pain only dimly reflected in the loss of a loved one here on earth. In a very real sense, to taste of pain is to begin to experience the dimensions of God's love in Christ. That Jesus would suffer so for humans shows that he is utterly and totally committed to serving them in love. That is why, for the Christian, nothing, including pain and death, "will be able to separate us from the love of God in Christ Jesus our Lord" (Romans 8:39).

The biblical perspective on death is radically different to the humanistic outlook. Death is annihilation for the humanist. For the Christian, death is the end of this earthly life, the moment of divine judgment, and the passage to eternity. The hope of annihilation cannot compare with the hope of eternal life in a community of mutual love relationships.

Consideration of the Basic Arguments

We are now in a position to reflectively consider the two main arguments for voluntary euthanasia. You will remember that the arguments were based on compassion and autonomy. The first argument maintains that compassion demands the practice of euthanasia in those cases where death is the only way of alleviating extreme pain. The second argument affirmed that individuals have the freedom and right to decide whether they live or die.

There are a number of myths that are circulated in relation to the alleviation of extreme pain. One such myth is that terminal pain is inevitable and cannot be controlled. Dame Cicely Saunders is one of a number of recognized palliative care specialists who testify from extensive medical experience that the claim of inevitable pain is a myth. As long ago as 1980 she could proclaim "that so many patients still suffer unrelieved pain is inexcusable and is more often due to lack of knowledge and prejudice than lack of staff and money" (Saunders, 1980, p. 89). This quotation leads us into another myth. This is the myth that governments cannot afford good terminal care. In the last decades the development of successful home care programs means that only a small percentage of patients need to go into specialist hospice care. Biblical ethics would encourage home care programs where the patient can be with members of their family, who can provide the love and support necessary to give the patient a sense of personal worth at this difficult time.

A great number of palliative care specialists testify that the number of people suffering from untreatable pain is very, very small. A number of palliative care specialists responded to the statement of Bob Dent cited earlier in this chapter. There was some surprise that his condition and pain had not been managed more effectively. For those few with untreatable pain, euthanasia might have a great appeal. But the appeal is only at the level of the individual, and it cannot easily be converted into a more public and general appeal. Arguments presented in the next section will show that the legalization of euthanasia would put many more people in danger than it would help. The individual appeal is countered by the biblical affirmation that killing is morally wrong and by the negative affects euthanasia would have on the quality of life of the elderly. The negative affects would flow from the attitude to old age fostered by the practice of euthanasia. In this regard Saunders highlights the benefits of a positive attitude to old age.

> The best way to live on is to remain as active as possible and
> to receive the respect of others; the worst way is to be told
> continually how sad and undignified old age can be and how
> we should be free to ask to be rid of it (Saunders, 1980, p. 90).

The claim that love demands the practice of euthanasia where death is the only way of alleviating extreme pain trades on one particular set of moral values. The essence of compassion and love is a commitment to the good of others. The question is what is the good for those suffering extreme untreatable pain. Enlightened individualism declares that the good is the alleviation of pain by death. The Christian gospel, which speaks of the love of God and the hope of eternal life, sees the good to be found in resting in the love of God and the hope of heaven. Because the words 'love' and 'compassion' refer to a commitment to the good of others they are tied to the notion of what is good. The logic of the various uses of the words 'love' and 'compassion' changes with the different assumptions about what is good. For those operating on a biblical ethic, love does not demand the practice of euthanasia for those suffering from extreme untreatable pain, no matter how few in number they be. In the end, the real debate is not about euthanasia but which set of values is the true one. There are many competing perspectives alive in the world today and each of these generates their own values system. Unlike the perspective of enlightened individualism, not all perspectives generate support for the practice of euthanasia. Choosing between these perspectives is not easy. Christians would argue that the biblical perspective more adequately accounts for the experiences of life than any other perspective. Alasdair MacIntyre and others have demonstrated how the perspective of enlightened individualism has proved less than adequate.

The second main argument used to support the introduction of euthanasia is the argument from autonomy. As we observed in an earlier section of this chapter the word 'autonomy' can have a weak and a strong sense. The biblical worldview rejects the strong notion of autonomy. People are creatures and they are not free to create their own world of values. Any set of values they create independent of the generic and telic order revealed in the Scriptures will be a false set of values and they will ultimately have a detrimental affect on the lives of those who operate on them. People are not free to take their own lives nor are they free to instruct another to do so. Life is the gift of God; he is the only one free to give and to take. In a somewhat extraordinary fashion, the biblical writers would want to claim that people are not even free to choose the wrong course of action. Maintaining that people without the Spirit of Christ are slaves to sin, writers like Paul would consider people as locked into wrong choices. It is not hard to comprehend that people who have committed themselves to the cluster of beliefs and values we have called 'enlightened individualism' are not free to follow God's system of moral values. It takes the miracle of conversion to bring about a shift in their grid of beliefs, values and commitments.

Individual Interests versus Communal Interest

There is no doubt that the practice of euthanasia will appeal to anyone who agrees with some of the cluster of ideas we have identified as enlightened individualism. In the English-speaking world, with its history of individualism, this number will be significant. Arguments based on the Christian Scriptures will have little impact on these people since they build their knowledge of the world and personal life on a different foundation. Many of these people have not carefully worked out a consistent grid of beliefs. Some will have remnants of Christian doctrine scattered among their 'enlightened individualism'. Perhaps it is possible to trade on these remains of a former culture to convince these people that euthanasia is morally wrong; perhaps not. But there are other factors that provide arguments against the adoption of the practice of euthanasia. These are consequential arguments. They trade on the fact that biblical morality is faithful to the generic and telic order of creation. It was argued in the chapter on homosexuality that if our account of biblical morality was true then those who deny the generic and telic order of creation and set up their own goals and purposes would suffer as a consequence.

Somerville (1995, p. 3) points out that the present conditions which the pro-euthanasia lobby see as warranting the introduction of the practice of euthanasia have been around for hundreds of years. The four basic conditions are (i) that people are terminally ill, (ii) that they are suffering extreme pain, (iii) that they want to be killed, and (iv) we have the ability to kill them painlessly. Yet for thousands of years people have held that it was wrong to kill each other even for reasons of mercy and compassion. It is not the case that all killing has been considered wrong. Killing was seen to be legitimate in war, self-defence and capital punishment. Questions must be asked. What has changed? 'Thou shalt not kill' has been one of the most fundamental rules upon which society has been based. What will happen to the fabric of society if this fundamental rule is changed? Two things come immediately to mind. The first is that community attitudes towards life and the value of life would change. Life would be less sacred. The quality of life would be diminished and the demarcation between justifiable killing and unjustifiable killing would become less clear. Society would be the poorer for the change.

Another question must be asked. What would be the impact of legalizing euthanasia on the medical profession? At this point we do not have to speculate. The evidence from the experiment in the Netherlands is conclusive. The government of the Netherlands did not legislate to make euthanasia legal. Rather it was agreed that if medical practitioners followed the strict guidelines implicit in a 'narrow' definition of euthanasia then they would not be prosecuted by law-enforcement agencies. The 'narrow' definition of euthanasia had two components. Euthanasia was (i) to be restricted to those who asked for it, and (ii) it had to be for the relief of suffering.

Fleming (1992) provides evidence from official Dutch reports that over half the patients 'euthanased' were not killed at the patience's request. The killings were not 'euthanasia' under the narrow definition, because they were not voluntary. This evidence shows that a great number of doctors who killed patients because they asked to be put to death for the relief of suffering moved from the double criteria of 'being voluntary' and 'for the relief of pain' to operating on just one criteria; the relief of pain. Having been given the *power to kill* at the request of the patient for the relief of suffering, many physicians abandoned the voluntary component and relied on their own judgment about who should receive relief from suffering. Acquiring the power to kill changed these physicians' attitudes to the life of their patients. The patient's wishes became irrelevant. The doctors assumed total responsibility for the lives of their patients. The patients were 'dehumanized' even under the terms of enlightened individualism. They were robbed of their autonomy. Under the biblical ethic, God was 'robbed' of his agent in the world. Sadly it is not hard to imagine this new attitude to human life spreading out from the medical community into the community at large if it has the sanction of the law.

Even if it is conceded that the practice of euthanasia might meet the needs of a small group of individuals in the community, the pro-euthanasia pressure will not be validated. Adopting the practice and enshrining the beliefs behind it into the legal structures of the community will have public consequences. These consequences will be dangerous, and place many more people at risk than the few whom the practice of euthanasia would help. Biblical moral values count against the practice. The reality is that the adoption of the practice would bring more harm than any possible good. A rational community cannot endorse it despite the emotional pleas of individuals.

Conclusions

The biblical ethic does not just call upon Christians to morally evaluate the practice of euthanasia in negative terms. It calls upon the Christian to be loving in character and deed. Christians must make every effort as a group to provide for the welfare of the terminally ill and to relieve their suffering. In doing so they will not only witness to the character of their Lord but give dignity and worth to the dying.

Section Four

PRACTICAL APPLICATION

The study of biblical ethics is useless unless it
finds its expression in the life of the believer.
This section makes suggestions about how the
insights gathered together in this book might
nurture the believer's moral life.

CHAPTER FOURTEEN

How to Live a Moral Life

The Dimensions of the Moral Life

There are two aspects to living a moral life. One has to do with making moral decisions, and the other with developing a moral character. The development of character is an essential element because morality has to do with personal relationships. If a person hides their character behind their actions then no true love relationship can develop. Being and doing must correspond or the charge of hypocrisy will be a valid one. We shall begin by examining the process of moral decision making. Beginning at this point should in no way imply that decision making is the dominant aspect of the moral life. The formation of character is equally important. Decision-making cannot be isolated from character formation. The adoption and nurture of moral virtues found in the Bible will affect moral decision making. The endorsement of the virtue of truthfulness, for example, will embody a disposition to apply the rule 'tell the truth'.

Making Moral Decisions

Start with the Big Picture

Making moral decisions is a multi-stage process. It begins with looking at the Bible as a whole and seeing the direction and purpose of God's activity in history. Biblical ethics starts with doing biblical theology. From the study of the Bible, we not only get an understanding of God and salvation history, but we get the basics for developing what many have called a 'world-view'. A world-view is a set of beliefs about what exists and how it all operates, including a set of values. As long as we recognize that acquiring a biblical world-view or Christian perspective is an on-going process there will be no problems. Problems only occur when people think that they have a complete and perfect set of beliefs and values. Perfection is not possible this side of heaven.

The Bible is not an ethical textbook. The biblical writers are interested in revealing God's plan of salvation. They were not concerned to integrate the scattered moral elements into a systematic whole. Moral ingredients are dispersed throughout the text of Scripture and when these ingredients are gathered together they do not in themselves present a totally comprehensive picture. There are many gaps, and these do not allow us to correlate everything into an entirely comprehensive arrangement. While the creation accounts inform us that God created various kinds of things and ordered the relationships between these kinds, there is no systematic account of these kinds and their goals. The complete purposeful pattern is not available to us. The Mosaic Law provides some information about God's intended order through its regulations and rules. The overall scheme of things is given substantial shape when Christ is revealed as the goal of all things. Nevertheless, there are still many topics and issues not mentioned. In regard to ethics, the biblical portrait is like a jigsaw puzzle with quite a few pieces missing.

New Testament writers like Paul seem to hint that given a knowledge of salvation history and the final goal in Christ, Christian people can work out the bits of the jigsaw that are missing. Working out what is right or wrong is part of living in the Spirit. The Spirit and the Word of God are inseparable. The Spirit applies the Word. The letters of Paul are littered with his examinations of situations in the light of God's Word. A significant part of the application of the Scriptures is dependent upon a good empirical knowledge of the situation. However, biblical knowledge and theological insight play an essential part. The logical process of this integration is called abduction. Abduction is the process of putting all the clues together using imagination and intuition. Abduction is the skill used in seeing how the isolated parts of a jigsaw fit together. The fact that it is based on imagination and intuition does not discredit it. Many modern scholars have demonstrated that modern science relies on abduction. It is the first step that enables scientists to come up with a theory. While abduction includes a subjective or personal element the objective shape of the pieces of the jigsaw precludes putting things together in any way we like.

There is no reason to think that any particular individual might have all the right beliefs, understanding and values. In fact, the Bible leads us to believe that none of us will understand fully until the Kingdom is consummated. In the meantime understanding the Bible and the world around us is a fellowship activity where we all learn from one another. Many elements of a biblical world-view will only be worked as new situations are confronted. If we continue the analogy of the jigsaw puzzle then we could claim that Chapters Four to Eight of this book have mapped out the borders and highlighted some of the main features in the picture. As we take up specific moral issues we will fill in some of the details of the picture relevant to the particular topic.

Draw Out the Principles and Values Involved

In 1 Corinthians 8, Paul gives us a great example of moral reasoning. A problem has arisen in Corinth. Corinth was a pagan city and most, if not all, of the meat offered for sale in the market place came from animals that had been offered to idols. The individual Christians in Corinth were faced with a moral question—what ought I to do in relation to meat offered to idols?

The way Paul deals with this question is very illuminating. The very first thing he does is to get the Corinthians to focus on love (1 Corinthians 8:1–3). It appears that many of his readers gave a great value to knowledge. Paul does not deny that knowledge is important. Rather he shows that if one gives first place to knowledge then it is likely to make one conceited. Knowledge is something that we must possess. But focussing on the possession of knowledge can make people conceited. By way of contrast Paul points to love. Love is a commitment to others. Love does not puff up but builds up. In so doing, Paul is suggesting that the Corinthians get their values right before they begin to examine the issue. Love is the central value.

Drawing on his world-view Paul states certain facts. It will be helpful to list them.

(a) An idol is nothing (v. 4).
(b) There is no God but one (v. 4).
(c) Food does not bring us nearer to God (v. 8).
From these facts he draws the conclusion,
(d) A Christian is free to eat meat offered to idols (vv. 8–9).

Yet this is not the whole picture. Because Christians are to be for others, they are to consider the consequences of their actions even if in principle the action is correct. Another factor from the situation is introduced. Some Christian brothers and sisters have a weak conscience. Their intellectual convictions have not been fully absorbed emotionally. Although they have knowledge (8:1—we all possess knowledge), their habitual contact with idols (8:7) means that they still feel the reality of the false god when they eat meat offered to idols. At the level of thinking, they know that an idol is nothing and that there is no God but one. Following the example of the strong Christian they might eat meat offered to idols and then, since their consciences are weak and uneducated, experience a strong sense of guilt. Such an experience of the reality of false gods is not good. The moral convictions, which arise from their new relationship with Christ, are overridden and defiled. There is a very real possibility that they will fall back into idolatry and their faith will be destroyed (8:11).

As a matter of principle, a Christian is free to eat meat offered to idols. But the use of this freedom is always determined by the context. If, by exercising his or her freedom, a Christian encourages a brother or sister with a weak conscience to eat meat offered to idols then that Christian has placed a stumbling-block in the path of their brother or sister's relationship with Christ. At this point, Paul brings into play another principle—do not become a stumbling block to the weak (8:9). This principle leads him, at the practical level, to operate on the rule—don't eat meat offered to idols (8:13).

It is important to see that Paul understands the context in Corinth in terms of his theology or the big picture provided by the revelation of God's purposes in Christ. It is possible that Paul could conceive of a context or situation where the application of the principle 'do not become a stumbling-block to the weak' would not issue in the rule 'don't eat meat offered to idols'. For example, if Paul knew of a context where there were no brothers or sisters with weak consciences then he might not advance this particular rule.

Paul's method is quite clear. He understands the particular context in Corinth in terms of the big picture given to him by Scripture. He places his understanding of the particular context within his understanding of the big picture. This enables him to see how love for God and love for his neighbour will be worked out on this occasion. In doing this, Paul has to pick out the relevant facts from the big picture that will help him to interpret the particular situation correctly. Not only this, but Paul has to pick out the values and moral principles that apply. In this case, he does not disvalue knowledge but sees its true value as being found in its employment to serve others in love. Some of the Corinthians had failed to see the true place of knowledge within the bigger picture provided by revelation.

Find a Place for Rules

Many of the rules in the Bible are applicable today, but some are not. Rules that are very particular in nature become inapplicable when the context changes. The command in Leviticus 19:9 to leave the gleanings of the field is a case in point. It is too particular. But it is derived from a higher principle. That principle is the principle of care for the poor and alien (Leviticus 19:10). This principle is but a more particularized expression of the very general command to love one's neighbour as oneself (Leviticus 19:18). Both these later principles are directly related to God's present and ongoing purpose to establish his Kingdom and so they are applicable today.

On the other hand some commandments were only ever indirectly related to God's ultimate and overall goal. These commands seem to have had a specific place in salvation history and there is no carry-over into the present. The Sabbath command might be one such command. The Sabbath commandment seems to have been related to the overall notion of taking possession of the

land and enjoying fully one's relationship with God through the
blessings of the land. The notion of Sabbath rest is developed
further in the New Testament. God's rest has come in Christ. It is
through Christ that we fully possess and enjoy our relationship
with God the Father. The Sabbath command which anticipated
and symbolized rest in Christ is now no longer necessary. The
command is not repeated or recited in the New Testament.

The command in Leviticus 18:19 which forbids sexual relations
with a woman during her monthly periods also seems to be a rule
which is no longer applicable. This rule is based on the clean/unclean
distinction in Leviticus that was employed to teach the Israelites
about holiness and unholiness. We saw earlier that Jesus overthrew
the clean/unclean distinction. Indeed, the New Testament is bold
enough to say that the blood of Jesus saves us. If blood were still
ritually unclean then this very thought would be out of order. One
might still have aesthetic or hygienic reasons for adopting the sexual
prohibition today. But it would not be a moral rule unless it could be
shown to be related to the good of people in general. Clearly, other
commandments, like the four mentioned by Paul in Romans
13:8–10 are still related to the good of neighbours and are still
applicable. Adultery, murder, stealing and coveting, all harm one's
neighbour's interests and do not fulfil the command to love.

The Bible knows nothing of the modern aversion to rules made
popular among Christians by Joseph Fletcher in his book *Situation
Ethics*. Jesus invokes rules against anger and lust (Matthew 5). Paul's
epistles are littered with moral imperatives exhorting Christians to do
this or that. The letters of James, John and Peter all contain moral
imperatives. While many of these moral imperatives are not framed in
terms of a rule, they can be summarized by a rule. A rule is merely the
particular application of a principle to a specific context. In following
the rule in the context, a Christian is just employing the principle.
The moral life would be difficult, if not impossible, without rules.

Developing a Christian Character

As we have seen, the Bible provides us with a big picture of God's activity in history. A picture of God's overall goal is established and the details of this picture are gradually developed. The goal is achieved in Christ. God's goal is referred to in many ways, but chiefly it is referred to as the Kingdom of God. The Kingdom of God, as we have seen, reveals itself to be a community of mutual love relationships. The principles governing mutual love relationships, and many of the rules that flow from the principles, are presented in various ways throughout the Scriptures. Neither the principles nor the rules can be divorced from the goal of mutual love relationships. Those who operate on the principles and rules with the intention of forming mutual love relationships with both God and man must internalize the values contained in the rules and principles into their own character. These internalized values are the virtues that all the saints are called on to display. A knowledge of the virtues listed in the New Testament will be vital if we wish to develop a character that consistently reflects the character of God in Christ.

Moral Virtues in the New Testament

The Bible contains many lists of moral virtues and vices (for example, Ephesians 4:2; Colossians 3:12; Titus 3:2; 1 Peter 3:8). A study of these lists would show that many, if not all, the virtues are directly or indirectly orientated towards the creation or maintenance of mutual love relationships. That is, the virtues are qualities of personal relationships. A study of the vices suggests that they destroy mutual love relationship. These lists of virtues and vices do not appear to be exhaustive. The examination of some of the virtues listed in the New Testament will enhance our understanding of mutual love relationships and give us biblical moral values to work with.

Patient Endurance

Believers living in this present evil age are like plants living under hard and unfavourable conditions. In the light of this fact the New Testament writers use a Greek word (*hupomone*) to map out the nature of an essential virtue. This Greek word was used of the endurance in the face of grief or the coming of death. It referred to

a capacity to carry on and get through the time of trial. The New
Testament writers use this word of Christians facing the trials and
afflictions of this evil age (Romans 5:3; 2 Corinthians 6:4;
2 Thessalonians 1:4). Patient endurance is something that springs
from faith and it confirms and strengthens faith (James 1:3).
Because faith keeps the vision of the inheritance of heaven in sight,
it supplies the hope to continue under the most trying circumstances (Romans 5:3, 15:4; 1 Thessalonians 1:3). Since faith and
hope know that the inheritance is secure in Christ, there is a sense
in which they share the joy of the future in the present (Colossians
1:11–12). Christians are to endure everything in order to share in
the salvation to come (2 Timothy 2:10). Moreover they are to live
out the future now in the present despite the hard conditions found
in the present disordered age. They are to patiently do good seeking the glory and immortality to come (Romans 2:7). Patient
endurance is an aspect of faith, hope, and love (1 Corinthians
13:4). It enables the Christian to live life in a positive way even in
the face of trials and tribulations. It is the spirit that sees beyond the
present pain and suffering to the glory which is yet to come.

There is another Greek word that is seldom used outside the
New Testament. It seems to refer to a peculiarly Christian virtue.
This is the word *makrothumia*. Like *hupomone*, it refers to the
notions of patience and long-suffering. It is a disposition or attitude
that will not give in even under duress. It is used of people who
never give up their hope in God and belief in his faithfulness to his
promises (James 5:7–11). This attitude can bear the delay and suffering in this evil age while it awaits the Kingdom to come. But it
is also an attitude that extends to neighbours. It is the spirit that
will never retaliate. It is a fruit of the Spirit (Galatians 5:22) and
without it Christians will never walk worthily of their calling in
Christ (Ephesians 4:1–2; Colossians 3:12–13).

Gentleness, Kindness, Forbearance, Consideration
There is a Greek word (*epieikes*) used by the New Testament writers
that defies an easy translation. Behind the use of the word is the idea
that laws and principles can be defective because of their generality.

THE HOW AND WHY OF LOVE

The ancient Greek world recognized that a person could claim something that was legally justified but morally wrong. The New Testament writers use this Greek word to insist that in such cases the claimant should not press the claim. In this sense the word refers to a loving other-person-centeredness that is not demanding. Behind this notion is the character of God as revealed in Christ. In his humility Christ displayed great gentleness (2 Corinthians 10:1). Indeed if God was not gentle and forbearing then no-one could stand in his presence. James tells us that this virtue is an aspect of wisdom (James 3:17). Wisdom comes from having correct knowledge and the right value system. Wisdom only comes with a gospel-centred understanding of the Bible. In the light of this understanding, masters are expected to be considerate of their slaves (1 Peter 2:18), and Christians in general are reminded to "avoid quarrelling, to be gentle, and to show perfect courtesy toward all people" (Titus 3:2).

Meekness and Humility

There is another Greek word that takes up the idea of gentleness and develops another aspect of the concept. This is the word *praotes*. It refers to humility. Behind this idea of humility is the concept of a wild beast that has been tamed. For example, once a horse has been tamed, it can be mild and gentle in manner. Even children can ride upon such animals. The essential idea behind this word is that of strength under control. In Matthew 21:5, the word is used of Jesus' entry into Jerusalem upon a donkey. Jesus is the King of Heaven and has all the power of God at his disposal, but he enters Jerusalem in this way to show that his strength is under control and being used in the service of others. Meekness is a facet of Christ's character (2 Corinthians 10:1). Paul offers the Corinthians the choice in the area of discipline. He can come with a stick or with meekness (1 Corinthians 4:21). The choice is between strength not under control and strength under control. Christians are summoned to clothe themselves with meekness (Colossians 3:12) and to live worthily of their calling in Christ (Ephesians 4:2). Meekness is especially appropriate when disciplining opponents (2 Timothy 2:25) or making a defence of the gospel (James 1:21). But it is to be displayed on every occasion (Titus 3:2). A good life is manifested in works done in meekness born of wisdom (James 3:13).

The controlled strength manifested in meekness is motivated by an attitude of humility. One's strength is controlled in order to serve others. For this reason the Greek word is sometimes translated as 'humility'. Humility is that aspect of love that counts the other greater than oneself. Humility delights in doing good for others. It may be contrasted with another Greek word *tapeinos* that speaks about a condition of poverty. If one is born with no social status then one may be of humble birth. Or, if one lacks the material possessions one may be in humble circumstances. Humility in this latter sense may even include someone who lacks confidence in himself. A condition of poverty may lead to a lack of self-esteem, but this should not be confused with humility. A person can have a healthy self-esteem that does not devalue their capacities and achievements and still count others greater than themselves.

Self-control

In the ancient Greek world self-control was a key virtue of the soul. For Plato the soul consisted of three parts: the mind, the emotions and the desires. A person exercised self-control when the mind governed and controlled the other two parts of the soul. However the biblical writers had an integrated and holistic view of the person. The thinking, feeling and choosing aspects of a person were centred in the heart. The threefold activity of the heart issued in intentions. Intentions could be good or evil. They could be in accordance with the will of God or they could be against his will. In the New Testament self-control is seen to be the fruit of the Spirit (Galatians 5:22). While the exercise of self-control involves the activity of the mind it also involves the activity of the emotions and the will. Self-control in the Bible is not a matter of bringing the emotions and the will under the control of reason, but of bringing all three aspects—the mind, emotions, and will—into line with the will of God.

Sincerity and Purity

The two Greek words *eilikrineia* and *katharos* refer to the virtues of sincerity and purity. The logic of these two virtues is such that they can be treated together. Sincerity designates an openness of character. If one is sincere, then the innermost thoughts and motives can be displayed because they are pure. Hence the Greek word for sincerity can also be translated purity. *Katharos* basically means cleanness, but when it is applied to the human heart it refers to purity. The pure in heart are those whose thoughts and motives have been sifted until there is no evil element to be found. Love comes from a pure heart, a good conscience and sincere faith (1 Timothy 1:5). Peter tells us that Christians have purified their souls by obedience to the truth (1 Peter 1:22). The consequence of the purifying process is that they experience a genuine mutual love. This love comes from the heart. (We need to note that the words 'heart' and 'soul' are used almost synomously on this occasion.)

Other Virtues

It will not be possible to provide a complete list of the virtues found in the New Testament. Lists of virtues are found in the following passages: 2 Corinthians 6:6–7; Galatians 5:22–23; Ephesians 4:2–3, 32; Philippians 4:8; Colossians 3:12; 1 Timothy 4:12, 6:11; 2 Timothy 2:22, 3:10; 2 Peter 1:5–7. Some of the other virtues mentioned in the New Testament include:

> Compassion, excellence, faithfulness, godliness, goodness, knowledge, that which is lovely, that which is noble, peace, perseverance, praiseworthiness, truthful speech.

These virtues seem to be universal in nature. They are addressed to many different congregations in many different places. Christians must seek to secure the virtues in their own lives. Habitually operating on biblical principles and rules will see the appropriation of these virtues.

Vices

On the other hand Christians must root out vice. Repeated repentance, recommitment, and prayer in the context of fellowship will eventually witness the overthrow of vices through the power of the Spirit. Lists of vices are found in the following passages: Mark

7:21–22; Romans 1:29–31, 13:13; 1 Corinthians 5:10–11, 6:9–10; 2 Corinthians 12:20–21; Galatians 5:19–21; Ephesians 4:31, 5:3–5; Colossians 3:5, 8; 1 Timothy 1:9–10; 2 Timothy 3:2–5; Titus 3:3; 1 Peter 2:1, 4:3, 15; Revelation 21:8, 22:15. The vices mentioned in the New Testament include:

> Abusiveness, adultery, anger, arrogance, bitterness, boastfulness, brawling, brutality, carousing, coarse joking, conceit, cowardliness, criminality, debauchery, deceit, depravity, discord, disobedience to parents, disorder, dissension, drunkenness, envy, evil desire, evil thoughts, factiousness, filthy language, folly, foolish talk, foolishness, (being a) God hater, gossip, greed, hatred, homosexual offence, hypocrisy, idolatry, immorality, impurity, insolence, irreligion, jealousy, law breaking, lewdness, lying, love of money, love of pleasure, love of self, lust, magic arts, male prostitution, malice, meddling, murder, not loving the good, obscenity, orgies, outbursts of anger, perjury, perversion, pride, quarrelling, rage, rashness, rebellion, selfish ambition, sexual immorality, sinfulness, slander, slave trading, strife, swindling, theft, treachery, unbelief, (being) unforgiving, (being) ungodly, ungratefulness, unholiness, vileness, wickedness, witchcraft, (being) without love, (being) without self control.

Educate Your Conscience

The word 'conscience' refers to something that comes with knowledge. It has to do with an awareness of one's own actions. Records from the earliest times suggest that people always had an awareness of the fact that the actions they were doing, or actions they were contemplating, were morally right or wrong. In every age consciousness or awareness of the rightness or wrongness of the act seems to have come with the awareness that one was doing or had done a certain action. The Scriptures give a real place to the activity of conscience. Although the word is not used in the Old Testament the idea is found there. 1 Samuel 24:5 records the fact that David's heart smote him after he cut off the corner of Saul's robe. The Greek word for conscience is found numerous times in the New Testament.

Roman Catholic theology, with its adoption of the doctrine of Natural Law, seems to have followed an old Greek view of conscience. According to this view conscience is legislative. That is to say, conscience gives you the principles and rules of morality. According to this approach everybody has access to the moral law. In this regard there is no need to have a knowledge of Scripture if one desires to be moral. Scripture is merely a moral reminder. Human thinking or reason can read moral values from the order of creation. But studies of the notion of conscience as it is found in Scripture strongly suggest that the conscience is judicial and not legislative. That is to say, the conscience takes the principles and rules of morality from some place, like the local society or the Scripture, and applies those principles and rules to a person's actions. Conscience, in this sense, is a judge.

As conscience is judicial it needs to be educated. Christians need to educate themselves with the moral principles and values of Scripture so that the conscience will operate properly. Education of the conscience is part of developing a Christian character. Conscience also needs to be heeded. If one ploughs ahead and over-rides one's conscience time and time again then it will become seared. It will be like the brakes of a car that is driven with the brakes on. It will burn out and become ineffective. Paul can speak about those who renounce the faith in this way (1 Timothy 4:2). Deceitful hypocrites have had their consciences seared by their renunciation of the truth and their hypocrisy.

Conclusions

Developing a truly moral life is a complex on-going process. The range of contexts that demand a moral response require a constant shift of focus and approach. In the regular course of daily life, operating solely on a set of moral rules will be inadequate. A new situation may provoke examination and deliberation. The situation may require the location of relevant moral principles. Bear in mind that the Christian life is a fellowship activity. Talking through moral predicaments with others can inspire new insights into the way that the situation is to be interpreted. The way things are viewed depends upon the character of the viewer. So mature Christians who have had a long relationship with the Lord may be able to discover elements and factors missed by others. Thinking through an issue can cause one to reshape one's ethic and adjust ideals and paradigms.

Personal disappointment with the morality of one's own actions, or the rebuke of another Christian, can lead to the discovery of character traits that are ungodly. Envy and greed, for example, can be very subtle vices. The desire for a new car can be triggered by a neighbour's acquisition. Self-examination may be old fashioned, but it is an essential part of being faithful to Christ and living by faith.

The Christian's relationship with Christ provides the power and the instruments of change. All the things mentioned in this chapter cannot be done without a personal knowledge of God and of his Word. The study of the Scriptures and the nurturing of a personal spiritual life are essential to right living. When immorality is encountered in our own lives, whether it be in action, thought, or trait of character, it should be met with prayerful repentance and a zealous recommitment of obedience to a loving Saviour and Lord. While deep personal changes can be difficult, those in Christ are not alone in the struggle. They can call upon Christian friends and find the strength of fellowship. More importantly they can call upon the name of the Lord and receive the power of his Spirit.

Notes

1 The ESV translates Mal 2:16 differently from most other English translations (see the ESV footnote for the more common rendering). Even in the ESV translation, however, God's firm opposition to divorce is clear.

2 In his classic study Sherwin Bailey discovered that while the Hebrew word 'to know' occurs over 900 times it is used less than fifteen times with this sexual connotation (Bailey, 1955).

3 'A concubine was a slave woman, in a very different and inferior relation to her master compared with his wife' (Wright, 1983, p.176).

4 See note 1.

5 I have argued in this book that the Bible writers in general take a teleological approach to ethics. Elsewhere I have argued that Paul in particular takes a teleological approach (Hill, 2000).

6 By the way the integration of the body and soul would also explain the necessity of the resurrection unto eternal life.

Bibliography

Bailey, D. S. (1955), *Homosexuality and the Western Christian Tradition*, Shoestring Press, London.

Batchelor, E. (1980), *Homosexuality and Ethics*, The Pilgrim Press, New York.

Bayer, R. (1981), *Homosexuality and American Psychiatry: The Politics of Diagnosis*, Basic Books, New York.

Boswell, J. (1980), *Christianity, Social Tolerance, and Homosexuality*, The University of Chicago Press, Chicago.

Bradley, F. H. (1927), *Ethical Studies* (2nd Ed.), Oxford University Press, Oxford.

Bright, J. (1960), *A History of Israel*, SCM, London.

Brown, W. P. (1996), *Character in Crisis*, Eerdmans, Grand Rapids.

Cannold, L. (1998), *The Abortion Myth*, Allen & Unwin, St. Leonards.

Carter, A. (1990), 'On Individualism, Collectivism, and Interrelationism', *Heythrop Journal*, Vol. XXXI, pp. 23–38.

Cooper, J. W. (1989), *Body, Soul, and Life Everlasting: Biblical Anthropology and the Monism-Dualism Debate*, Eerdmans, Grand Rapids.

Countryman, L. W., *Dirt, Greed and Sex*, SCM, London.

Dixon, P. (1993), *The Genetic Revolution*, Kingsway, Eastbourne.

Dumbrell, W. J. (1985), *The End of the Beginning: Rev 21-22 and the Old Testament*, Baker Book House, Grand Rapids.

Dumbrell, W. J. (1988), *The Faith of Israel*, Baker Book House, Grand Rapids.

Dumbrell, W. J. (1997), *Covenant and Creation: A Theology of the Old Testament Covenants*, Paternoster Press, Carlisle.

Dwyer, J. C. (1987), *Foundations of Christian Ethics*, Paulist Press, Mahwah, N.J.

Elliot, R. (1991), 'Environmental Ethics', in P. Singer (ed.), *A Companion to Ethics*, Basil Blackwell, Oxford, pp. 284–293.

Evans, C. S. (1977), *Preserving the Person: A Look at the Human Sciences*, IVP, Downers Grove.

Fairweather, I. C. M. & McDonald, J. I. H (1984), *The Quest for Christian Ethics*, Handsel Press, Edinburgh.

Ford, A. L. (2000), *The Beginning of the Human Individual: A Response to Norman Ford's Decisive Moment*, Unpublished Moore College Project.

Ford, N. M. (1988), *When did I begin?: Conception of the Human Individual in History, Philosophy and Science*, Cambridge University Press, Cambridge.

Fleming, J. I. (1992), 'Euthanasia, The Netherlands, and Slippery Slopes', *Bioethics Research Notes Occasional Paper*, 1, Southern Cross Bioethics Institute, Adelaide.

Frankena, W. K. (1963), *Ethics*, Prentice-Hall, Englewood Cliffs.

Giddens, A (1976), *New Rules of Sociological Method*, Hutchinson, London.

Goldsworthy, G. (1981), *Gospel and Kingdom: A Christian Interpretation of the Old Testament*, Crossroad Distributors, Rydalmere.

Goldsworthy, G. (1991), *According to Plan*, Lancer Press, Homebush West.

Goldsworthy, G. (1997), 'Is Biblical Theology Viable?', in Gibson, R. J. (ed.), *Interpreting God's Plan*, Open Book & Paternoster Press, Adelaide & Carlisle, pp. 18–46.

Gorman, M. J. (1982), *Abortion and the Early Church*, IVP, Downers Grove.

Hauerwas, S. (1984), *The Peaceable Kingdom*, SCM, London.

Hauerwas, S. (1981), *A Community of Character: Toward a Constructive Christian Social Ethic*, University of Notre Dame Press, Notre Dame.

Hays, R. B. (1996), *The Moral Vision of the New Testament*, T&T Clark, Edinburgh.

Hebert, A. G. (1950), *The Bible From Within*, Oxford University Press, Oxford, 1950.

Hill, M. (1994), 'Homosexuality and Ethics', in Webb, B. G (ed.), *Theological and Pastoral Responses to Homosexuality*, Open Book, Adelaide, pp. 123–143.

Hill, M. (1997), 'Biblical Theology and Ethics' in Gibson, R. J. (ed.), *Interpreting God's Plan*, Open Book & Paternoster Press, Adelaide & Carlisle, pp. 91–109.

Hill, M. (2000), 'Theology and Ethics in the Letter to the Romans', in Bolt, P. & Thompson, M. (eds), *The Gospel to the Nations*, IVP/Apollos, Leicester & Downers Grove.

Janzen, W. (1994), *Old Testament Ethics*, Westminster/John Knox, Louisville.

Jochemsen, H. (1995), *Euthanasia: A Christian Evaluation*, Latimer Studies Pamphlet 49, Latimer House, Oxford.

Kinsey, A. C., Pomeroy W. B., & Martin, C. E. (1948), *Sexual Behaviour in the Human Male*, Saunders, Philadelphia & London.

Kinsey, A. C., Pomeroy W. B., & Martin, C. E. (1953), *Sexual Behaviour in the Human Female*, Saunders, Philadelphia & London.

Layman, C. Stephen (1991), *The Shape of the Good*, Notre Dame Press, Notre Dame.

Lukes, S. (1973), *Individualism*, Basil Blackwell, Oxford.

Martin, N. D. (1987), 'Ecology', in *Encyclopedia of Biblical and Christian Ethics*, Nelson, Nashville, Camden & Kansas City.

Meilander, G. (1996), *Bioethics: A Primer for Christians*, Eerdmans, Grand Rapids.

Mitchell, P. (1997), 'Medical and Psychological Perspectives', in Gibson, R. J. (ed.), *Theological and Pastoral Responses to Homosexuality*, Openbook & Paternoster Press, pp. 105–121.

Murray, J. (1957), *Principles of Conduct: Aspects of Biblical Ethics*, Eerdmans, Grand Rapids.

O'Donovan, O. (1986), *Resurrection and Moral Order: An Outline for Evangelical Ethics*, IVP & Eerdmans, Leicester & Grand Rapids.

Polanyi, M. (1958), *Personal Knowledge: Towards a Post-Critical Philosophy*, Routledge & Kegan Paul, London & Henley.

Robinson, D. W. B. (1955), *The Hope of Christ's Coming*, Evangelical Tracts and Publications, Sydney.

Robinson, D. W. B. (1997), 'Origins and Unresolved Tensions', in Gibson, R. J. (ed.), *Interpreting God's Plan*, Openbook & Paternoster Press, Adelaide & Carlisle, pp. 1–17.

Rowley, H. H. (1956), *The Faith of Israel: Aspects of Old Testament Thought*, S.C.M., London.

Sarna, N. M. (1987), *Exploring Exodus: The Heritage of Biblical Israel*, Schoken Books.

Satinover, J. (1996), *Homosexuality and the Politics of Truth*, Baker Book House, Grand Rapids.

Saunders, C. (1980), *Caring to the End*, Nursing Mirror, Sept 4, pp. 89–90.

Schmidt, T. E. (1995), *Straight or Narrow? Compassion and Clarity in the Homosexual Debate*, IVP, Downers Grove.

Scobie, C. H. H. (1991a), 'The Challenge of Biblical Theology (Part 1)', *Tyndale Bulletin*, Vol. 42.1, pp. 31–61.

Scobie, C. H. H. (1991b), 'The Structure of Biblical Theology', *Tyndale Bulletin*, Vol. 42.2, pp. 163–194.

Simkins, R. A. (1994), *Creator and Creation*, Hendrickson Publishers, Peabody.

Somerville, M. (1995), *The Real Implications of Euthanasia*, Foundation Genesis Pamphlet, Lane Cove, August.

Spencer, C. (1995), *Homosexuality: A History*, Fourth Estate, London.

Spohn, W. C. (1984), *What are they saying about Scripture and Ethics?*, Paulist Press, Ramsey.

Vardy, P. & Grosch, P. (1994), *The Puzzle of Ethics*, Fount, London.

Webb, B. (1994), 'Homosexuality in Scripture', in B. Webb (ed.), *Theological and Pastoral Responses to Homosexuality*, Openbook, pp. 65–103.

Wennberg, R. N. (1985), *Life in the Balance; Exploring the Abortion Controversy*, Eerdmans, Grand Rapids.

Wright, C. J. H. (1983), *Living as the People of God: the Relevance of Old Testament Ethics*, IVP, Leicester.

Bible Passages Index

Authors Index

Subject Index

ABOUT MATTHIAS MEDIA

Matthias Media is an independent, evangelical, non-denominational company aiming to produce books and other resources of a uniformly high quality—both in their biblical faithfulness and in the quality of the writing and production.

For more information about our extensive range of Bible studies, books, evangelistic tools, training courses, periodicals and audio-cassettes, visit us at **www.matthiasmedia.com.au** or contact us in any of the following ways:

Mail: Matthias Media
           PO Box 225
           Kingsford NSW 2032
           Australia

Phone: 1800 814 360 *(tollfree in Australia)*
           9663 1478 *(in Sydney)*
           int + 61-2-9663 1478 *(international)*

Fax: (02) 9663 3265

Email: info@matthiasmedia.com.au

❀ MATTHIAS MEDIA